Written in the Sky

Written in the Sky

LESSONS OF A SOUTHERN DAUGHTER

PATRICIA FOSTER

THE UNIVERSITY OF ALABAMA PRESS
Tuscaloosa

The University of Alabama Press
Tuscaloosa, Alabama 35487-0380
uapress.ua.edu

Typeface: Arno Pro

Cover image: Photograph by Patricia Foster
Cover design: Michele Myatt Quinn

Cataloging-in-Publication data is available from the Library of Congress.
ISBN: 978-0-8173-6096-2
E-ISBN: 978-0-8173-9466-0

For my mother, eternal muse
1922–2020

Contents

Prologue ix

PART I. RECKONINGS, 2018

Written in the Sky 3

PART II. FAMILY LESSONS, 1929–1968

Nowhere 19

You Girls 33

The "Orig" 45

Silence 59

Sleepwalking 61

PART III. HISTORY LESSONS, 1933–2019

Alabama Triptych 73

What Needs to Be Needed 83

If I Could Write Postcards to Mary Hamilton 95

Native Daughter 100

CONTENTS

Club from Nowhere 124

A Dark, Unruly Space 126

Fingering the Scars 139

PART IV. LESSONS OF LEGACY AND LOSS, 1996–2020

Umbilicus 151

Amends 161

Pilgrimage 180

The Custodian 189

PART V. RECKONINGS, 2018

Archive of the Dead 203

Acknowledgments 209

Notes 211

Prologue

IN MY EARLY TWENTIES, AFTER I left Alabama, I worked as a caseworker in a swampy part of western Tennessee known as the Bottoms. My clients— mostly poor white people who sharecropped, hauled junk, and cleaned houses—put no truck in the happy ending or the quick fix. They wanted to eat, to work when work was available, and to indulge in the few pleasures open to them: smoking and drinking beer on their front steps, swimming in the creek in summer, hunting deer in the fall, and buying moonshine when they could.

Two or three days a week, I made home visits to wooden shacks with barren front yards full of scrawny chickens scratching in the dirt. Teenage boys watched me warily while their mothers, often unemployed and depressed, cleared a place at the table for me to sit. I was grateful for their generosity, and though I believed I could be of help to these families, in truth I knew just enough to keep them from starving. It took me three long months to realize this, wedded as I was to good intentions and the beauty of a vase of wildflowers near a kitchen window rather than the sober facts of poverty and the southern caste system.

Later, I'd see this job as a reality check to the sentimentality of easy solutions, do-gooder notions, and the up-by-the-bootstraps mentality that fueled so much of popular philosophy. I had yet to understand the sour meanness and desperation, racial injustice, ill health, and lack of resources that so often accompanied poverty. But more than that, I understood little of myself. Both success and failure seemed to elude me, darting around me like exotic fish, unknowable and vicarious. Instead, I lived in a state of waiting: waiting for my inner life to make sense; waiting for my disappointment to clarify; waiting for something to happen. And then, like an avalanche, it did: My marriage fell apart and took me with it.

As I struggled through a difficult divorce, my life split open. I couldn't work. I couldn't eat. I couldn't sleep. I was afraid of everything. Even afraid of being afraid. Unnerved, I quit my job and sat in my bedroom, staring at the small crack between the closed curtains, watching how, with a slight breeze, sunlight made a timid jab into the room. In my drawer one morning, I found a clothespin I'd brought from Alabama, and I eliminated the crack. Now darkness filled the vacuum where ordinary life had been. Though my old life was broken, I didn't want to leave this room. Not yet. I didn't want to leave, because I'd begun to ponder what I realized was an essential question: How does one keep the broken part from shattering the whole?

I'm still pondering that question, even as it has expanded beyond my divided attachments to the historical and the cultural. The broken part isn't just in me but in the world of the past and the present, a world of great beauty and brutality, of promising errors and tragic liberations, a world that requires not only skeptical musing but also the pursuit of spontaneity and pleasure. Of course, I never found a satisfying answer to my question. And yet because of that question, I discovered a way of thinking, an awareness of my own organizing intellect's ability to observe and to experience and to insistently ask what lessons need to be needed.

And so, I begin.

I try to tell my stories. Stories of class and race, of gender and caste, of silence and ambition, stories of reckoning after my first visit to the National Memorial for Peace and Justice in Montgomery, as well as stories of childhood longing and family loss. My stories are always about the South, both as a place and as an inheritance that stretches inside and beyond me, a place I'll never understand and yet will never let go. A place that will never let go of me.

"All over Alabama the lamps are out," James Agee wrote in *Let Us Now Praise Famous Men* as he watched the warm southern night descend, the leaves soften, the winds cease, and a vigilant silence reign.

As do I.

Unable to sleep, I pull back the curtain of my life and wait for dawn.

PART I

Reckonings, 2018

Written in the Sky

Letter to my great-niece after visiting the National Memorial for Peace and Justice in Montgomery, Alabama

D EAR ADDIE,
I've tried to write this letter several times, first to my sister, your grandmother—you called her Beanie—but the words shimmered, then vanished. I wanted to talk to the dead about the dead, to tell my sister how the shadows of our southern past have always haunted me, but it seems I can only talk to the living. And so, I'm writing this letter to you, but also to me, or me meeting me as you, a thought experiment as real as Einstein's curvature of space or why the sky is blue.

You're five (going on six) and have all the awe and swagger of our family, an ambitious, fierce, and sometimes troubled people. They will most likely think I'm crazy to write to you about such a hard subject: racial violence, lynching, segregation, hate, the meanness that bites into our country. But then again, how can we teach you to love our country if we don't also explain our country's oppressive history, its duplicity and sin, its guilt and blood? How else can we encourage you to hold us to a higher standard, consistent with the rules you wrote to me in the *LOVE BOOK: How to Love Peppol?* (1) *You have to lern how to be kind* (decorated with red hearts). (2) *You have to get frens* (two girls with defiant hair holding hands). (3) *You have to see yourslf* (two big eyes). *And then you will no how to love peppol.*

As I sit at my desk in Iowa, I worry about what I can say. Because it's late at night and there's so much silence around me, I stare into the edge of my feelings, dark roads that meander into darker alleys, a thicket of melancholy trees. On the simplest level, what happened is this: I went on a trip to Montgomery in August 2018. I came back to Iowa. And in between is a story of what I experienced, what I saw and didn't see, what I thought and couldn't say. Maybe this isn't a letter to you at all but a letter to history in the only way it can be written, with the tears and sorrow that should belong to us all, using the instructions of a child.

The air in Montgomery is hot, suffocating, any breeze a prayer. My fair skin pinks and sweat bubbles above my lip as I stand in line with my ticket, listening to a drawl of voices, slow and deliberate, both familiar and foreign. "Y'all get over here," a mother orders her daughters, fussing with them. "No need all that bickering. Hush now." Then, "God bless you," an old man, white-haired and bent, nods to a woman who's stepped aside to give him a little shade.

The line snakes forward to the National Memorial for Peace and Justice, a six-acre site that pays tribute to 4,400 Black victims of lynching by white mobs in the United States between 1877 and 1950. I think its subtitle might be: *How We Learned to Hate People.*

Once inside, I stare at the first row of eight hundred oxidized steel columns suspended by long dark rods as thick as rope, each representing a particular county in the Deep South and the Midwest, each bearing the names of the men, women, and children who were lynched in that county. I move to the next row, then the next, a seemingly endless number of columns the color of a wound. Will I be able to look at all these columns? Will I be able to read all these names? A few days ago, the simple steps of *How to Love Peppol* seemed clear and obvious, but now I'm engulfed in an epithet of currency that is anything but.

Instead of kindness, my mind confronts sadism, a laundry list of atrocities Black men and women, but particularly Black men, suffered at the hands of a white mob: Not only were they hung, they were burned at the stake ("barbecued"), maimed, disfigured, castrated, blinded, ears and tongues sliced, skin blowtorched, fingers and toes cut off, their knuckles for sale as souvenirs in the town square the next day. Unfortunately, I can imagine a young white boy, seven or eight years old, mesmerized by the gore, the slime and thready goop of knuckles crammed together like pickles in a jar, and begging his father for a few pennies. *"Please. Just so I can get one! So I can show Bobby."* Simultaneously, I try to imagine the terror of a young Black boy when he hears this story, but when I attempt to conjure his anguish, the tumult of his mind, the grip of his fear, something buckles in me. I can only flinch at such savage trauma.

Sometimes the corpses, charred and mutilated, were dragged through the streets as a gratuitous thrill for white onlookers. Sometimes church services were interrupted, white Christian worshippers hurrying from their pews, unfinished hymns still vibrant on their tongues as they rushed to get a good "spot" for the lynching spectacle. Sometimes white newspapers wrote hysterical, sensational editorials based on hearsay and innuendo, trumping up charges against Black citizens, whipping up the ire of the white populace.

I move on through a geography of terror.

Jefferson County, Alabama
Fulton County, Georgia
Webster Parish, Louisiana
Hernando County, Florida
Florence County, South Carolina
Dallas County, Alabama
McLean County, Kentucky

Column after column, I read the names: Lewis Scott, Sam Townes, Jennie Collins, Dave Harris, Frazier Baker, Julia Baker, Sam Howard, Cairo Williams, Arthur Davis, Red Haynie, Mrs. Martin, James Sweat, George Burden, William Fambro, Marcus Westmoreland, Penny Westmoreland, Essex Harrison, Jeff Darling, Oliver Wideman, Bennie Thompson, Robert Davis, my eyes tracking the list, first and last names sliding through my brain like silk, soft and slippery and then unrecoverable unless I write them down. Many, I imagine, were sharecroppers, trapped in the tenant system that kept both Black people and poor white people in debt, dependent and easily controlled in a bleak, agrarian life. Perhaps some drudged in coal mines or on chain gangs, and maybe a few had more prosperous jobs in barber shops or mortuaries or as local professionals. After all, Thurgood Marshall, after trying a case for the NAACP in rural Tennessee in 1946 was almost lynched on his drive back to his Nashville hotel. That night he, the other trial lawyers, and a reporter were stopped by three highway patrol cars, the officers edgy, their hands twitchy on their guns. In minutes, Thurgood Marshall was arrested for drunken driving (he had not been drinking), put in the back of one of the cop cars, and driven away. The other three passengers were waved off, warned to drive "right on to Nashville," though luckily they ignored this directive and followed the cop car down a deserted road to the deserted bank of the Duck River where, in unending darkness, a group of white men waited.[1] It's possible the very presence of Marshall's companions saved the life of a future (and first African American) Supreme Court justice. Who can know how such a perilous experience sharpened the private instincts and legal clarity of Thurgood Marshall himself, what improvisations of self-making it triggered?

At the very least, his system of reality would have been burdened by an instant, anguished upgrade.

Baldwin County, Alabama
Colquitt County, Georgia
Callaway County, Missouri
Shelby County, Tennessee
Lamar County, Texas
Alexander County, Illinois

The night before I drove to Montgomery, I stayed with my ninety-five-year-old mother, your great-grandmother and namesake, a woman who, as you well know, makes the best red velvet cake in southern Alabama. Unsullied by age, her lipstick bright and blotted, her voice as strong and clear as if she were in her sixties, she's still "running the roads" to doctor appointments, weddings, and funerals and caretaking the family tribe. After dinner, she and I talked late into the night about ordinary things: a new leak in her roof, the delight of her great-grandson's graduation, our mutual fatigue (we were both yawning and apologizing), and only as we were agreeing "that yes, it's time to get our beauty sleep," did she mention my upcoming trip to the memorial. "I can see you're interested in these things," she said, "and that's good. That's never been my interest, but I know you need to go." I nodded, pleased that in the last few years we'd been able to speak about our differences. We hugged, then parted to get ready for bed.

And yet as I lay in bed that night, a thought vibrated like a telephone wire in my brain: *Maybe you either have the gene for fighting racial injustice or you don't.* Of course, I knew this was absurd. I'd be the first to admit that the aches and sorrows of daily life are exhausting and need tending, and yet a part of me worried that ignoring our oppressive history could allow a tacit avoidance, a kind of hallucination of innocence, maybe even a preference *not to see.* And doesn't "not seeing" cast the other into oblivion, allowing for illusions and delusions when the story is right before your eyes?

"The record is there for all to read," James Baldwin wrote about racial injustice in America. "It resounds all over the world. It might as well be written in the sky."

In the sky. Yes, I thought as I shifted and settled in my old girlhood bed, trying to get comfortable in a place I'd left fifty years ago. I couldn't help but wonder if not feeling deeply about how discrimination affected both the Black psyche and white psyche (to say nothing of the Black body) was . . . well, a failure of the imagination. *You have to lern how to be kind,* you wrote in the *LOVE BOOK.* Certainly, kindness is a willingness to risk something of the self for the other, and thus, an act of the imagination. And certainly, discomfort and anxiety are necessary to the very idea of risk.

I want to think so.

As these thoughts swarmed my brain, the clock on the bedside table ticked toward midnight. I heard the lonely hoot of an owl hidden somewhere in the nearby trees, the skittering of insects against the screen. I should sleep. My three-hour drive to Montgomery would come too soon and I'd wake, yawning and groggy, and be tempted to reset the alarm. I turned out the light. But I'd barely adjusted to the darkness when I felt the hard pinch of reality: *You're not risking anything. You're just going to the memorial. Don't get on your high horse.*

When I visited you in North Carolina, you were all charged curiosity and eager intention. You read, you sang, you wrote about ghosts, about love, about Jesus. You rode your bike, racing ahead, wild hair flying in the wind beneath your helmet. You made rules about what your younger brother could and could not do, snatched cookies, decorated your face with stickers, teased, and laughed. And of course, you pouted, wanting your way. "But I want to," you huffed with each demand, eyes impatient, pupils darkening, at first charming, then defensive. When denied, you stomped off, yelling, "It's not FAIR," your bottom lip stuck out, your whole body sulking.

Assertion. Insistence. I think about how fiercely you resent being subordinated, a trait I hope you retain, as I walk deeper into the memorial, the floor sloping gradually downward, the columns now higher, like motionless bodies dangling above me. Inevitably, I stop, breath held, staring at the endless forms as symbol and reality intertwine. I can't move. Other people stop here too, the air cooler, the light dimmer, the columns eloquent and sad and oddly intimate. *It's not fair.*

"Disempowerment is the very *premise* of segregation," I whisper as if you're beside me. "Lynching was the de facto corrective and fear the conduit. Fear as big and ugly as an unpredictable beast. A cold breath of hate."

I can't yet expect you to understand either the words or the premise, you who live in a family and a culture that loves you, where you thrive in a white, privileged life of tenderness and attention, enhanced by healthy food, good schools, private lessons, and family support, a life you don't recognize as privileged, only normal. And like all the people who love you, I'll fight hard and long to keep you from experiencing hostility and abuse and hate, but I also want you to know that it exists. Everywhere.

> Miller County, Arkansas
> Franklin County, North Carolina
> Tulsa County, Oklahoma
> Grant County, Indiana
> Warren County, Mississippi
> Wythe County, Virginia
> Logan County, West Virginia

As I descend into the last section of the memorial, I have a queer, dizzying moment. I'm tired and suddenly hungry. I chew on a ragged fingernail, slightly bored, shifting my purse to ease its weight. A headache threatens, and I want to flee. I've been here for less than two hours, but already the hyper-focus and heat have depleted me. I don't bother reading the names on the columns anymore, the words and dates a blur, my attention dispersed. I stare at a woman's gold lame high-top tennis shoes and the paw print tattoos that accessorize her calves. I stare at a young girl with delicate pink rosebuds attached to her flip-flops and a beautiful woman absently twirling her blue-and-green-striped umbrella as she lags in front of me. There is a mix of white, Black, and brown people here, of young and old, of hair woven, ponytailed, bunched, and bald. Teenagers wear cutoffs and tank tops and chew gum just as they do at the mall. Elderly men hunch and stop to rest. When I gaze out at the hot, humid day, the grass looks absurdly green, the clouds drifting in a white sky, and I want suddenly to be where people are chatting and casually drinking water from paper cups. That's what I want. *Get me outta here.*

And yet I don't leave. When I see a raised platform of concrete steps where other people sit, I plop down beside them. A few minutes later, I note the reason for the steps. A high granite wall shimmers with a cascade of water endlessly baptizing words carved in stone: *unknown victims of racial terror lynching.*

Because there were so many more. Unreported. Unnamed. Undocumented. Unknown to history. Lives destroyed though (I want to think) still mourned.

Looking around me, I'm relieved that others look as bruised by the heat and the experience as I feel. They fan themselves, slouching, shirts pulled out of pants, shoes slipped discreetly off, purses open to glance at phones. Some close their eyes, resting. Others gaze vaguely at the wall. I yawn and rest my head in my hands—I should have gone to bed earlier last night—and when I look up, I see a little girl in a green sundress, about your age, snatch her father's iPhone and dash toward that wall of water. As nimble as a dancer, she zigzags between people, moving in close to click her picture, then turning back to us with a bold, capricious smile.

We all laugh.

"Lord, we needed that!" A woman sitting below me, glances up, her smile wide beneath her colorful sun hat.

"Absolutely." I grin.

"Praise God," someone else sings out.

A five-year-old brown girl. The future. A little splash of hope.

If you were here, I know you'd grab my phone and rush off to play with her. *You have to get frens.* You'd want to show her what you could do and see what she could do, the two of you comparing and testing and sharing and showing off. And you'd have no sense of restraint, a reassuring thought to someone who grew up, as I did, in the formalized separation of the segregated South.

And yet even as I think this, I realize this is a white woman's vision, a moment based on knowing your easy friendliness rather than the adventurous brown girl's readiness to play. What if, even at such a young age, she's been touched by the racism of our culture? What if she sees you rushing toward her and instead of pleasure, she feels a roar inside her head, a need to turn away, to tell you to stop?

Chastened, I watch as the little brown girl, her sundress flashing in the dim light, runs smiling back to her father and hugs his knee.

Exhausted by the memorial, I walk back to my hotel in the thick June heat, getting lost, then finding my way past an empty lot and onto the main drag. Once in my room, I slump on the clean, white bed, feeling a vague disquiet. Through the walls I hear the drunken sounds of a wedding party I saw in the lobby, the trills of laughter, the ding of the elevator, whoops of celebration. Joy. I wish I had a reason to dress up in fancy clothes, to leap up and dance.

Instead, I go to the desk, open my laptop, and wait for my thoughts to emerge. But nothing comes. No images flash across my retina. No stories ricochet in my brain. My mind feels dull and flat, as pale and thin as a piece of old cardboard. I can't think of one thing that hasn't been said. So, I eat two cookies, lick my fingers, and drink the last of my Diet Coke.

I wait.

Nothing.

Why did I come here? I ask myself, as if I can ambush my thinking even as I slump in my chair. I wanted to tell you a story. I wanted to tell myself a story. But what I haven't dared admit is that I might return from the memorial, my mind numb, emptied, my imagination depleted. A dry husk. With no stories. Do I even have a right to a story? I slip deeper into the chair. What does it matter what I think about kindness or bigotry or the horror of the past if I can't feel?

I stare at the blank screen.

Then I close my laptop.

When night descends, I turn out all the lights and stand at the window, looking out at Montgomery. *Set your watch back one hundred years*, my friends used to say about this city. I always laughed. But now I don't. From here, the city looks dark and empty and unknowable, a deserted shell. Only the lights of the capital—once the capital of the Confederacy—glimmer in the night, small sparkles of brightness. I lean into the window, feeling the cold rush of air from the air-conditioning, letting it flutter my shirt as if I'm a tree with drooping leaves.

Why *did* I come here?

I think about James Baldwin's enduring voice, his anger, his persistence, his ability to discover hidden meanings, to unravel contradictions, to speak a personal truth. And yes, I know the record of injustice may be written in the sky, but it's not only the record that matters but also the sensibilities of the person reading that record, the mind attuned to both the bitter and the sweet.

The bitter and the sweet.

Maybe I just need to sleep. Maybe . . . I reach up to draw the curtains, to get ready for bed. Somewhere in the distance, a security light blinks, and for a brief moment I'm surprised by a palimpsest of another self, the faintest shadow.

A girl. An early morning. A memory.

I was eight years old, small and fair and thrilled to be on vacation with my family in the mountains of North Carolina. Huge trees sprang up, green-bright and thick as we lurched around mountain curves. The sky was a fairytale blue, the air so cool chill bumps pimpled my arms. We were sequestered in a tiny town, *a secret nowhere*, my sister and I whispered, with other white families who'd driven to this secluded place for a southern medical convention. It was the summer of 1956, Eisenhower was president, the cost of gas was twenty-two cents a gallon, and all was right with the world. This was what we knew.

I'd never been to North Carolina, and the thought of hiking in *real* mountains, riding horses, and learning to clog shattered all pretense of sleep that first night. My sister and I (the girls) had twin single beds in the back room of a three-bedroom cabin painted white with dark shutters and a wide front porch dotted with rocking chairs where our parents would entertain at night, visiting with other doctors and their wives, talking about anesthesiology, the flu vaccine, about china patterns and shopping excursions, things that didn't interest us in the least. Awake that first night, I pretended I was walking alone up the wide front steps to the porch, barely touching the white wooden banister, and then I was through the door, proclaiming everything as my territory: my table, my chair, my knotty pine wall, my picture of a bucolic landscape, my bed, my bureau, my closet, my window. Out the window, there was even more to claim—honeysuckle, oaks, sycamores, the odor of horses, the sweet smell of grass, the chatter of crickets. Our cabin was perched on a hillside with a tiny apartment tucked beneath the second story.

"This is the best place I've ever been," my brother insisted the next day.

"Yes!" my sister and I yelled.

It was on the second night that everything changed.

As we were returning to our cabin from dinner at the lodge—where everyone was served family style—we were surprised to see a light on outside the apartment door. We were dawdling, my father and mother talking, my sister and brother and I picking up pebbles and tossing them behind us, listening to them snap and ping on the path, each trying to outdo the other, bragging and egging each other on. That is, until my mother stopped. "I don't understand," she said, her voice quiet, but tense, and it was her muted apprehension that made us turn. In the distance, we saw a Black man in the white shirt and tie worn by the kitchen help open the door to the apartment beneath our cottage. Except for his white shirt, he was a mere shadow. He slipped inside. The outside light went off, and an inside light flared, soft yellow warming the space.

That was how we learned that two of the kitchen employees lived in the apartment beneath our cabin.

"Don't worry," my father said. "I'm sure it's a mistake. I'll ask for a new cabin tomorrow."

Once in the cozy realm of our cabin, I didn't think any more about it. I slept.

But the next morning, as I was sneaking around the side of the house, hoping to find a dead beetle or something to scare my sister, I was surprised when the apartment door opened and a young Black woman, small and neat and dressed in a starched white uniform, emerged. When she saw me, she smiled, an easy smile of friendly acknowledgment. And yet for me, time became suspended. I didn't move. I barely breathed. Instead of returning her smile, I froze, staring, my gaze locked to her gaze. As if reacting to my silence, her face went still, then blank, her mouth pressed closed, her eyes averted. She turned quickly, locked the door, and walked away from me toward the lodge. And yet it was as if everything had altered, everything changed. The man last night had seemed mythical, imaginary, barely there. But this woman was real. She was pretty. She was young. She had paused, smiling, and for the first time I was aware that she slept in a bed in a room beneath my room, that she put on her nightgown and brushed her teeth and combed her hair no less than twenty feet away. I could imagine her drinking a cup of coffee, just as my mother did, and looking out the small apartment window, listening to doves, hidden and cooing in the trees. I could imagine her laughing, her body loose and uninhibited, surprised at something the man said, then saying, "oh, hush, you," and washing out her coffee cup and setting it on the rack to dry. I could imagine her hanging up her clothes, tossing off her shoes, eating raisins from a tiny red carton, then turning on the radio and humming.

But was that right? Was it right that she lived so near?

What I felt was a tangle of feelings: curiosity, surprise, sadness, confusion, but also the insecurity of my family, the belief that we must never be different from the other white middle-class families who were here. I knew that being different was a danger, that it could mark you, blur you into invisibility. Difference was a stain, a slippery path, a mouth twisting in disgust. But there was something else, something new and unpleasant and suspicious idling below my consciousness. Did I want the Black woman to envy me, to want what I had, to turn back, her eyes hooded, slightly afraid, while I stood in the yard, my eight-year-old white self already enhanced by the vulgar pleasure of power? Was I drawing strength from that old cliché of superiority? Or did I simply want the Black woman to go away so I could make this cabin imaginatively all mine again?

I turned sharply and ran back into the cottage, forgetting all about scaring my sister.

I'm still at the window. My hand still holds the curtain. I'd like to think I was merely a confused southern child enmeshed in the mores of my culture. Better yet, I'd like to imagine that all my conditioning about race vanished the moment the young woman smiled, the gap between us eclipsed by surprise. But it's not true. It's never been true. Power is presumptuous. Some part of me thought I had a right to judge her, to make her turn away and feel distress. Even at eight, I was no innocent. I'd been trained in the psychology of prejudice and power and now this memory hangs suspended, raw and burning, in my consciousness.

Maybe I came here to remember.

To remember and call out the beast in me.

"Do you ever meet yourself?" you whispered as we drove to a farm in North Carolina where you'd picked strawberries last summer. You looked solemn, serious. You held my hand, waiting.

At first, I was surprised by your question, but you've always been quick and intuitive, curious about what's hidden. *You have to see yourslf.* I gazed into your dark brown eyes, then looked away. I wanted to tell you that meeting yourself can change you forever. Or simply be an elbow in your side. I wanted to say that it's like tearing yourself apart, but so is *not* meeting yourself and wanting to. In the moment of seeing, you may have a secret desire to think, *wow, that's me,* but the instant such a thought snags your consciousness, the meeting's over, the self as opaque and elusive as ever. Maybe that's why meeting yourself, actually seeing yourself, is often accidental, your ego pushed slightly askew, your lipstick smudged, your breath thick with onions.

I wished I knew how to tell you, Addie, that the self is slippery and unstable and that these moments of seeing can disturb the peace, can shatter the status quo. And this, I think, is what the memorial is meant to do: to act as a wake-up call, a timely alarm to our national consciousness, reminding us that the legacy of terror—and the tolerance of that terror—must be exposed if the *LOVE BOOK* is to rule. And yes, talking about racial violence is hard, but ignoring it is craven, an ignoble kind of hiding.

"Well?" You shook my knee, your brow furrowed. You were afraid I'd drifted off.

When I gazed at your face—your eyes could slip from earnest to dismissive in a split second—I smiled. "Yes," I said, "sometimes I do. And it usually surprises me. Because it reveals something I didn't know I knew about myself, something that makes me wonder, *who am I?*"

You nodded, eyes grave, studying me. And then, as if you wanted to contemplate this on your own or maybe just to watch the sky, you turned abruptly and fluttered your hand out the window, feeling the soft rush of air.

PART II
Family Lessons, 1929–1968

Early morning dampness, dew glistening on the grass, the car windows sweating. Everywhere there's silence, except for the rustling of a tree branch and the cooing of doves. I drive quickly down the road away from my family home, staring nervously into onrushing grayness, the sky and earth a muted smear. Though I must hurry to the airport, I pause longer than necessary at the stop sign, the motor humming, my foot on the brake, my hands tight on the wheel. I look back. I always look back.

Nowhere

I.

SHE CAME FROM NOWHERE. NOWHERE retreating to brush and bramble, stubble and weed, the ground red and fertile, then wet and marshy after the autumn rains. Nowhere meant biblical places, isolated bad luck hamlets where the Scots-Irish settled: towns like Maben, Littleton, and Praco, barely a scratch on the map of Alabama. Such places made her vigilant, eyes keen to every rustle, every flicker as if she had tiny mirrors implanted in her head.

Even now she perches on the edge of a chair. Alert, ready.

When I can't sleep at night, I think about my mother growing up, a child in the late 1920s, her mother and brothers in the fields growing tomatoes and cucumbers, milking the cows, bagging pecans from twenty-odd trees, her father walking the roads, looking for work. It was the eve of the Depression, the mines shut down, wages eroded, trust evaporated, the economy soon to become more crippled and broken. To make do, her family sharecropped near Littleton where wild daisies and dandelions bloomed along the dirt roads and irises sometimes brightened the fields. On the shelves sat stacked jars of pickles and tomatoes in the late spring of 1928, when she was five. What, I wonder, will such a beginning make and unmake in her?

II.

On Saturday she woke shivering, a late March wind rattling the windows, the sun not yet up, the baby crying. Her mother was already in the fields when she jostled her little sister, tickling her toes to make her squeal, and then, on impulse, put the baby's white leather shoes on top of the coal-burning stove. That would make the baby coo and giggle, toddling around in all that warmth. "Play pretty, pretty baby," she sang as she fixed the bottle, staring out at the trees, watching a leaf flutter, two leaves stir, then the whole live branch shake violently, yellow leaves twirling and shivering as two crows cawed, their feathers flying as they sprang from the tree. They circled the air. She laughed and pressed her face to the glass, hoping to see those tiny black specs, high up in the sky. When she turned, she smelled them before she saw them, a brownish scorch creeping up one side. Though she rushed to their rescue, the shoes were hard as wood, seared rusty-black on the bottom.

"Play pretty," the baby said, reaching for the shoes. But they were no longer shoes. They were toys to be rolled and kicked around on the floor.

Only in the late afternoon when her mother arrived, red-faced, her hair slipping free of its knot, her feet already swelling, did the girl realize her mistake: She'd left the baby's shoes by the table, in plain sight. One glance and her mother went livid. "Stupid!" she yelled, her arm already swinging. "You stupid girl!"

Whirling just out of her mother's reach, she streaked out the screen door, stumbling through elderberry and blackberry bushes, not caring that thorns raked her legs. She hid beneath the ash tree, flies buzzing, her breath ragged. An hour later she crept to the porch, climbing quietly into the big wooden swing, hugging herself. The afternoon was warm, the air thick with the scent of goldenrod and bluebells, the rind of a watermelon left drying in the dirt by the porch, ants crawling over its pink-lipped edge. She was not a good girl. She was stupid. She would always be stupid. She would never be cherished or loved. Only Sweet Child, barely eleven months older, was loved, because he was good.

From the swing, she watched her oldest brothers tramp in from the fields, sunburned and wiry, mere boys forced to grow up too fast, their adolescence narrowed, their futures trapped and splintered by what they'd already sacrificed. They wore faded overalls and no shirts, their chests sweaty, dirt ringing their necks, edging their jaws. Their pants legs were wet from the grass, their feet barefoot, their toenails hard as pennies. Sometimes they made her touch their big toes just to watch her squeal. Sometimes they fought with their father, a fury of fists and snarls and crashing bodies as if they were possessed by demons. Today they sank onto the swing beside her, sighing, grunting, one on each side, damp muscled arms and stained fingers. They idled the swing with their feet, and she rallied with the little shift of air. "Your weight holding us back, Sis," the older brother said, teasing. "Better hop off."

He pretended to push her. She pushed back, knotting her hands into fists. He laughed and they shifted again.

They didn't call her Stupid. They called her Sis.

And they liked to play games. If she could touch their knees before they caught her hand, they'd give a big, glorious swing. Now she looked coyly at one, then pounced on the other's knee. She won!

"Aiiiiiii!"

She glanced up at the porch ceiling where the old swing creaked, the hooks rusted and flaking, some twine bundled around the bolt. She let herself wait and wait, her brothers' attention waning, then she grabbed both of their knees. *Surprise!* They laughed, pushing the swing all the way back till they were almost standing. "Ready? *Here. She. Gooooes!*" the older brother said, then let it fly! It was as if she was slipping free of her badness, a scent of forgiveness carried in the sudden cool air as she glided back and forth, back and forth, a dizzying, terrifying relief. She wasn't stupid at all!

"Again," she begged.

"One more," the older brother said. "Then we wash up."

She thought to play the first trick again, gazing up at the sunburned cheek of the younger brother whose whiskers hadn't yet sprouted. Like lightning, she snaked out a hand. But the older brother grabbed it, and before she could react, he moved her hand inside his overalls, his big hand clasping her small one, his dark eyes holding her hazel ones as he guided her palm over the damp skin of his stomach, then lower, lower, to something hard, probing, and alive, his hand pressed tight against him. Instinctively, she wiggled her fingers, but he grasped her tighter. The younger brother laughed. "Stop," she said, but confusion stymied her.

"You lost," the older brother snapped. Suddenly, he seemed angry as he pinched her hand. The younger brother's eyes were closed.

When finally he let go, she ran.

Inside the house, oblivious to trouble, Sweet Child stood on a stool, drying the spoons in the kitchen and stacking them with care on the counter. "You want to help?" he asked, moving over. Outside, the brothers were silent.

III.

This much she knows: Stupid is punished. Weakness is derided. Obedience is required, a hickory switch freely used. She is sent to school. To church. To the table. To bed. She eats when told to eat. Sleeps when told to sleep. Bathes when told to bathe. Listens when told to listen. One day as she's bringing laundry into the front room, the pretty woman from the next farm rushes through their front door, her right eye a bloom of colors, her blonde hair streaming loose from its catch, the shoulder of her house dress ripped, exposing skin. Bruises circle her wrists and there's an odd stain at the front of her smock. Her name is Georgia. "He's trying to *kill* me," she cries out. "Next time he'll kill me, he'll . . . I love him but he's going . . ." and then she sobs on the sofa while her mother says, "Shhhh now, hush that, stop that now," and tells her to run for ice because "look what Joe Preacher just done." Even as she does what she's told, opening the ice bin and dropping pieces of ice into a cloth, she's amazed at what this woman has said. She's never heard anyone say the word "love" in relation to other people. Does that make the unhappiness easier or is it the reason for the unhappiness? She stares at the ice, hearing her daddy mutter in his tired voice, "Happy is for suckers." He went down in the pits at age fourteen, just like his daddy. He says other things too:

Damn mine owns you.

Fields own you.

Fellow who owns the fields owns you.

Even your damn stomach owns you.

Sometimes he says this while tenderly rubbing the loose neck folds of his dog.

IV.

She doesn't think much about being happy until the day she discovers what makes her special. At school, during recess, all the girls line up. At age five, she's the smallest and youngest and, thus, at the end of the line. While she waits, she watches, keen to see how the feet move, how the rope moves, how the two girls swinging keep the rhythm to the song—*"Five little monkeys / Jumping on a bed / One fell off / And bumped her head"*—sassy words floating in the air, sometimes a dare, sometimes a charm that can lull the jumper as they quicken the pace, dizzy the words until the jumper's caught, mouth open, the rope coiled between her feet. When it's her turn, she listens with her feet and her ears and some sixth sense inside her—*"Mama called the doctor / And the doctor said / 'No more monkeys / Jumping on the bed'"*—the words singing through her body, announcing that only now is she born.

That night, she badgers Sweet Child to find her a rope. "You *have* to," she pleads, "'cause you're the reason I go to school." His first week of first grade, Sweet Child sobbed inconsolably, his face swollen, his thick lashes stuck tight together, a flush spreading like a burn across the back of his neck, hot as a fever, until the next week, she was sent too. Sweet Child just needed a companion.

And now every day she practices jumping rope, stopping in a grassy spot near school while Sweet Child listens for the clang of the bell. She curls up the rope like a prize in her lunchbox, flattening the biscuits and blackberry jam her mother packs, leftovers from breakfast. But on Wednesday, she forgets to remove the rope, and seeing it, her mother tosses it into the backyard. "No time for nonsense." Only at dusk, her mother busy with the baby, does she sneak out, searching on hands and knees until she finds it beneath the clothesline where her brother's overalls hang faded and shapeless, drying in the cool air.

On Friday afternoon, the day bare and bright, she decides to practice all the way home, though she's been told not to dally, chores always waiting. "I won't be wasting time," she tells Sweet Child, giving him her books and her lunch pail, insisting he hurry on while she jumps her way down the path, which isn't a path at all, just mashed down weeds. It's still summer hot, only the late nights filled with a coolness that sweeps through her bedroom windows, fluttering the curtains. And yet nothing can touch her as she step-jump-steps through the spread of green. It's like being alone in a secret part of herself and at the same time showing that secret part to the world, even if the world is just the fields and the trees and the yellow yolk of sun. She doesn't tell herself this is happiness, because it's enough to concentrate on this special thing. She's singing the song the other girls sing, the rope slapping the grass, rising and falling, a slender thread in the air. *"Five little monkeys/Jumping on the bed."* She's half the way home, concentrating on the path as she chants and jumps—*"One fell down"*—noticing only as the rope flies over her head a flash of color, a ribbon of orange and black, something coiled and writhing caught on the rope. The snake sways aimlessly as the rope rises, then aggressively, imperiously, it reaches out, tongue flickering. She sees it in a yellow haze as if she's drowsing motionless in the sun, and then, waking, she shrieks, losing her step, her happiness, her life.

Why doesn't she run to Sweet Child and let him hold her hand? "Just a snake, a doggone snake," he'd say, softening the words. "Nothing bad now." Why go instead to the older brother, his hands greasy as he bends over a broken engine in the backyard? Her breathing is ragged as she tugs on his overalls, her hand nervous as she touches the stiff, stained material. "What?" he says annoyed, but then he grins, sliding his greasy hand over hers. She doesn't look at him. She looks at the distant sky. So blue. So cloudless. That's why the birds flew away.

V.

For months, she flies away too. Aimlessly soaring and circling, then finally pivoting into the work assigned at school, reading and numbers, spelling and history, penmanship and storytelling. She doesn't think of this as escape to another realm, release from the gloom and torment of home, her life unconsciously split into good and bad, curious and shamed, competent and stupid. She still thinks of the world as all of one piece, a beleaguered path from home to school and back home again.

And so she's surprised when Miss Allison, her pretty, soft-looking teacher, a pleasantly plump woman who wears dresses printed with tiny pink flowers and thin blue stripes, invites her home for a night to the house where she lives with her widowed mother. She doesn't know why Miss Allison chooses her, why she's sitting thrilled in the plush front seat of her car—she's never ridden in a car—cruising through the town of Dora to see the grand old brick churches, Episcopal, Methodist, and Presbyterian, and the US Post Office, its flag waving in the breeze, and then walking up a flowered path to a large white-framed home with dark wooden shutters surrounded by a smooth green lawn and entering the "vestibule" (a holy word to be whispered) with its full length mirror, mahogany chest of drawers, and bookcase full of books. She stores up every detail: the gold framed mirror with a fleur-de-lis at each corner, *War and Peace* shelved next to *Miss Post's Etiquette*, so that she can brag to Sweet Child, she the worldly, the extravagant one.

Miss Allison's mother, also a small plump woman, dressed in a dark navy dress with a brooch of pearls that glimmers in the light, nods at her but doesn't rise from her chair. That slight nod takes in her rush of dark hair, her thin, slipping socks, her washed-again dress, her small hand holding tightly to the paper bag with the clean cotton nightgown tucked inside. Instantly, she understands that this woman is Above her, understands that Miss Allison's mother can deny or dismiss her, her small body already stilled by the woman's unflinching gaze.

As the girl looks away, she remembers the thin, puny girl who rushed toward her at recess last week while she stood with the other girls in her pale pink coat, a new coat with tiny loops of nubby cloth to make it look furry. Secretly, she called it her princess coat! She was surprised by this flapping creature with dishwater hair and pale blue eyes who clutched at her arm and said happily, "We look alike!"

As she pulled her arm free, she saw that the girl was wearing the very same coat, though it was stained with dirt and little streaks of greasy yellow that matted the loops near the neckline, mashing them flat. Twigs tangled in the girl's hair. She wore boys shoes. One of her ears looked squashed flat.

"We have the same coat," the girl beamed, grinning, pointing back and forth. "We're the same. Just alike."

"We're *not*!" she said quickly. "Yours is dirty." It was her first lesson in the way of the world, of who's above and who's below. Only those Above were allowed to judge. She wanted to push the puny girl away, but the other girls had gone quiet, watching, and so she turned back. "Whose turn?" she said as if they'd been playing a game.

Now my mother can't move, can't speak, and longs suddenly to be home on the back porch with Sweet Child, washing Buster, the suds splattering, flying in the air as the dog shivers and shakes, swishing its tail.

"Sit, dear," Miss Allison says.

But choosing a place to sit is risky business. There's the elegant cream-colored sofa with its high curved back that's already inviting her to trail her fingers along its smoothness. There's the small Victorian chair with its upholstered seat and a larger high-backed chair in soft mauve velvet. Uncertain, she waits for Miss Allison to motion her to a chair where she will sit carefully, crossing her legs at the ankle, prim and quiet, the visit suddenly bewildering, even oppressive.

This, I imagine, was my mother's first encounter with the perverseness of generosity, the kindness of condescension, the compromise and error of performing the self.

She sits.

That night at dinner, she watches the way the mother cuts tiny bites of broiled chicken and lays her knife, blade inward, across the side of her plate. She notices the drops of water glistening at the bottom of her iced tea glass and the slight clinking of ice when she sips. She notices the crease in the linen napkin, the mother occasionally wiping daintily at the side of her mouth. This woman is a mystery. What does she do all day? Does she sit in each chair? Does she lie on the sofa? Does she wash and fold the napkins? Does she stand at the window, tallying the mistakes and idiocies of the people who walk by on the sidewalk? Miss Allison and her mother talk about meeting Eula Pearson at the library tomorrow and about the stands of lilies at Mr. Frederick's funeral. "He was sent away so nicely," the mother says, pressing the napkin again to her lips. "Like a perfect gentleman."

"Which he was," Miss Allison agrees. "He once bought me a chocolate crème when I looked sad."

During a lull in the conversation, the mother glances at her plate. "My goodness, *someone* has an appetite," said in a tightening voice.

She'd expected praise for eating everything on her plate, even the round sweet pickles she doesn't like, just as she's required to do at home. Only now does she notice that Miss Allison and her mother have left small portions of mashed potatoes and the crust of a roll with a smidgen of butter on their plates. Her plate looks as if it's been licked clean. She nods and then politely refuses dessert, generous slices of peach pie, the crust lightly brown, juices bubbling from tiny pricks of a fork, as if denial will even the score.

"I'll run a bath," Miss Allison says after dinner as if it's the most ordinary thing in the world. She stands at the bathroom door, excited as Miss Allison kneels beside the tub, turning a handle, water gushing from the spigot. She's so startled by the sudden flood that she gasps, stepping back. Miss Allison turns her head, grinning, her gums pale pink above small white teeth. "Not too hot, I promise," she says, thinking she's worried about the temperature, not knowing that it's the sheer novelty of the tub that excites her along with the flush toilet like the one at school. "It feels so wonderful to be all clean,"

Miss Allison says breezily, chatting away and then absently brushing her hair and setting the brush on the vanity.

Once alone in the tub, my mother is as regal as a princess in all that lovely warm water. She soaps herself up, making peaks and valleys and saying softly to herself, "I'm not afraid of snakes. I'm not afraid of my brothers. I'm not afraid of being stupid." And then she immerses herself in the water, washing away any dirt or stain or mistakes that might remain. Though she intuits there are other things to be afraid of, other things that will require a cleansing, tonight she is clean enough. Tonight, she is free. While drying off with the white towel, she hears the cheery laugh of Miss Allison, her teacher who has chosen her, claimed her. She eyes the brush, and on impulse, she selects a strand, surprisingly soft, and winds it around her finger for luck. And yet, once in her nightgown, she longs for that piece of pie, wishes she hadn't been so proper, so sacrificing, wishes she could . . . and then she remembers the butterscotch candies piled in a small crystal bowl on the side table beside the sofa. She imagines them being offered to her—"of course, dear"—even as she tiptoes into the room, selecting three and holding them tight in her hand. In bed, she feels happy because of her secret. She will give one piece to Sweet Child and keep the other two for herself.

On the drive home the next morning, they pass Georgia's house, more faded and ramshackle than her own. Georgia is sitting outside, slumped on her porch steps, her face in her hands, the very picture of misery. "Goodness, what's wrong with that woman?" Miss Allison asks. "She looks all worn out."

She thinks of Georgia's face, how her pretty blue eyes—"cornflower blue," her mother calls them—are sometimes framed by bruises, but the girl is too ashamed to admit this to Miss Allison, as if knowing Georgia's story might reflect badly on her. "I don't know," she says, which is also true. To reassure herself, she looks down at her pink furry coat folded in her lap. Her prettiest thing, the candies tucked carefully inside the pocket along with the strand of hair. It's too hot to wear today, but even in her lap, it feels like a prize. Outside the leaves shiver in the breeze. A dog barks as the car passes. Goldenrod blooms in the ditches. Miss Allison begins singing in a whispery soprano as they drive up the hill, *There's a church in the valley by the wildwood/No lovelier place in the dale.* Her voice is soft, calming.

And then, too soon, there it is, her house.

"No spot is so dear to my childhood."

She prays that Sweet Child will be on the steps waiting for her. Though shy and sometimes flustered, Sweet Child makes people want to protect him and, by extension, her.

"As the little brown church in the dale."

But when Miss Allison stops in front of her house, she sees her older brother sprawled across the porch swing. When he sees the car, he jerks upright and saunters to the steps, leaning against the railing, his hair matted with sweat.

"You coming in, Little Miss," he calls out, then turns and spits tobacco juice into the bushes. "Come on in now, and we can play some games."

She blushes, confused and suddenly angry. She looks away, so ashamed of her brother's taunt that instead of properly thanking Miss Allison, she lurches from the car, almost losing her footing and dropping her precious coat, catching it by the sleeve and spilling the candy, the three pieces of butterscotch rolling beneath the front right tire. She wants to reach down and pick them up, but Miss Allison is watching her, a frown puckering her softness. "Well, dear," she says with false brightness. "I'll let you go. I see your brother's waiting for you. I guess he's looking forward to playing with you."

"Yes," she murmurs. "Thank you." And quickly, she steps away from the car, lifting her hand in a wave. She's still waving as the car backs up, the wheels rolling over the candy, pushing the pieces deep into the earth, grit piercing the plastic as if her butterscotch is just another useless piece of rubble, contaminated by the world below. But even as she waves, a kind of rage flares up in her at Miss Allison's ignorance, her kindly unknowing about the lives of girls like her.

"There is no wildwood," she yells as the car disappears down the hill. "There's no church in the vale. There's nothing, nothing."

VI.

Alas, there may be no wildwood, but there will always be Above and Below. Even as a child, I grew up with that simple dichotomy, knowing intuitively, as a child often does, how the distinction plays out in white, small-town culture. Those Below wear cheap clothes, have crooked teeth, and often present themselves with a posturing swagger or a deferential nod. There's Bud McKenzie, a shrimper, waiting patiently outside our back door, whistling under his breath, his jeans sagging, a faded fishing hat on his head, his feet in muddy tennis shoes. "Come on in, Bud, and have some iced tea," my mother says, opening wide the door.

"No, oh, no ma'am, not dressed fur it. Just bringin' you these shrimp."

Or Linda Prochatska pulling her son Pete back from the church door where he'd been folding his church program into an airplane so that my mother could pass, though there was plenty of room. Or Buster McBride shaking his head at the excess of Christmas decorations in my mother's shopping cart. "You thinkin' Santa won't find you this year?"

And yet what I remember most keenly aren't the constraints of Below but the incredible fragilities of Above. Instead of the confident ease of middle-class families I read about in books or saw on TV, my family was circumspect, on guard, alert to every slip in status. Anything could happen! Reversals. Disappointments. Ruin.

Above, I realized, was provisional, slippery, and thus, we had to be impeccable, flawless, avoiding mistakes. Even as a child I understood that uncertainty is incorporated into the story of overcoming, that tenacity must claim the nagging beat of our hearts. I knew that my mother and father had jumped class, had moved from Below to Above, knew that because of their hard work and education, my brother and sister and I had been naturalized into the middle class, slipping in free but with obligations. We had to look and act appropriately. My sister and I wore velvet dresses with white lace collars to concerts in Mobile, listening to someone from somewhere play Liszt and Brahms in a hushed concert hall, or appeared in silk sheaths with single strands of pearls and tiny high heels to watch the Alvin Ailey Dance Troupe perform in Pensacola, their choreographed contortions so exhilarating that I laughed. We had our teeth straightened, our hair styled. We went on a trip to Bon Marche in New Orleans to be properly fitted for brassieres. We depended, as so many had before us, on creating our identity through education and enrichment. Why else sit at the dining room table listening to vocabulary records, endlessly repeating, *"Anomaly. The man in the coonskin cap is an anomaly in the congressional cloakroom"*? That sentence still boomerangs inside my head, calling up the experience of the room, the dimmed chandelier, the pastel aqua carpet spreading out into the living room, the tiny recessed lights above the credenza, my mother calling out to my father from the kitchen, "Oh, Johnnie, please don't use toothpicks. They're so uncouth."

When I look at my mother's pictures from my childhood—perhaps the one from the "Birmingham News" with the heading *"Alabama's Most Gracious Lady"*—I see a woman with a confident, pretty face and elegant posture seated in a 1950s upholstered chair, the very portrait of middle-class ease. She looks as if she's been hustled to dancing and music classes throughout childhood, taught to walk across a mahogany floor with a book, perhaps *Jane Eyre*, balanced on her head, straightening her shoulders and practicing "the walk," as my sister and I did when we imagined being led by the captain and the co-captain of the football team out onto the field to be crowned homecoming queen. How different that picture is from her memories of harsh words, whippings, and family violence.

In our small southern town, we were Above, and yet to our surprise the larger world promised a more intricate caste system, gradations of hierarchy like graveled roads branching into highways, then highways into interstates that circled and sprawled great distances with many exits between Above and Below. Intuitively, we learned to defer to anyone who inherited money and wore the cool gloss of entitlement. "She has an income from timber," my mother whispered to me at a bridal brunch, seeing a woman at the head table in a cream-colored suit take off ivory kid gloves to eat her chicken salad. "Their children have china from *both* sides of the family, china that's been 'put away' for years."

"They have maids full time," she said, once we were home, sitting on the sofa, carefully slipping out of her shoes. "She's never mopped a floor." She rubbed her instep inside her stockinged feet, then went to the kitchen for an ice-cold Coke.

We had maids, but not full time, had china and silver, but not inherited, owned a house, but not land, not timber or beachfront or farmland leased out for soybeans or cotton. We had no accomplished history, no ancestral portraits, no wedding veils passed down from grandmother to mother to daughter. We were Above, but precariously, a threat that terrified and emboldened us, making us ambitious, watchful, intent on accumulating more.

Even as a child, I began to worry. My nerves burned. My fears quickened. I lurched up from sleep, panting, frightened. I got rashes. Headaches. Pimples. Leg aches. Before performances I had panic attacks. What if I didn't win first or second place in a talent show, didn't receive special applause at a dance recital? Just thinking about the possibility, I suffered an avalanche of guilt, a deep, anguished shame. Only distinction mattered. I became withdrawn, a brooder, all those expectations tightening me into a knot. Who was I?

Down deep, I feared I was from nowhere too.

Later, I'd understand nowhere as a metaphor for the invisible, the irrelevant, a trope for the social psyche of those who stand outside of history. Its calling card is duty and shame. For most of my life, I've longed only to slip free, to be clever and immune, standing to the side, neither Above nor Below. And yet lately, I've begun to see nowhere as an opening, a doorway to grasping the weight and worries of my inheritance, my psyche. Directly or symbolically, we writers explore what is done to us, what is done to our families, to our most intimate cultures and thus, inevitably, we become the interpreters of our particular tribe. How could it be otherwise? How could we not mourn and mock and push against the past? Of course, we want more clarity, more recognition and reconciliation for the troubled ways that we've survived. I was meant, I believe, to inhabit a broader, a more capacious space than nowhere, to reside squarely in the middle class, secure and confident, embodying acquisitive appetites. And yet I must have watched too closely, listened too attentively to the nuances of failure while feeling keenly the unfathomable yearning to succeed. Perhaps I was secretly enraptured by my mother's story, the way it seemed to shimmer above us, a transparent cape, never quite visible but always there, a threat, a warning. Or perhaps I saw the wheels rolling over her candy while I stood watching, uncertain what to do.

VII

"I can stand anything," my mother used to proclaim. And I believed her. Nothing could break her. Nothing could cast her back. She'd survived Nowhere. Survived and triumphed and progressed to Somewhere, to new houses and pink bedrooms and gardens overgrown with lacy ferns and yellow roses. Every morning the smell of brewing coffee, of bacon frying, pancakes on the griddle, orange juice in a cut-glass pitcher beneath a window of African violets. She'd left that bad luck hamlet at age sixteen, naive and unprepared, and stepped into the world of college. Having learned early in life the many ways the world can break you, she knew to be vigilant, to listen and watch, to be clever, an inner eye strained open. She noticed shadows, gaps, dark corners, voices in empty air. She would never be seduced by lazy yellow light, by moonlight, by the pull of pleasure.

Perhaps this is why she perches on chairs, never relaxing her guard, always standing at the periphery, listening, waiting.

And yet what eventually breaks her is so sly, so unexpected. It is neither treachery nor humiliation; not a disastrous mess, embarrassing and defaming. Instead, trouble envelopes her like a mist, a fog rolling in from the ocean, subtle and slow, covering the yard, the trees, the azalea bushes, sweeping over a woman walking toward her car. What she'd never expected was invisibility, the vanishing of the self in plain sight, as if she didn't exist, had never been, a contradiction of realities. At age ninety-four, when she goes to the store, she isn't noticed. When she puts her bananas and yogurt and Kleenex on the conveyer belt to be scanned, she isn't seen. When she walks out of the store, pushing her cart with small, tottering steps, she's already vanished, been inexplicably erased, forgotten. And finally that day in March when she falls in the parking lot of Winn-Dixie in the early afternoon, her legs quietly buckling, betraying and surprising her, she isn't the girl from Nowhere who went Somewhere but just an old lady with scraped knees, a purple bruise spreading its hurt across her arm and a blood-filled hematoma rising on her forehead. And in that moment, she lies on the ground, neither watching nor listening, only needing.

VIII.

Some days it hurts to be this close to my mother's life, to write the stories of a child trapped in a family, a history, and a class. And yet there's also a personal pleasure in trying to fit the pieces of her life together, as if I'm blazing a trail of redemption, rhetorically evening the score. Of course, I'm not saving her at all. Quite the contrary. I'm merely using the stories she's told me to imagine a sequence that will make sense to me.

Make sense to me. There's the rub.

"When I think about the past," she tells me one morning at her kitchen table, "I recall what I don't want to recall." There's a sadness in her voice.

Let it go, she seems to be saying.

But I can't. For me, the past isn't just a room crowded with shame and hardship. It's also a story, a place where I can be alone with my mother, where I can hold her hand and imagine the shape of her shifting thoughts. It's the place where I come closest to knowing her.

You Girls

W E WERE ALMOST THERE. AFTER we crossed Fish River Bridge, then passed the migrant workers hauling burlap sacks of potatoes out of the dusty fields and onto flatbed trucks, it was only ten miles to Mama Dot's. Usually when my mother, sister, and I arrived, Mama Dot would be sitting in the green straight-backed chair beside the piano, listening intently as she finished up a lesson with Susie or Trudy or Anne-Marie, or she'd be in the kitchen scraping carrots or mixing organic flour with milk and blackstrap molasses for her molasses cookies, the ones we craved at recitals.

But today—the day I'd slip free of my ordinary life—we raced up the steps, across the screen porch, and through the open door to find Mama Dot slumped on the rattan couch with its faded tangerine cushions, her legs crossed at the ankles, one arm crooked behind her head of cropped gray hair. "You girls come on in," she said, raising her head but not sitting up. She closed her eyes as if retreating to her afternoon nap. "There are cookies in the kitchen, girls. Go on and get yourselves a plate."

From the kitchen we heard Mama Dot talking with our mother, murmuring about stomach cramps and aching breasts, about soiled morning sheets, all things that happened on her "female days," symptoms that made her take to the couch, more resigned than resentful, her face pale, exhaustion circling her eyes with deepening shadows.

As I ate my cookies, I had no premonition that today would be any different from other lessons. I simply stared out the window at the rough woven baskets perched on the mossy brick wall perpendicular to the back door, baskets often full of dried cotton bolls, gray-white hairy pods that were oddly beautiful, or bunches of yellow and purple wildflowers, or old machine parts that Uncle Kenny, Mama Dot's husband, collected. Beyond the wall, pecan trees and fig trees and apple trees rose beside a sprawling vegetable garden and a clothesline strung between two jack pines. And beyond that, a mystery of live oaks and brush known as "the woods."

I knew when we came back into the living room that Mama Dot would be sitting with her knees bunched together and wearing her uniform of olive or khaki Bermuda shorts (earth tones, though we wouldn't have used that word back then) and a knit shirt—not a T-shirt—with a small, rounded collar that lay limp against her collarbones. Always she wore brown, lace-up orthopedic shoes that made her look sturdy and sensible, as if she'd cast aside frivolous things—high heels and open-toed sandals and even flip-flops—for more solid footing. Though I wouldn't have said so back then, it seemed to me she'd cast aside femininity as well—or at least the florid femininity that held sway in the 1950s South, where women favored dresses that revealed a swell of breasts and hips, tapered skirts that fit snug over firm, girdled buttocks (I almost wrote "butt," but we wouldn't have used that word either). Mama Dot never wore girdles or stockings or plunging necklines, never put on lipstick or mascara or rolled her hair. Her hair, cut short with a thicket of bangs like Mamie Eisenhower's, accented her high cheekbones and fierce hazel eyes. And yet I knew she was beautiful, not because of her fine, chiseled features—the aquiline nose, the clean arched brows beneath a high forehead, the small bud of a mouth—but because of the intensity of her gaze: those alert, penetrating eyes that said, "I *see* you. I see what no one else can see."

After our mother left, Mama Dot made a cup of tea, and we started our lesson as if the "female days" had never been, as if only music and pleasure held sway, the downstairs windows opened wider, the smell of honeysuckle and lemon in the air, the small piano light turned on. I know this can't be so . . . and yet in my memory the adult world was instantly swept away and we girls claimed center stage, gabbing easily to Mama Dot about our day at school, telling stories about the neighbor's runaway beagle, about Mrs. Peak's hissy fit over commas, about some serious but baffling dream that had lifted the roof off the house. After our stories, Mama Dot settled into her green chair and I sat at the piano, warming up with scales and arpeggios, my mind sinking down into my fingers, my body humming, then still. Beside me, Mama Dot crossed one leg and leaned toward me, listening. Once I'd finished my scales, she picked out a piece of music—maybe Debussy, maybe Liszt or Brahms—and placed it on the piano rack. For a moment we both stared at the notes. "Notice the adagio here," she said, pointing to a notation on the passage. "Let yourself feel that, the slowness"—she leaned closer—"like sitting in the dark during a summer rain."

And I'd think about that. I'd imagine the dark, the close heat of the air, the rain not heavy or wild but slow, steady, a drizzle that blurred the windows and softened the air. I imagined putting my head lightly against the window. A secret quiet.

I began to play.

And yet today, this day, something else happened. Something unexpected. After my sister and I had both finished our lessons, Mama Dot went out to the kitchen to get another cup of tea and a plate of sliced apples, and when she came back I could feel the change, the air charged, her face flushed with excitement. "I'm feeling better," she said, a smile pushing at her lips. "You girls are making me better." And even as I took a handful of apple slices, I sensed an idea forming, a destiny about to be revealed. We were the girls, her students, the ones she loved, the ones she imagined would someday burst out of our cocoons, our heads filled with remarkable, even magical ideas even though we'd been raised to be well-rounded and well-groomed, to observe the proprieties, to write thank-you notes and get-well cards and prove our competence on standardized tests. We were meant to get straight As, to obey authority and not make a mess.

"Let's try something new," Mama Dot said, her eyes brightening. "Let's not be bound by the ordinary." And then she looked at me. Freckles dusted my nose. My hair billowed, a halo of smoke. I was nine years old, small and skinny with tiny feet and big front teeth. I didn't smile much. I often came to my music lesson from my dance class, dressed in my black leotard with its three thready runs down the front. "You have such natural grace," Mama Dot said, taking my hand and holding it lightly. "Let's put you on top of the piano and have you improvise while Jean plays."

I must have looked uncertain, even scared, as she closed the top of the baby grand so that it lay smooth and flat and polished, no more than five feet at its widest. I wasn't bold. I wasn't a show-off. I liked spelling words but not spelling bees. I didn't like the mad dash to the board to compete in an arithmetic problem, anxiety scratching at my ribs. I thought of myself as lurking in the shadows, someone who liked to watch. I *wanted* to be bold. I lusted after the limelight, but the strategy of getting there baffled me, left me hugging tight to my knees.

"Here, we'll get a chair and I'll help you up." Mama Dot was suddenly decisive. Her eyes narrowed as if sizing me up, and then they softened, her lips parting as if in anticipation. I could feel something new let loose in the air. *I would dance on the piano.*

I was surprised by my own excitement.

"Just get a feel for it," she said as I slipped off my shoes and climbed on the chair, then onto the piano. "I won't let you fall."

The height felt huge. If I reached up, really stretched, I could touch the ceiling. When I looked out the window, I saw squirrels scampering across a neighbor's roof, watched a dark bird soar high into the pale white sky, slowly disappearing from view. Then I stared at my sister's hands with the clipped fingernails, small and white on the keys. Mama Dot smiled and my sister began to play a Chopin ballad. As in dance class, I pliéd, my body sinking, rising. I gazed with surprise at my knees, at how easily they bent and straightened, as elastic as rubber bands. I turned slowly—a ballerina's turn—spotting the clock above the fireplace, never breaking my gaze as I'd been trained. And then I lifted one leg in an arabesque, balancing carefully as if I were a figure in a tableau, a pretty girl in a music box. When I glanced down at Mama Dot, she nodded, her dark eyebrows rising in approval as if she were proud of me but also proud of her own inventiveness, the risk of doing something adventurous, even a little crazy, something no other music teacher would do. I knew this was a whim, a fancy, and simultaneously an opening, a prelude to something more. I looked at the top of Mama Dot's gray head, at the slight fold of flesh beneath my sister's T-shirt, and some tension inside me shifted. A quiver at first; the sweating of my bare foot against the wood. And then suddenly I felt as if I were swaying in midair, not flailing or trembling but needing a new center of gravity. Quickly, I folded myself down to a squat, both feet close together, my hands touching the piano, my heart wildly beating, my shoulder blades tightening like newly clipped wings. When I closed my eyes, I imagined one foot slipping over the edge, my body held by nothing but air. Who would catch me? Who would . . . ?

I shivered.

But when I opened my eyes, Mama Dot gazed at me as if this too were simply part of the improvisation, this pause, this uncertainty, this private fear. *This too*, her eyes seemed to affirm, *will make you stronger*. I looked beyond her to the wisteria blooming outside the open window, bursts of lavender pushing against the glass, a bee lazily buzzing. The world going on. Without thinking, I slid one leg out behind me, the other forward until my body bisected the piano in a split, my torso floating above. For a moment I forgot to think, aware only of my body, my legs resting on polished wood as sound vibrated beneath me, my toes warm and weightless in the sunlight, my eyes almost closed. When I looked again at Mama Dot, her own head was tilted, watching, and then very quietly, she nodded with a look of such intense pleasure, I instinctively raised my arms, curving them in a circle above my head, the fingers not quite touching.

Who was she, this maverick teacher, this confident, eccentric woman: a music teacher whose fame spread no more than sixty miles in any direction? For four years, we drove twenty-five miles three times a week from our small farm town with its three dinky traffic lights to Fairhope, Alabama, where Mama Dot taught us music and theory—summers included—though it wasn't just music and theory that we learned. Instead, she became a part of our lives, part of the story we told about ourselves, a point of view we embraced because of her particular history, her particular troubles, her essential grasp of possibility.

"Dot had push," her ninety-one-year-old sister Helen tells me many years later, after Mama Dot's death. "People always said I had talent, but Dot had push. She had a strong character like my mother." As Helen talks, I think about that word, "push," a word I like so much better than ambition because it implies grit, a private desire nudged by both longing and defiance. *Push.* Some people have it. Other people don't. Though it seems as simple as that—drive, intensity, intent—I know it's not. In some ways, talent is less interesting, if only because it's always discussed as a given, something one "has," not by accomplishment but by possession, an entitlement as mysterious as grace. But grit straightens the spine, stiffens the jaw, deepens the crease lines around the eyes even as it rivets the gaze.

I look at a picture Helen shows me of Mama Dot sitting on a piano bench in front of a restored upright piano at the Organic School Museum in

Fairhope, a picture taken when Mama Dot was in her late seventies or early eighties. She's wearing a white tailored dress (the first dress I've ever seen her in), and she looks regal and fierce and proud, that chiseled chin tilted upward, those hazel eyes that neither flinch nor stray, a queen in her own country, accepting her due. But of course, she didn't start out that way. Or did she?

According to Helen, her parents, Mr. and Mrs. Beiser, moved from Chicago in 1917 to Fairhope, Alabama, after hearing the educator, Marietta Johnson, speak only once about "her grand experiment with organic education."

Only once? I think. But why should it surprise me, a family picking up and moving a thousand miles because of the ardor of one speech? I remember Mama Dot returning from the kitchen with her cup of tea, her face flushed with possibility, an idea igniting in her head.

"Mother was ambitious and sophisticated," Helen says in her soft, confiding voice. "She ruled the roost. If she wanted to move to Fairhope, we moved."

I know from my reading that Marietta Johnson, a zealous high school teacher from St. Paul, Minnesota, opened a small progressive school in Fairhope in 1907 based on an egalitarian pedagogy and philosophy aligned with John Dewey's belief that "education is growth." And I try to imagine *that* Fairhope in the early twentieth century: a small utopian town set on the red bluffs of Mobile Bay populated with bohemians and farmers and fishermen and artists and ordinary tradespeople who believed in the cooperative experiment of the economist, Henry George, that land must be common property, not private property. Amazing! "Fairhope was a community built on the idea that American society must be *shaken up*, wrested from its old fetters and given a new direction," Paul Gaston, historian and emeritus professor at University of Virginia, wrote in his book on Fairhope. And he should know. His grandfather, disgusted with the excesses of the Gilded Age, led a group of Midwesterners to Fairhope in the 1890s to begin this socialist experiment in, of all unlikely places, the Deep South, a place where *shaken up* didn't yet include African Americans.

Helen tells me her parents bought a grocery store in Fairhope and leased six acres of land from the Fairhope Association where they built a house, where they had horses, a cow, a chicken yard, and a garden. "When sugar was rationed during the war, Mother gave it away," Helen says with obvious pride, her eyes behind her bifocals dark and blinking. "She believed in fresh vegetables." And I remember Mama Dot always pushing us toward a plate of carrots and celery and apples and cookies made only with molasses or honey at a time when we craved Nutty Buddies and Devil Dogs, when white sugar lined every middle-class cupboard.

I settle back on the wicker love seat beside Helen and gaze past the jack pines and palmettos to the bay. Sometimes I think it all circles back to the mother. A mother with push. A mother who believes in a radical education. A mother with a strong will, who says, "*Let's go.*" But if that were the only requirement, then Helen too would have been ambitious and demanding, driven in the same way as Mama Dot. And Helen freely admits that she wasn't. "Oh, goodness, I liked to dance. I liked to have too much fun," she says, smiling such a girlish smile I imagine her entertaining beau on the veranda while, inside, Mama Dot sat at the piano, playing a Chopin nocturne.

Perhaps the difference is that Mama Dot had two mothers, two mentors, two high priestesses with visionary passion, two women with big ideas and a great deal of confidence who claimed and mentored her. Certainly, the biological mother encouraged and supported Mama Dot's musical interests. "I used to ask Mother why she didn't make Dot clean up the kitchen or set the table," Helen tells me. "'Dot's practicing,' she'd say and that was that."

Weeks later, I visit the Marietta Johnson Museum with its oiled, wooden floors, its noisy ceiling fans and wide school-teacher desks. I can almost smell the chalk dust in the air, hear the creak of wood as the windows are raised to let in fresh air. I stare at a framed picture of Marietta Johnson, a pleasant-looking woman with soft folds of dark hair, dressed in a Victorian-style dress and seated with a book on her lap on the lawn beside her students. In article after article, I read that she was charismatic and charming, a driven, resourceful woman, and I know she was a teacher and a model for Mama Dot, who attended Organic School from the ages of four to eighteen, then took two years of teacher training under Mrs. Johnson's supervision. And yet I confess that Marietta Johnson never becomes quite real to me; she's all ideas and early morning energy, and I want to see her laughing—a burst of jovial hilarity—or gently teasing a friend, slippery and soft-voiced and smiling. I like to think of her as a straight shooter, a woman who had the gift of oratory, a grand, even riveting, public voice, but also a woman who liked to tell stories about her teaching in St. Cloud, Minnesota, while kneeling in the garden, pulling weeds. What seems clear is that to Marietta Johnson, education wasn't a means to an end but a natural form of enjoyment, a personal discovery. She might help the older students present Shakespeare's *As You Like It* on Friday night and take them sailing the next day on the catamaran her husband had built. She didn't believe in grades or rewards or recognition for success or punishment for failure—no carrots, no sticks—but in improvisation and passion without all the standardized hoopla of report cards. She refused even to send reports of any child's progress to parents, believing such things interfered with the "sincerity and unself-consciousness of the child."

"Every child had a garden, in which he planted what he pleased and as he pleased; he cultivated it or not as he pleased," she says in one of her articles, suggesting that individual motivation was the real ticket to learning. She started the first kindergarten in Alabama, and it's been said that children could climb out the windows and splash about in the wading pool. Whether true or not, the thought makes me laugh and secretly long for a childhood education that emphasized such spontaneity. Johnson believed that education should be joyous. Not permissive. That's a different thing entirely, implying lack of supervision. What she practiced and taught was the development of each individual child.

One child she literally rescued. A ten-year-old boy ran wild in town, a boy whose father had died and whose mother was bedridden with TB, a boy the city fathers wanted to pack off to reform school before Mrs. Johnson interceded, determined to save this rambunctious child.

And here, I think, is the knitting together and unraveling of Mama Dot's life. While a student at Organic School, Mama Dot would fall in love with the wild, orphaned boy who had been saved by Marietta Johnson, the beautiful boy who would grow into a wild, beautiful man, his face framed by a thatch of blond hair, his blue eyes alive with pleasure as if the word had been invented just for him. He adored Marietta Johnson, this woman who had rescued him from truancy, who had seen something special about him, had noticed his uncanny ability with machines and tools, his intuitive understanding of mechanical structure. She took him to the school's industrial shop run so competently by her husband, a place where the boy could tinker and learn to build and repair to his heart's content. I imagine that at age eighteen or nineteen,

Mama Dot—like most of us—saw only a glorious future: love and work and family and pleasure. Hadn't Mrs. Johnson started a school in Fairhope, then another in Greenwich, Connecticut, toured the country as a lecturer and fundraiser, and managed a happy marriage and family? Hadn't Mama Dot learned from Marietta Johnson to make her own decisions, to follow as often as possible the logic of the heart, even when that meant disobeying her family's wishes by marrying the orphan boy, the one so close to their teacher, the one who understood machines, who liked whiskey, whose particular skills would take years to come to fruition? This too—risking her mother's disapproval—might have given Mama Dot the "push" she relied on for the rest of her life, a determination to follow the insistence of her thoughts. The writer and critic Carolyn G. Heilbrun once hypothesized that some "gifted women unconsciously and indirectly take power over their lives by committing an 'outrageous act,' a social sin that frees them from the constraints of conventional society and its expectations—defying parents, rejecting religion, leaving a marriage." Or, I would add, agreeing to one. Maybe this man's hand on her thigh both softened and emboldened Mama Dot. Maybe this defiance tapped into a deeper, more elemental energy.

As a girl, I didn't yet know that it's often the shape and handling of adversity that structures a life: what doors swing open or slam shut, where the eye lights and the mind tilts when surprise saunters into the room. Adversity, like sudden good luck, is often a balancing act, the fear of falling as you sway and stiffen and flutter your hands. For Marietta Johnson, the first disaster came in the death of her second son, a lively toddler who died from a freak accident. And then, within months, her Fairhope benefactor suffered a fatal stroke. Devastated, Mrs. Johnson—after months of grieving—found recourse and sanity only in work. "Work was the best antidote," she said, taking on more and more obligations, pushing herself because she needed to and could. For Mama Dot, the first fevered slip also came with her second son: At age ten, he was diagnosed with a brain tumor, benign and operable but resulting in epilepsy, in grand mal seizures, in life on the edge. To complicate matters, her husband—that lovely boy-now-man—turned to alcohol, drinking heavily in his workshop, sequestered and unholy, tools rusting on the shelves. He lost his job. He drank. He was probably deeply depressed. For Mama Dot, I imagine every day required a new vigilance as her son's seizures worsened, as more doctors were consulted, as more money was needed. I imagine her husband withdrawing, silently seething at all their blighted promise. I imagine fights and recriminations and quick, ardent reconciliations. And then when the son began to improve, Mama Dot collapsed, went quiet and still. Months later, when she rose from her bed, she sat down at the piano and played Bach and Beethoven and Schumann late into the evening, letting all that sadness work its way through her fingers, letting pleasure loose in her veins. And then one day, she moved to the green chair and pulled out stacks of music, inviting her students to come back.

The world goes on.

She turned her energy, that penetrating gaze, on her students. I was one of the girls who came to her during this period, when one world had ended and another had begun, a world that brought a different kind of wisdom and a silent vigilance. Perhaps she *saw* me, saw an orphaned psyche, a child running amok. Perhaps she sensed not talent but desire, a barely visible hunger. Or perhaps she sensed my confusion: how deeply I'd internalized my mother's need for safety and status, for a beautiful house and female virtue, and how uncertain I was that this would be my fate. Years later, Mama Dot would remind me of a confession: One afternoon I admitted I felt like myself only before sleep. I don't remember it. I must have said it quietly, feeling ashamed, staring down at the piano keys, my hands in my lap. Perhaps that thought had spawned her later impulse to put me on top of the piano. I imagine she said, "Don't worry, just see what happens," knowing that a child doesn't simply drop the burden of a conflicted self but that given a chance to play she might momentarily lose her self-consciousness, might relax to pleasure and discover an intuitive boldness.

As a child, I couldn't have said that I longed for adult support, would have felt ashamed of my craven need for attention. I certainly didn't know the word "mentor," nor could I have said that I—like most girls—needed two mothers, needed not just the smart, curious biological mother who worried about my well-being and my education but also the artistic, liberated woman who disliked hierarchy and fancy privileges, who allowed big, loose enthusiasms to carry the day. It wasn't that Mama Dot made me feel differently about myself but that she made me think that someday I *might* feel differently about myself.

And then suddenly, after four years, our music lessons stopped as abruptly as they had begun. Uncle Kenny, Mama Dot's husband, was diagnosed with TB and sent to a sanatorium, and Mama Dot insisted her focus must now be devoted entirely to him. Miraculously, it was in the sanatorium that this man had the time and the encouragement to design what he'd always longed to build: a telescope. I imagine the ghost of Marietta Johnson sitting quietly, attentively in his room, nodding her approval as she tucks a gray hair back into her bun and watches his progress. Two years later, Uncle Kenny and Mama Dot traveled the country in an old camper, marketing the telescope he'd designed along the coasts of Florida and California. They formed a business that in ten years would become wildly successful.

I don't remember much about the day of the recital. I know I was nervous. Even thinking about it now, I can feel my throat tighten, my breath catch. I can feel the heat of a summer day, the heavy weight of the air on my fair skin. But I don't remember if I wore the black leotard with its scooped neck and long sleeves and the three thready pulls down the front or even the black ballet slippers with their scuffed heels and tight pleated front that covered and curved around my toes. I don't remember what piece my sister played, whether it was a Chopin prelude or something lighter, maybe Tchaikovsky or Mozart. I don't remember the students who were there, sitting on cushions on Mama Dot's floor, cross-legged and hot and anxious about their own prepared pieces. I don't even remember Mama Dot, where she sat or how she introduced my sister and me, how I must have climbed—with her help—up onto the piano. What I remember is only a single thought as I stood on the piano, my heart beating wildly, my hair curling in the humid air, a single thought that calmed me enough to make my arms and legs move. I don't know why this thought came to me, why my mind reached into last year's memory and saw Mama Dot walking beside a group of us girls out into the blue-gray water of Mobile Bay, Mama Dot in her plain cotton bathing suit with its wide straps and boxy legs, her face tilted toward the sun. The tide was so low we could wade far out into the bay, past the end of the piers with their rusting crab traps and barnacled pilings. It seemed we might go on forever, the cool, clear water rising to our knees, then our thighs, then the bottoms of our bathing suits. Mama Dot looked at me. She smiled. The next minute she dove into the water, slipping into another world as if called there by invisible gods. I stopped, waiting, aware of the water glistening and still, the sun emerging from behind white, drifting clouds. When Mama Dot surfaced ten or twelve feet away, she turned, her hair slicked back, her white neck rising stalklike from the sea. Her voice called to us, exhilarated, impatient. "C'mon, girls. What are you waiting for?"

The "Orig"

WHEN THE CURTAIN OPENS, SHE lingers at the edge of the stage, half-smiling, half-musing as if surprised by a pleasant thought. Perhaps a hot fudge cake waiting on the kitchen counter. Perhaps the final chapter of *Exodus* still to be read. Perhaps the memory of green-eyed Mark Trevor sneaking into Ivy's party, two bottles of beer tucked inside his coat pocket. Before her the grand piano gleams, its mahogany finish polished to a high gloss except for the scarred, slender legs and the stubby ankles trapped in dust. No matter. She'll play Chopin. The audience will politely applaud. And then she'll escape into the cool, dark night, feeling reckless and triumphant, ready to heap chocolate-chip ice cream into a big, crystal bowl.

She is fifteen.

She turns once to glance at the audience: students from her classes, neighbors and friends of her parents, teachers and principals and teacher's aides and PTA members, and all the little kids who couldn't find anything better to do on a Friday night than to be dragged to a high school talent show. *Geez! Not even popcorn!* She sits at the piano, looking down at the keys, so familiar, so ordinary, little poker-faced whites and blacks. But as she lifts her hands to begin the Chopin étude that will put Mr. Crenshaw, the State Farm Insurance man, and Lila Schneebaugh, his secretary, and all the bored football players to sleep, she freezes. Her smile vanishes. Her right foot, near the pedal, goes numb. Her brain, usually crammed with colliding ideas, remains empty and still. *Just like that* she can't remember the first notes to be played, notes she's practiced endlessly, played with both ardor and abandon, half singing to herself, *mmmh-mmmh-mmmh*, as she leaned into a feeling as sharp and light and transparent as summer air. Now, the notes have tiptoed out the door and she's stuck here on this hard piano bench, her thighs sweating beneath the pretty aqua sheath her mother just bought at Raphael's. She lifts her head higher, like a child drowning. Someone coughs in the audience. Someone yells out "Hey!" as if she needs a reminder that, well, people are *waiting*.

She thinks of a tooth wiggling loose in her mouth in first grade . . . the surprise of it. She thinks of the small naked baby, its feet turning blue, its breathing thin and labored, that she saw in the ER with her father last week. Nothing is certain. Nothing can be counted on. Nothing except that she's here, onstage, sitting absolutely still in front of everyone she knows. She shivers, then steadies herself, and before she can think another thought, she stands to her full height and faces the crowd. "I'm going to *play* this thing," she says, and she brings her right hand down fast and hard, slapping the keys as if *they* are the offenders.

Shocked, the audience goes silent, and then a ripple of laughter.

She laughs too, and before all the laughter slips away, she sits down and plays the Chopin étude as if she is back home in her living room, alone and enthralled by how the melody flickers and holds, how the touch of her little finger feels like a bird's wing brushing the keys.

Almost forty-five years later, she's walking behind me with the little dog, the one always sniffing ice plants and barking at seabirds. I plunge ahead with Bud, the half-crazed lab mix who runs toward the sea. Following him, I rush into the waves, white foam lacing my ankles as he romps in the shallow water, then turns in lazy circles. When I look back, my sister's a still life: woman and dog on the beach, staring at the sand. But then she glances up and laughs, her hair blown up in a short, gray ruff. She's been sick lately, her hips aching, and now walks slower than I do. I'm yanked around by Bud, who's spied a sand crab scuttling out of its hole, but I pull on his leash, holding him still until my sister and the little dog catch up. Together, we walk on, the dogs between us, a southwest wind caressing our backs.

Inside her beach house once again, she dusts sand off her feet and picks up a book before I've even unleashed Bud and gone to the bathroom. And this is the way I remember her: lying on the couch or the bed, a book propped up in her lap. In our girlhood room, books sat in uneven piles on the floor, in stacks on the dresser beneath socks and underwear, in boxes pushed up against the closet, and in the car, sometimes on the seat, usually on the floor with gum wrappers and flip-flops and broken pencil stubs. In 1965, books arrived in a plain cardboard box from Duke University addressed to Miss Jean Foster: books by John Updike, Graham Greene, Flannery O'Connor, Albert Camus, Arthur Miller, a freshman reading list—insight wrapped in the ordinary, tragedy hidden in the cautionary tale. I can close my eyes and still see her lying on our queen-size bed in khaki shorts and a T-shirt reading *Rabbit Run*, her eyes barely blinking as she followed Harry Angstrom from the sweaty basketball court into the dark, predatory hall.

"How is it?" I asked.

She didn't look up. I slouched down beside her and picked up a book of my own.

In the afternoon, we sit in rocking chairs on the deck, sipping hot coffee. We're on the bay side of the beach house where a sultry light reflects off the water, the tips of the sea oats almost silvery in the glare. The little dog is sleeping inside, but Bud lies between us, his tail thumping. He's hoping we'll throw the slimy tennis ball lying near his front paws so he can lope across the deck and retrieve it.

"Don't even think it," I tell him. But occasionally we relent. We drink coffee. Everybody's happy.

It's one of those lazy days, the sky blue except for wispy scarves of white. I've driven to Alabama from Iowa City where I teach English at the university, and Jean has taken three days off from her medical practice to meet me here. Sometimes a car ambles down the road that separates the house from the sand dunes, but mostly it's quiet except for the distant cries of gulls, dark shadows in a September sky.

I don't know why I ask my sister about her four years at Duke University in the late 1960s, the years she majored in music, the years she rarely talks about or talks about in digressions as if the point is to confuse and distract. Maybe it's because this is the first time we've been together in a decade with no agenda (no wedding, birthday, Christmas celebration, graduation, hospitalization, or funeral) other than to make ourselves happy. Maybe because

Duke was the first place that separated us, the first place she ventured out all alone.

During high school, it seemed we were always together, reading in our beds or racing Mother's car down the two-lane blacktop in the late afternoon, thick heat rising from the potato fields, the sawgrass almost white in the estuaries near Mobile Bay. We went to music lessons, dancing lessons, writing lessons, movies, concerts, bakeries, dress shops, pizza parlors, shoe barns, anything lively that bound us together, that gave us a thrill or a competitive edge. Back then I thought of her not only as my older sister but as the *original* smart girl, the one who set the terms, the tone, the thrust for what we were meant to be, the one who was so talented and determined, it never dawned on me she could ever fail. Whenever I'd mutter to myself, *think fast, think fast*, I'd conjure her image beneath a cartoon bubble of flashing light bulbs, their beams brightening. If someone had asked me what I meant by smart, I'd probably have ticked off the usual things: National Merit Scholar, National Science Foundation Scholarship, valedictorian, while thinking *that's not it at all!* For years, I believed it was because she sat close to the family nervous system, her fingers on our pulse, her eyes narrowed in concentration as if she, and only she, could perceive our fate. But that wasn't it either. She wasn't a seer or a prophet. She was funny and quick but also impulsive, undisciplined, and totally incapable of keeping secrets. "I shouldn't tell you this," she'd lean across the table, eyes shiny with forbidden knowledge. Then she'd pause as if for effect, picking up a brownie and stuffing it in her mouth. She liked to eat too. "But you got tapped for National Honor Society even though you bombed on that chemistry test."

What I understand now is that early in life she learned to trust herself, to shake off intrusive influences, following the path of her instincts through numerous open doors. "I want this," she'd say, and turn toward it (whatever it was), grab it, and give it a close-up scan. If she wanted to lie on the couch reading *A Tale of Two Cities* instead of going swimming at Pirate's Cove with the other girls, she'd nestle down at one end of the brown sofa with a coke and a blanket and mutter, "Leave me alone." If I told her those new glasses with the rhinestone fins were "freakin' ugly," she'd push them further up the bridge of her nose, dimpling and saying "I love them!" If she went utterly blank onstage—as she did at fifteen—she'd fess up and get on with it as if she knew the score because she'd decided it. Alone. A decision burrowed deep inside.

Now how did that happen?

For a long time, I believed the gods simply favored her, giving her an enormous appetite and a sheltering wit, stuffing her head chock-full of ideas. In contrast, I often felt cautious, constrained. While she turned the pages of *Life* magazine, gazing at photos of the Eiffel Tower or Audrey Hepburn or fly-covered orphans, pot-bellied and starving in Sudan, I sat watching her, pale, nocturnal, at loose ends. As a child, I chose gray socks as if already claiming a metaphor.

But of course, it was never that simple, that much of a cliché. In the end, I was the one who needed the wild scent of new places, the one who slipped away, hungry for more and more and more. And yet I have a vivid memory of my sister sitting beside a group of girls at a softball game, her head bent over a book as a batter's foul ball rose, spinning in the air, and then landed—smack!—in her lap, knocking her book to the ground. "What?" she gasped, as if she'd been hit by a meteor. The whole grandstand burst into laughter. But she didn't get it. She just didn't get it. "Where's my book?" she said, staring frantically into the damp, rough grass below. "What happened to my book?"

When I look back at childhood and adolescence, she seemed—already—set apart.

We are eleven and twelve and getting ready for a piano recital at Mama Dot's house. We have a thirty-minute drive to Fairhope, the place of the recital, and as I sit in the front seat beside my mother, terrified of performing, panic scratches at my throat.

Outside, a stark, creeping light brightens the soybean and cotton fields, a checkerboard green and white landscape that goes on for miles and miles. My only relief is seeing the rising crest of Fish River Bridge above the pale skirt of water that flares out toward the horizon. Sawgrass and bamboo crowd the shore. A few crippled piers jut haphazardly out into the bay. I fix my eyes on the water, on its endlessness. I imagine opening the door and throwing myself out, out into the air, the heat, the blur of water—anywhere to escape the recital to come. While I'm fretting, my sister's in the back seat with our neighbor Susie, who's also in the recital. When I turn to look at them, my sister's exploding with laughter, her arms clutching her stomach, dark hair falling into her face while Susie's eyes are squinted shut as if she's trying to button down the hysteria. *They're going berserk*, I think. And I want to go there too.

Twenty minutes later, my sister sits quietly before the black and white keys, her eyes nearly closed, her body shockingly calm. Softly, she begins a Beethoven sonata, fingers floating across the keyboard as she leans into the music, leaving the room, the students, behind. I glance quickly at Mama Dot, our music teacher and our guide to intensity and obsession, the world of aesthetics. Mama Dot sits to the left of the piano, watching, lips compressed, her hawk-gaze following the music and the girl playing the music, knowing the two can never be separated, never wrestled apart. Outside, the sky is blue with white, sagging clouds. A hot breeze sweeps through the open windows and our legs stick together on the chairs and cushions, the sweat cooling our underarms. When my sister finishes, she doesn't move. She only gazes out the window at the purple blooms of wisteria brushing against the glass. And then she smiles at me.

But I don't smile back. Playing the piano fulfills no private longing, opens no secret grace note inside my head. It's simply something to be done, scales, arpeggios, the smooth progression of notes, something I must do to please my family, to round out the "idea" of me. Though performing terrifies me, it never occurs to me to say, "No, I won't!" I'm too caught up in doing the right thing.

My sister seems oblivious to doing the right thing. She eats too much. She talks too much. She argues too much. She pees too much. She doesn't even like to run her own bathwater but tries to get into the tub with me when I turn away to add more hot water. I feel her creeping toward me, her body hunched. "Get away!" I yell, kicking at her with a dripping foot.

"Selfish," she yells back, then stands up straight, wrapping herself in a towel and leaving me in peace. She'll probably forget to take a bath. It's happened before. She'll wander into the kitchen, sneaking a brownie, picking up a book.

That's the way I remember her, blurring the boundaries, resisting the rules, sometimes insistently, sometimes unintentionally as she did in seventh grade, the only girl who danced with the Pinhead, thinking that, well, surely, he was lonely. Of course, he wasn't really a Pinhead, just a boy, Walter, whose head was dented in on one side, a boy left alone, avoided, known to be "slow." That year, her blouses came untucked and her bangs hung crooked, too long at one end, waving in the middle. She wore braces over bunched-together teeth, gleaming silver wires tightened by tiny, clinical rubber bands.

I try to imagine the day, a late afternoon, a slight drizzle from the overcast sky. It is October, and Mrs. Newman, the seventh grade teacher, has planned square dancing for PE, telling the students to push back their desks and "pair up." To Mrs. Newman, who still has the taste of onion in her mouth from the tuna salad at lunch, dancing is mere exercise, a release of excess energy, not physical contact. "Pair up!" Mrs. Newman commands again, clapping her hands together as she looks benignly at her students' oily foreheads, their sharp elbows and pointy knees. Nobody notices when my sister heads toward Walter, who stands alone near the back windows, the glass already fogged and streaked with rain, but miraculously she's in front of him, holding out her hand. What can he do? Usually he dances with Mrs. Newman, who's like holding a thick cushion, but now my sister is before him. Of course, she's not the most popular girl in class. Not like the blonde beauties with their deep blue eyes, their cheerleader legs, but she's there, her wavy brown hair falling to her shoulders, her plaid, pleated skirt just above her knees, her white blouse hanging loose in the back. I imagine a silence humming inside his body, a soundless ocean that could easily drag him down. For a moment he stands there, frightened, uneasy, and then suddenly he takes her hand, pretending she's Mrs. Newman with a bag over her head.

Perhaps we all put bags over our heads in the early 1960s, those years crammed tight with positive thinking, with ranch-style houses and cream-colored station wagons, with Maytag washing machines and dryers and upward mobility—for white folks, that is. Though the Cold War fixed its angry eye on Washington and from there radiated a turbulent fear of bombs and war and radiation sickness, we still had our milk and mail delivered, still crowned the annual beauty queen and the homecoming court, still had dramatic storms in early September with wild winds and floods, the pine trees snapping beneath a hot, yellow sky while the ground, saturated with water, rose alarmingly, almost to our doorsteps. There might be the Bay of Pigs fiasco, the Cuban Missile Crisis, and the beginning of the Vietnam War, but in our town, politics and history seemed as far away as Katmandu.

And yet our household was anything but tranquil. We meant to outrun ordinary life, to push past the slowpokes, the dawdlers, the TV watchers, the couch-sitters, rushing forward if not necessarily upward, eternally busy, always on the move.

After our dancing lessons in Mobile—where we performed tour jetés and plies in a large, mirrored room overlooking Government Street, then front walkovers and back flips in the lush spring grass outside—my sister and I inhaled a pizza in the back seat of the car or feasted on sloppy meatball sandwiches followed by a sticky pastry we called "elephant ears" or thick slices of German chocolate cake, the gooey icing dripping between our fingers. My mother drove along the causeway, the bay dark and silent, until finally we were on the narrow back roads hemmed in by pastures, an hour to our house. We ate in the car so we'd be ready to do our homework as soon as we pulled into our driveway.

Though we didn't know much about the larger world, we were hell-bent on getting there, excited by the college catalogues my sister collected— Antioch, Sarah Lawrence, Yale, Duke, Emory, Mary Washington, Northwestern —thick, smooth, reassuring catalogues with glossy pages of happy coeds eating apples on a grassy quad or chatting with other girls in front of the library. My sister spread these out on our bed as if the pages contained magic. Maybe they did. They represented, in fact, the future that would tilt and press her life into a new shape, a shape that darkened but also deepened her philosophy of self.

"Duke," my sister says now, watching Bud gnaw on the tennis ball. He bites down, attacking it with gusto as if it's a new and surprising activity. "Oh, God, it was such a surprise to me. I couldn't wait to get there. None of the girls from Mobile got accepted, but *I* did." She smiles, nodding with pride. "But I had no idea what a private college would be like, and I registered for courses based on what Elsa Britain (a retired doctor's wife who'd gone to Stevens College) said I should take: logic, French, biology, English Literature, and European history."

I can't bring Elsa Britain into focus, but I remember the day my sister left, how we all stood around her, eating the leftover popovers Mother had made for breakfast, excited and anxious and exasperated with the reality of her leaving, wanting and not wanting her to go. Of course, I knew she'd do well, would become a star, and as she waved goodbye, she grinned, flashing a victory sign.

"Those choices," my sister rolls her eyes, "I mean, *those courses* were a disaster. *Total.* French? I'd never studied French, but I was in classes with girls who'd had at least two or three years of high school French and vacationed in Paris. Logic? *That* was a mistake. But I didn't know who to turn to for help. Who could I have turned to?"

I know what she means. We'd attended small-town public schools, southern schools known for their unremarkable academic achievement, schools where sports demanded more loyalty than scholarship, where the football team's victories defined our status. Who cared if half of our teachers were coaches with bristly crew cuts and physical education degrees and maniacal strength, coaches who had a minor in history or literature and liked True/False tests? Though my sister and I had risen to the top of the heap, we weren't prepared for the concentrated focus of a mental life. We didn't know how to be nerds, how to think, think, think, how to sustain an argument or determine the terms of mattering. We didn't know that our possibilities might be limited by class and gender or that a small-town education might seriously cripple our options.

Though we read constantly, we never analyzed or dissected a work of literature, never considered the social or political theories of our time, but focused on plot and character, two things we could talk about at the dinner table: how Jane Eyre lived wildly, intensely, resolutely in her own mind until she met that arrogant Rochester; how Addie Bundren *ruined* her smart, sly son Darl and he went crazy. In our house, a discussion of political or cultural issues was perceived as troublesome, anxiety provoking, unnecessary. I'll always remember the night we were discussing the spiritual conflicts of different religions when my father, a busy small-town doctor, intervened. "That's enough of that," he said, clearly agitated, the veins at his temples visible. He was so rarely home from the hospital and clinic for dinner that we didn't want to upset him. "Let's hear some good stories about your friends."

Friends. More than anything, we were expected to be social, to be popular, or, at the very least, to enter the realm of stories, mythmaking, to read character and motive, to know, for example, that pious Mr. Huston, a Church of Christer who refused to let his daughters dance, *disliked* his near-sighted, bookworm of a son even as he boasted of signing him up for basketball. We were meant to understand the self-deceptive follies and raucous hopes of people in our town, to know instinctively when scorn was disguised as politeness, desire as courtesy, hurt as obligation, to know when power was lost or gained, when love was defeated or aborted. We learned to smile, to please, to seduce, to tease, to slip into the sleeve of another's thought, but we didn't know how to sink into solitude, to sit at a desk and study abstract ideas, to push a line of thought until it spread into a swirl of possibilities, pursuits that required a disciplined nature.

"Sometimes I think it all started with that history tutorial I took," my sister says, screwing up her face, then sipping her coffee. "Dr. Pierce's European History. Four hours of credit and four years of my life. I always thought if I read the class assignment the night *before* I'd be prepared. I mean half the time in high school I didn't read assignments until during class. I really felt this was an improvement."

I smile into my coffee. It's so like her. In high school, she'd finish *East of Eden* or *My Antonia* late at night instead of her history assignment, and then do her homework at breakfast.

"And it was tough reading. Plato, Aristotle, Descartes, Hobbes, Sartre, those guys. Before I went to Duke, I thought history was about facts, you know, like that Gradgrind guy in Dickens. And after a few months, I was lost, completely confused." She gives me a wry, cautionary smile. "I wanted it to be so different. You know, it was beautiful there."

As she talks, I can see her riding back to Duke after Thanksgiving, fall leaves still coating the ground in a carpet of rust and gold, the Smoky Mountains in the distance edged with snow, such a relief after the dull, faded greens of southern Alabama, where it never snowed, where in autumn, the leaves never turned a brilliant, ruby red and the forests of scrub pines were full of kudzu and brush.

"But in history class the next day we were reviewing Aristotle's theory of the golden mean and its relationship to other theories. Immediately, the professor called on *me*: 'Miss Foster,' he said in this annoying adenoidal voice. 'In what ways does Aristotle see Plato's second wave as flawed?'

"Well, I couldn't remember much about Plato except that he was against the possession of objects and private property. I'd forgotten about his prejudice against the nuclear family and other stuff, so I just said what I knew, how Aristotle was against Plato's communal system.

"At first the professor seemed bored, slightly skeptical. 'Continue,' he said. 'Try to be specific if you can.'

"I thought of the history book on my desk, how it took thirty minutes to find it under a pile of sweaters and skirts, how I read late into the night the new assignment—Sartre's theory of art and history—never dreaming that today would be a review of earlier readings. I could see the page numbers on that book, blocky, Helvetica type, the way the headings were indented, bold and square. I remembered the sudden peace I felt while reading Sartre, the beginnings of an understanding that people could think so differently than those from back home. But Plato? Plato Resistus, I'd called him all semester. I shook my head. I had this sinking feeling in my stomach, a flutter of defeat.

"Then he said quietly, 'Miss Foster, perhaps it's time for you to consider whether you really belong here.' When he paused, I looked out the window at the snow. It rained like ashes from another world. To me his voice became small, tinny, a crackerjack voice. What I heard instead was Mother's voice calling out gaily, 'Rise and shine,' and Daddy saying, 'Come along with me to the hospital, Jean.'

"I think Dr. Pierce implied I might not be, you know, 'smart enough' for his class. The stinker!" She paused, staring at the sky. "And then, oh, I don't know... I was like some leaf blowing southward, tumbling over and over, like trash in the wind."

We don't say anything for a while. I listen to the gulls screeching, the swish of the wind in the sea oats, the *clack-clack-clack* of something rattling down the side road. I think of my sister sitting at that desk, not moving, unable to move, a paper bag over her head.

When Bud groans in his sleep, I glance at him, his front legs spread, his eyes twitching behind closed lids.

"My English teacher was the only person who was kind to me," my sister continues. "When he read my first essay, he said, 'Jean, I'm going to let you write this again before I grade it.' He tried to give me some pointers and I ended up making a B in his class, the best grade I made at Duke."

"That's awful," I say, but then we look at each other and burst out laughing. I see her striding onto our high school stage at age fifteen, forgetting her Chopin étude, and then suddenly standing up and doing the unexpected. Didn't she always know how to pull the rabbit out of the hat?

"Fucking A."

"I'd have freaked out," I admit. "Never left my room. You know, they'd find me at the end of the semester still in bed, my blankets covered with chocolate kisses wrappers."

"Wimp!" she laughs.

"What about science class? You always liked science." I remember when she won a science scholarship in ninth grade, her picture was taken looking into a microscope, her dark hair puddling in waves near the base.

She closes her eyes, then opens them wide, staring out at the bay. "I went a few times."

That sentence hangs between us. "Why didn't you go back?"

She shakes her head. "It didn't work out that way."

I feel shocked. Where is the original smart girl? Where did she go? The one who danced with the Pinhead, the one who read at ball games and was always the star at Mama Dot's recitals. "Piano?" I ask. "Didn't you do well in piano?"

Now she turns and stares at me, her gaze narrowed, head tipped to one side. We are no longer laughing. "I was fair . . . well, mediocre." She picks up the ball and tosses it. Bud wakes and scampers across the deck, bringing the ball back in the cage of his front teeth. "Good boy," she says, petting him. "Good boy." She sighs. "Actually, I think I was the worst one in the department." She pulls the ball from Bud's wet mouth. "So, I decided to concentrate on my social life."

"I hope that was good."

"It was *great*. But then, I devoted myself to it."

And I can see her dancing wildly at a fraternity party to "Papa's Got a Brand New Bag" or "Jumpin' Jack Flash" or flirting with someone she's just met at the Ratskeller in Chapel Hill, with its sawdust floors and crowded tables. She was thin and pretty with dark, wavy hair and a wide, happy smile. Who could resist?

It's not a new story—the substitution of a social life for an intellectual one—but I can't stop wondering how she survived the Big Diversion, as I've come to think of it, without losing all self-respect. "Really, how did you survive?"

She seems not to have heard me. She taps the floor with one foot and rocks. She yawns. Then fiddles with a button on her shirt. "I don't let things get me down too much," she says finally, shrugging. "I know it's weird. But I don't. And I divert." Though she grins at me, her eyes remain serious, intent. "Then after a period of diversion, I can go *back* to the problem."

I feel a brief moment of indignation as if my sister has betrayed her role, kicked over the pedestal, smashed the light, and walked out the door. How dare she disappoint me? But this thought is quickly replaced by the realization that she too has suffered . . . suffered for not being perfect, for being unprepared and innocent, for not knowing how much she didn't know, and then not knowing what to do about it. And perhaps the very fact of her failure is what surprises me most: I never expected her to experience pain or discomfort or incoherence, having too easily believed that everything—for her—would be easy, accessible, within arm's reach. Later I will think how my sister's story reveals a difficult truth: Intellectual readiness is often a mystery, some confluence of desire and luck and sufficient preparation, a feeling of being on the scent of one's own inevitable interests. My sister entered Duke with a fantasy narrative, one primed by girlish expectation, by brochures of happy co-eds laughing beneath a flowering cherry tree, by a provincial culture that kept its eyes low to the ground of practicality, and by our family's mistaken belief that a little talent and high test scores are adequate preparation for achievement. But talent and test scores are seldom enough. Achievement requires a driving, restless need, an obsession, a who-you-are-is-what-you-do attitude of willful assertion. Achievement means hunger. A big, grabbing hunger.

I think of the years after my sister got her BA in music from Duke. For a year, she worked as a secretary for an investment firm on Wall Street, an ordinary year of late nights and early mornings, of riding subways and eating in delis and walking fast through crowded noon streets. After that New York adventure, she went back to college to get an MA in counseling, married, and moved to Vermont to work as a social worker at a boy's institution. It was while living in that small town, surrounded by a blanket of snow and the bleak, gray skies of a Vermont winter, that she felt the first agitation of desire: Why not go to med school? Why not aspire to another life? It was only then that she realized she'd subordinated this desire for years, had hidden it from herself while trying to convince boyfriends to fulfill the dream. But now, the idea grabbed hold. *She'd do it herself.* In six months, she moved back to Alabama, got a job as a counselor in Birmingham, and began attending University of Alabama at Birmingham (site of the medical school) four nights a week to get the math and science courses she needed to apply.

When she called my father to tell him her plans, he said, "Jean, I've always supported you in everything, but you didn't try very hard at Duke. You go ahead and sign up for classes, and I'm going to withhold judgment until you prove you are serious."

Fair enough. She wanted medical school, wanted it enough to sacrifice sleep and easy pleasure, enough to watch the sun rise on Sunday mornings just beyond her desk. When she made the highest grade in her bio-chem class and As in her other classes, she called my father. "I'm going to medical school," she said. "Count on it." Two years later, she did, and after that, she spent the next thirty years practicing internal medicine in Alabama.

Suddenly Bud is pushing at her chair, nudging the slimy ball against her knees. "Okay, okay," she says. "We've got to take them out for a walk again. 'C'mon, Bud. Let's go."

As we walk the dogs on the empty beach, the sun is beginning to fade. The air is soft, warm against my skin. I stand at the shore, watching the endless lap of waves, letting Bud sniff every crab hole and tangled bed of seaweed.

"Watch this," she calls to me. And I see the little dog running around in circles, sniffing the sand until suddenly he tires and walks on without looking back.

It's not until days later when I'm driving back to Iowa, through the boring flatness of Mississippi, Arkansas, and Missouri, that I begin to put my sister's story in perspective. In her late teens and early twenties, I believe she had enough confidence to bide her time, to sink below the radar of expectation and put herself out of reach. I'm quite sure she felt the hard slap of criticism, the taint of failure. We all do. But it's a misperception to think that failure, the literal fact of it, is the largest blow. The trauma of failure lives in its repercussions, its aftermath, the way it is incorporated into the psyche. *How will I feel about myself? How will I go on?* And this, I begin to see, is the difference between my sister and me. I brood over failure, get sweaty and hot with despair as if I have a fever. I don't move, can't move. I feel trapped by guilt and shame, the tightening of a noose, released only by writing about it. My sister responds differently. After the first sting of criticism, the first swoosh of fear, she grabs hold of something in herself, something old and familiar and comforting, and then she turns toward the window, to see, perhaps, if the wisteria is blooming, if the dragonflies are out, if someone—maybe she herself—needs to walk to the bakery to buy the sweet rolls just iced or the blueberry muffins steaming in their tins. She picks up a book and slides it under her arm, then grabs her purse. How warm it is outside! How exciting!

Silence

It's March 13, 1965, a Saturday night. My sister and I are "doing hair" for friends who lounge on the soft comforters of our twin beds or sit cross-legged on the floor in slips and flip-flops as we get ready for a party at the VFW club, our party clothes hanging from the closet doors. Tonight, there are only five of us, Jean rolling Linda's dark shoulder-length hair on orange juice cans while Joan sits under the beauty-style "hood" dryer my mother bought for us last year. Judy calls out "talk *louder*" from the bathroom where she's shaving her legs. Because it's Saturday night, we're giddy with anticipation as if we might slip through the world of contradictions, escape the ordinary, and be touched by divinity. We breathe in the coming night's happiness as if inside a dream: We know the Elberta boys will be there, tall, lanky boys, already tan and beautiful with unforgivably long lashes framing pale green eyes. They're farmers' sons. They drive their daddy's chicken trucks to and from dances, getting out in a feverish pack as if they have so much energy they absolutely *must* jostle and smack each other before ambling into those damp, crowded rooms. Already I can see them standing together by the refreshment table at the VFW club sipping Pepsi and 7UP from paper cups, then squeezing those cups into tight-wadded shards to torpedo each other.

As we flip through the pages of *Mademoiselle* or stare at the glitter of our newly painted nails, we believe that everything lies ahead of us. *Everything*. Not just tonight's party but awards, books, proms, concerts, recitals, and college followed by what we call "the rest of our lives."

Our lives. As we stand before the mirror primping, smoothing "Pretty-As-Pink" lipstick on our lips and sweeping a tiny brush of dark mascara through our eyelashes, we never think of our lives as a cloister of whiteness, a code of conformity. But it's exactly that: We're white girls with white girl-friends, boyfriends, teachers, mentors, preachers, doctors, coaches, neighbors, ball games, and parties. The only Black people we know are the maids who come into our houses once a week to mop the kitchen floor and iron our fathers' shirts and the Black men who mow our lawns or work as janitors at the public school. And yet, even as we curl and spray our hair, the civil rights movement is blazing through the once slumbering cities and towns of Alabama, marchers and activists demanding racial justice, planning sit-ins and teach-ins, giving speeches, registering voters, and even going to jail. Though the violence against them is brutal and televised, its reality doesn't penetrate our lives, as if we're enveloped in a fog of whiteness, a hush of silence, a cocoon of ignorance.

Tonight, as we gossip about the Elberta boys, wondering who'll be first to break from the pack and ask one of us to dance, no one mentions the six hundred peaceful marchers who crossed the Edmund Pettus Bridge in Selma last Sunday only to be met by a wall of state troopers, mounted deputies, and white spectators waving Confederate flags. No one mutters, "My God, did you *see* how horrible it was," how the troopers, their faces disguised by gas masks, rushed the crowd, striking men, women, and children with "sticks, clubs, whips and rubber tubing wrapped in barbed wire" to the riotous cheering of bystanders. In truth, no one has said a word all week about "Bloody Sunday," not at the dinner table, in the classroom, or from the pulpit, as if we aren't living in Alabama but in a place where goodness and mercy shine down and all we need worry about is who we'll become, never once questioning how that becoming might restrict or violate others' lives.

"C'mon." My sister nudges me as Joan waits patiently before the full-length mirror. "You do the back while I do the front and sides."

When I glance at Joan, her sudden beauty takes me by surprise: the soft curve of her cheek, the arched brows, the tumble of her chestnut hair as I unwind the rollers and stack them on the dresser. Not once do I think of her as white, privileged, and part of our silence. Not once do I think, *she can go to the public library and read anything she wants.* Instead, I begin combing out her hair, the strands luscious and thick, the ends loosely curled, smooth and lovely, their golden hue shimmering in the evening light. She will be chosen. I know it.

Sleepwalking

ON APRIL 4, 1968, A COLDNESS seeped into my elbows and knees as I walked toward Branscomb Quad, my dorm at Vanderbilt University, after a late class. It had rained earlier in the day, and at 6:30 P.M., the streets of Nashville were glazed with water, the air cool and thick with humidity, the leaves wet and glistening. I was a sophomore and I'd just switched my major from literature to sociology after a disastrous course called The Theater of the Absurd, a class in which I'd understood only vaguely the bleak self-determination of existentialism and the aesthetic minimalism of Beckett and Brecht.

When I arrived at my dorm's lobby, tired and hungry and eager for dinner, I sensed a tension, a wariness as if somewhere beneath the surface there was unrest, a parting of the air. "Curfew tonight," someone called out, a little too loudly, posting a note on the board. "We've gotta be in by *nine o'clock*." The normal curfew for women was 11:30 P.M. on weeknights and 1:00 A.M. on weekends. To insure this, each coed tallied her night's activities on a printed card in a glass paneled room in the reception lobby. When she checked out, she scrawled her destination and check-out time, then turned her card to OUT; when she returned, she noted the time and flipped it to IN. In this way, the dorm mother—paid for such surveillance—always knew our whereabouts.

Then, as I was wondering why in the world this new curfew had been imposed, another coed called out, "Oh, God, he's been assassinated," and began to cry.

"What?" Now everyone in the lobby stopped their conversations and turned toward the girl, confused and anxious to know what she knew.

"He was *shot*," she continued, sniffling, "just like Kennedy and we'll never know who put the scum up to it."

Simultaneously, an announcement blared over the radio: "Martin Luther King Jr. has been assassinated at the Lorraine Motel at approximately 6:01 P.M. Central Standard Time in Memphis, Tennessee. Four thousand National Guard troops have been called out in Memphis, Tennessee and a curfew will be in effect tonight in Memphis, Nashville, and in West Memphis, Arkansas." And with those words, the atmosphere in the room erupted with unspeakable anguish and excitement as only a disaster ignites. Upheaval. Despair. Panic. Riots were expected in Memphis and Nashville and at least a dozen other cities. Beside me, two freshmen began to wail, their shoulders shaking, their lips trembling, their books dropped, forgotten, onto the floor. Students started running toward the stairs and elevators, calling out to each other, rushing to their rooms to turn on TVs and radios and to phone their parents.

Later, I'd think: The modern gospel of American assassination keeps rolling on. Was this the future of America? This bloody terror? And yet that night, I worried mainly about what horrors might happen in the coming days as I grabbed a book, stuffed clean underwear into my purse, and reminded Vicki to flip my card to IN at nine o'clock.

As planned, my boyfriend pulled into the quad at seven thirty, and despite the curfew, we had no worries about spending the night together, studying and watching the news and then shamelessly curling together in his double bed. Who knew what the next morning would bring?

As we drove past West End Avenue, I noticed police cars lined up like cavalry, the streetlights blazing. Overhead, helicopters whirred. Our radio crackled with news: rioting in north Nashville; violence erupting in Memphis, DC, Chicago, Baltimore, and Detroit. And yet here, cars streamed past in a normal flow, eerily silent. *Martin Luther King Jr. is dead*, I thought, but I couldn't make myself *feel* the word, for I was alive, young and resilient, wanting only to lie down with my boyfriend in a darkened room, our bodies entangled, our words soft and murmuring, the voice of young love. Maybe death does that, stimulates an erotic energy, a sense of being intrinsically alive: breasts and hips, lips and thighs.

Suddenly, a police car zoomed past. Then another. And another. A siren startled the air. What would the police do, I wondered, if they caught you out after curfew? Would you be stopped, questioned, frisked, jailed? (I was so naive; I didn't think beyond that.) But then I gazed at my boyfriend's thick brown hair flirting with the collar of his shirt, his cheeks flushed, his left hand curled casually around the steering wheel. I moved closer.

In the last two years—as if the past had been a sprawling dream—my childhood was upended. I'd grown up in the post–World War II South in a small farm town near the Gulf of Mexico where the natural beauty of nearby rivers and creeks and bays left me dizzy with happiness as I swam and skied and paddled a skiff through the Narrows. For so many people, this had seemed an Edenic time, a healthy, prosperous decade in American life when a family would never imagine a bank screwing them with a bad mortgage or a company outsourcing their jobs to Mexico or China or a drug epidemic devastating a large part of the community. It was a time when my sister and I rode our bikes seven miles out into the country, carefree and independent, yelling gleefully at chickens and cows and fearing only chiggers and mosquitoes and seat-sore rumps. It was a time when small towns sported a gentle sense of humor. As you entered Daphne, Alabama, the official sign read: *"Home to 1500 good people and a few grouches."*

But of course, this is the story of the winners, the narrative of postwar white middle-class America, a story in which I was cocooned inside a privileged life, soaring through a vast interior space of possibility and unaware of the monstrous parts of our culture. Somehow, I'd failed to notice that my elementary school was segregated until one Monday morning in fourth grade as my mother drove me to school I watched a bus crowded with Black children, their faces peering at me through the glass, turn left at the stop sign while we turned right toward Foley Elementary School. Two little girls in pigtails waved, laughing, as if we knew each other, before their bus sped off down the road. I lifted my hand but wasn't sure if I should wave. "Where are they going?" I asked my mother, genuinely perplexed.

Newly awakened to the obvious fact of segregation, I still had no idea of the dangers and degradations that accompanied inequality, had no idea that the gas man, a white man, was "showing his privates" and "trying to get into Ora's house at her girls" while Ora was at our house, ironing my father's dress shirts. I knew only that Ora's doors were plywood-flimsy, the screens bowed, the locks cheap, the wood warped and patched. Terrified, Ora's girls, eight and ten, surely became one breathless shape hiding behind the sofa while the sun stood still. I had no idea that Cornelia, my father's receptionist, had attended school in a rural Black church from kindergarten to sixth grade, so many children crowded together in a sweltering space with few books, maps, or writing materials because the state provided only limited funds for educating Black children in our county. I had no idea that one of the *best* financial investments was to build and rent Negro shacks, flimsy, ramshackle constructions given minimal inspection, requiring no rent control and only incidental repairs. Who was going to protest?

It never occurred to me that *I* might protest. Even as a teenager I was sleepwalking through my life, anxious and distracted by competition for grades and honors and popularity and dates to the prom, earnestly working and self-absorbed by these private goals. Sadly, it never occurred to me to think deeply about my ignorance and indifference to the plight of others or to imagine that such indifference could be a subset of sin. If anyone had suggested it, I'd probably have laughed. *Are you crazy?* I didn't yet understand that indifference suggested complacency and complacency suggested passivity and that, in the moral realm, passivity is almost always tragic. Only much later would I recognize indifference as an ideological space, an acceptance of the status quo, a sense that the fate of others should be left to those in power as if an independent mind is dangerous, as if mercy is a wintry word.

And yet.

"Once you begin to awaken to the realities of what you know," Wendell Berry notes, "you are subject to staggering recognitions of your complicity in history and in the events of your own life."

During my sophomore year, as if startling half-awake from my dream, I had actually noticed the realities of my culture: The Vietnam War and the anti-war protests were raging, race riots ruptured the hot, restless nights of Newark, Watts, and Detroit, the civil rights movement pushed stubbornly forward not just in the South but in Chicago and St. Louis while an emerging women's rights movement pulsed with rebellious energy. And yet, alongside these changes, my own life seemed ridiculously ordinary and satisfying: a boyfriend, good friends, parties, classes.

And then, as suddenly, it shattered.

During that evening of April 4, my boyfriend and I pushed our chairs close to the TV and listened as President Johnson asked every citizen to reject "the blind violence that has struck Dr. King, who lived by nonviolence." Still in shock—who could grapple with this?—we devoted ourselves to the nightly news, ignoring our books on the kitchen table next to damp socks drying on a wooden chair. Images flashed and repeated on the screen. The second-floor railing at the Lorraine Motel. The blood-stained balcony floor. The drained swimming pool. The Cadillac idling below. Then, a montage that represented the biography of King's life. As I watched the tormented images from Birmingham and Selma, I couldn't help but think of the hate-fest of people who'd threatened to "blow out his brains." Well, now someone had. Some crazy person, some crazy white person—

That thought was interrupted by the ringing of the phone, probably a friend calling to grieve about the assassination. It was 9:30 P.M.

"I forgot to turn your card," Vicki said in a hushed voice. "I fell asleep. I'm *sorry.*"

I didn't move. I couldn't. The air inside was suddenly warm and close.

It seems ridiculous now. A silly rule broken. That's all it was. A curfew missed. But it mattered then. It matters now. Maybe you can never predict the moment your life will turn, when loss and worry about one thing bleeds into another. Five minutes earlier, I'd been wrapped in a protective cloth that secured me in its sheltering fold. Now it was coming unraveled. That's all it took: a tiny tear, a rent in the surface of protection, in the self I'd conjured.

I imagined for the first time the physicality of Martin Luther King Jr.'s death: shards of jawbone, splays of blood, buckled knees, his body crumpling, its thud solid, unforgiving on a concrete balcony, blood streaming from his nose and mouth, hemorrhaging from his neck wound, fast-flowing, then a darkening stain. His wing tip shoes were caught in the metal rungs of the railing, his necktie ripped from his shirt by the force of the shot, a hollow-point bullet, forbidden by the Geneva Conventions. Grit and dust and smoke rose into the cool evening air. I heard sirens, screams, a fog of terror. The ugliness and meanness of it sliced through me—"Kill the nigger!" segregationists had yelled at every civil rights march—as I stared fixedly at the clock: 9:34. 9:35. More than thirty minutes past curfew.

I was in trouble, but what did my puny humiliation count in the face of this larger national tragedy?

But it did. *It did.* And in that moment my mind split in two: One part of me wanted to protest the stupid rules for women as unfair and unequal, the rules relegating us to second-class status, an assumption that we needed protection, that we were "damsels in distress" even as we were being educated for so much more. "I'm going to protest," I insisted, indignant. "And what better time to do it than now." Why not be a courageous Hester Prynne instead of a cowering Dimmesdale, why not pursue heroic suffering instead of cowardly complicity? But the other part of me was frightened and pragmatic, already complicit with the lie of falling asleep at my boyfriend's apartment and missing curfew.

That night, I rode in the back of a Yellow Cab through the empty streets of Nashville, the lights now blurry, the barnacled trees silvery in the moonlight, the taxi an ironic sentinel, carrying me—a failed existentialist—back to a place I didn't want to go. As we passed police cars, I gazed at the profile of an officer at a red light. When he turned, his face looked worn, his shirt wrinkled, his sleeves rolled, a Styrofoam cup in one hand. He nodded to me. At 9:55, I arrived at Branscomb Quad and waited outside in the cool, wet air for the security guard to unlock the dorm door. By the time I took the elevator to my room on the third floor, I was so frightened, I'd almost forgotten about the tragedy of Dr. King's death.

Once alone, I pressed my nose to the mirror in my dorm room and saw every inch of white skin, every pore. Would I be thrown out of school? Would I be shamed, marched out of my room, the dorm mother eyeing my every move? Would I have to go home to Alabama, humiliating my parents? Fear surged through my body like a fever.

Two days later, I sat rigid before the ethics board, ready to affirm the lie I'd told, staring at the faces of the women sitting across from me. Particularly, I studied two upper-class women who held positions of authority on campus and lived on my floor. Calm and composed in their pastel shirtwaist dresses and yokes of pearls, they seemed untouched, untouchable, princesses applauded and revered and invulnerable. They smelled of coffee and Chanel No. 5, golden girls whose authenticity I'd never questioned. And yet I knew that they too had stayed out the night of Dr. King's death, that they, like me, were penned to Kappa Sigma's who'd let slip to my boyfriend this little nugget of truth. A shadow of lies lay between us. And so, I turned and spoke only to them: Let the guilty judge the guilty.

As I read my statement, I held their gaze, a blush creeping up my face. When I finished, the faculty advisor sitting across from me marked something swiftly, decisively, on a sheet of paper, her own hair untidy, her lipstick faded. "You must be more careful in your conduct," she chastised me, looking up, her voice fussy, her mouth prim. She stared at me as if waiting for a response or an apology, but everything inside me had shut down. "Well," she said, sighing and glancing inquisitively at my pearl-clad peers. The one with the sly, dark eyes nodded. And then the other. I waited, uncertain, aware of the soft green leaves of an elm tree fluttering against the window, showing their graying undersides. Silence. Somewhere in the distance, a dove cooed. A door slammed. The advisor capped her pen. Only when all the women stood, gathering their books, and one girl, tucking in a wayward curl, began talking about the upcoming memorial service for Dr. King at Gordon Memorial Church did I realize I'd been dismissed, pardoned. Given only a warning. I would not be asked to leave the university. I would not be sent home. Relief flooded my body.

I walked out alone, my nerves taut, the same soft green leaves now rustling in a sullen wind. I was still flushed, sweat at the back of my knees. But I had been cleared, let off, excused, pardoned! Surely, I'd soon feel at ease inside my own skin. *Pardoned.* I tried out the word, imagining how I'd tell my boyfriend and my friends and how excited they'd be. My boyfriend would hug me, pulling me so close I'd smell the scent of cigarette smoke on his collar, old coffee on his breath. We'd go right back to our old ways: driving to the Waffle House at midnight, drinking too much coffee, writing papers, going to parties, sleeping together and then eating scrambled eggs at the wobbly wooden table in his kitchen. And yet, instead of relief at this thought, I felt oddly burdened, as if my troubles were just beginning, as if existentialism was staking its claim.

What *was* this?

I stopped, then sat on a secluded bench facing an ivy-covered brick wall. The ivy was thick and dark green, almost gauzy near a second-story window. I stared at it, letting my thoughts loosen, my mind thick and slow. Before the meeting, I'd been too frightened of the outcome to think about the consequences, but now, well, now the consequences had dutifully arrived: Privilege and deceit had won, but what did that mean? I shifted my gaze from the ivy to the gray concrete where so many other feet had trod. As I stared at my black ladylike pumps, ones I'd chosen specifically for this meeting, I began to understand that I was irrevocably entangled in this story. A story of young love and sadness. A story of self-preservation and expedience, but also a story of historical tragedy and the beginning weight of disillusionment. A story of when innocence ends.

In truth, the sheltering cloth that held me had never come unraveled. As I rode in that Yellow Cab on April 4, 1968, toward Branscomb Quad, my white skin protected me, shielding me from suspicion, from danger and reprisals as if an invisible net surrounded me, valuing and sustaining me. Driven through heavily patrolled but empty streets, my security remained intact. Had I been a young Black woman, say a Black student at Fisk University in North Nashville in the same situation, would I have been so easily passed over, the cop nodding, institutional doors politely opened, the security guard gazing respectfully at me? Had I been a young Black man taking a friend to the emergency room or simply upset and disconsolate, devastated by the news, would the police have waved me by, have considered my dignity as a human being? I doubt it.

And yet oddly, it was this wide protective net that I came to resent, that prompted me in my mid-twenties to leave Alabama, to turn sideways and march off alone to California. And of course, the irony of that decision is that this choice had everything to do with my being young and white and educated. With having options. Even escape, it seems, is a kind of privilege. And this too was part of my racial education.

Only after escaping would I understand this simple thing: It is not always courage that awakens you. Sometimes it is shame. The shame of your own lies and ignorance, the juxtaposition of unrelated but conjoined events, the twinning of tragedy with minor transgression. In the coming years, when I thought about the night of Martin Luther King Jr.'s death, I'd remember yet again that I was white and privileged and that no one hated me for these things. No one wanted to harm me or kill me for such attributes. No one wanted me to suffer.

I couldn't change my whiteness or my privilege. Nor did I want to. What I could change was my indifference to the world.

I could stop being a sleepwalker.

I could wake up.

PART III

History Lessons, 1933–2019

There is no beginning. There is no end. There's only the middle, where silence and complicity shadow me, daring me to speak. Is it possible to write about race, to shape an essay that indicts and interrogates even if the writing will be flawed, possibly myopic? I sit at my desk and close my eyes, wanting to throw open the doors of the past and let in a flood of light. Not a birth. A haunting.

Alabama Triptych

FOLEY, 1961

IF NORMAN ROCKWELL HAD BEEN southern, he might have painted my hometown: a farm town, a two-stoplight town, the flat, pine-studded land wreathed with live oaks draped in Spanish moss, the outskirts marked by rows of potatoes and beans and corn. From February to June, azaleas sway with the breeze while skinny green lizards dart from the eaves, sprinting to patios where they lie still and patient in the sun. Ten miles away, sandpipers troll the beaches of the Gulf of Mexico, skilled retrievers of insects and crabs, pinpoints of constant motion, their footprints tattooing the white, glittering sand. Also in motion are colorful reports in our once-a-week newspaper *The Onlooker*, updates about the Posture Queen, the DAR speaker, the car lot stats for shipped potatoes, the Pony League wins and losses, and of course, the flash and noise of political news.

It's 1961.

On May 5, when Freedom Riders begin their trek through the Deep South, challenging local segregation ordinances that defy the Supreme Court's 1960 Boynton ruling (segregation on public buses is unconstitutional), I imagine the newspaper editor sits up, alert, his mind so focused he barely blinks as he stares at the TV news. Does he, in the days that follow, scrutinize the *Montgomery Advertiser* and the *Mobile Press Register*, constantly refilling his cup of coffee after the thirteen riders leave Washington, DC, for Virginia, winding their way through North Carolina, South Carolina, and Georgia, early summer leaves rustling on the trees, the sky a slate blue? Days later, do his eyes ache when the Freedom Riders arrive in Anniston, Alabama, tired and anxious, their stomachs empty, only to be welcomed by the Ku Klux Klan, whose greetings include shattered glass, slashed tires, and cracked heads, the blunt caress of hate?

Though the editor carries no steel pipe and swings no bicycle chain, he knows how to get down to business with his loaded pen, insisting it's *not* the KKK with an itch for violence but those nasty Freedom Riders, a pack of hotheads, sweaty and dangerous, who came down here "to stir up trouble." Don't we all know they're nothing but a bunch of "professional agitators . . . responsible for creating the trouble they set out to create"? Don't we all know the white mob simply "fell blindly into the plot and provided the action that made the violence-seeking tour a success"? Don't we all know these Freedom punks are "troublemakers" who "don't want an equal share of the hog, they want the whole thing"? Don't we all know their leaders are "tied to Communist front organizations" hell-bent not on "equality . . . but want to take over the country." And not just America. Heavens, no. They want to "delight the Kremlin and Red China."

Poor ole Alabama. Who knew a Greyhound bus full of men and women— Black and white, young and old, student and minister—passing through our state could ignite such wrongheaded change? Who knew the Freedom Riders would be in cahoots with the lily-livered Kennedy bunch or that "the White House should make a yo-yo out of Alabama to ingratiate itself with Harlem"?

But Alabama will *not* be a yo-yo. No matter what "President Kennedy . . . and his little brother, sitting at that big desk and barking orders over the phone and looking like Mickey Rooney just in from a game of touch football" try to do. Alabama will stand as straight and tall as the Posture Queen. Alabama will not lie still and patient in the sun while the "integration mill" grinds on, spreading its "left-wing programs," dependent on "federal intervention." Instead, Alabama will show the world its savage face. Alabama will leave its big brutal footprint. Alabama will snarl and thrash and jail its way to becoming the horror story of the nation.

And my town, Foley, is here to help.

TUSCALOOSA, 1963

History will remember an ambitious young woman in a pale, tailored sheath ascending the steps of Foster Auditorium on a blisteringly hot day in 1963 to register for classes. It had all been planned, approved, decreed, only the tap of her heels, the click of the cameras, and the heat-haze of the sun marking the moment, though four hours earlier, Governor George Wallace performed for the crowd, symbolically bandying his famous *"Segregation now! Segregation tomorrow! Segregation forever!"* as if offering the sharp claws of an animal on her first day in Tuscaloosa.

History will remember Vivian Malone with creamy pearls looped around her neck, moving with composure through the bustling crowd of TV crews, photographers, reporters, and a herd of white men: university officials, lawyers, police, and the Alabama National Guard, recently federalized to protect her. *Her.* A Black woman from Mobile, Alabama, entering an all-white university. History does not remember whether she glances up slyly, seeing the stern, averted gaze of a soldier, his mouth tight, spikes of perspiration tattooing his khaki shirt, his pale hands resting tensely above a holstered gun. Protect her. Will he? Does he have a choice?

History will remember her as a college student with dark hair and expressive eyes beginning her summer school classes on June 12, 1963, sitting upright and alert and separate, perhaps in Principles of Economics or Financial Accounting, alone in each university classroom. Years later, she will recount how the professor announced that anyone who did not want to be in the class that day would be excused, and one-half of the class got up and left. And yet to everyone's surprise, she is not the main story of the day, her fate usurped by an unexpected and more horrifying fate: In Mound Bayou, Mississippi, Medgar Evers, a civil rights leader, was assassinated in the early morning hours, gunned down by Bryon De La Beckwith, a fertilizer salesman and white supremacist Klansman. On any other day, perhaps she would think the words "white supremacist Klansman" were redundant, but today I imagine she needed *all* the words, all the familiar and foreign combinations that expressed what she was up against, what might hurt her.

History will not remember whether she wept at this devastating news alone in her dorm room where no one would hear, where no one would hold her, wrap their arms around her and comfort her. But perhaps she did not weep. Not yet. Perhaps the weight of this horror made her feel dizzy, so dizzy she breathed shallow breaths, then fewer breaths as she closed her eyes, becoming weightless, floating, floating to the ceiling, dissolving into nothing, dust in the air. Isn't it possible that no one seemed to know how she felt, just as no one seemed to know why the FBI and the police failed to escort Medgar Evers from work to home on this day as they'd done on every other day?

History will not remember whether she began to sob, relieved at the wetness on her face, dampening the soft white cotton of her blouse, or whether she opened her eyes and stared at the patterned curtains that had been pulled closed to keep her safe, to protect her from whatever was out there, from anger and threats and snarls of meanness, but also from sun and rain and the fragrance of newly mown grass. Even if she wept, she most likely heard shouts, bursts of laughter, bits of conversation, flirtatious teasing, and the constant footsteps of other people beyond the curtains. People who were alive. People who were safe. *Safe.* Would that word evoke something so quiet and defiant inside her she'd stop crying and think: *Go to your desk, turn on the desk lamp, and open your accounting book?* And would she dutifully flip to the first page of her assignment, the first page of tomorrow, resolved never to give up? Later, she'd learn that Medgar Evers was the first Black person admitted to a white Mississippi hospital, admitted only after having been refused treatment for being Black, admitted, and then dead within fifty minutes. Later, she'd say in interviews that his death made her more determined than ever.

History will remember that she did not give up. She did not give up when James Hood, who enrolled alongside her, dropped out after two months (to keep from having, he said, a physical and mental breakdown), leaving her the only Black student among more than eight thousand white students. She did not give up when the Sixteenth Street Baptist Church in Birmingham was bombed on September 15 and four little girls were killed, did not give up when three bombs went off in Tuscaloosa in November, one only four blocks from her dormitory, did not give up when "white students refused to make eye contact with her or return her smile," as reported in the *Guardian*, or give the slightest sign, even a sideways nod or a lifted eyebrow, of welcome. If the motif of her role was meant to be forward motion and perseverance, I can't help but wonder if many days it felt more like endurance and detachment.

History will not remember Malone's everyday worries, her deepening thoughts, her secret aspirations and private resentments. History, in this sense, is fickle, concerned more with measurable progress, with accelerations and reversals rather than with the intimate thoughts of a young college student. Still, I wonder if she puzzled over the way big things often overshadow small things and yet how small things can release a cascade of hormones, making of the heart a strangled bird beating too fast inside its captor's clasp. Was she able to speak of the small things alongside of the big things? Was she able to voice the institutional aloneness, the ostracism she experienced—alone in the elevator (the white students got off if she was there), in the cafeteria, at a study table in the library—or did she refrain from speaking . . . out of fear, nerves, rage, resentment, stubbornness, nonviolence, respect? Silence itself can silence you. And then the urge to speak, scream, laugh, mock, sing, wail.

History will not remember this moment: A young, ambitious white student tells me that in the summer of 1963, she was surprised when she rushed into an elevator at the University of Alabama and Vivian Malone stood there. This student looked carefully, almost shyly away as she pressed the button for her floor, then glanced up with a slow blink of her eyes. Did she smile? I wonder. Did Vivian Malone nod? Did their eyes meet and hold for longer than a few seconds, reminding them of the possible? For most of us, this exchange might seem a small thing, but I want to think it made both women wonder if more than elevator doors could open in their conflicted world, if day by day and week by week and month by month, the sharp stones of prejudice might be scattered from the white southern heart and the scales of justice prevail. For the young, ambitious white student, I imagine this as a brisk new thought, an awakening, a subversive recognition; for Vivian Malone, the idea is probably as old as her grandmother, as urgent and uncertain as the weather. Inevitably, the doors will close, and the elevator will rise while beyond them the world goes on, the light fading, the air cooling, the day ending as they shift their books, breathing in the stuffy air and waiting for the elevator to reach their floor.

TUSKEGEE, 1996

Steamy heat covers me like a blanket, my blouse wet with sweat from stepping out of the air-conditioned rental car to pump gas and ask directions. It's 1996, and I've driven from Iowa to Tuskegee, Alabama, to tour Booker T. Washington's house but also to talk to the librarian about teaching a writing class at the public library in late July. As I gather my bags in the parking lot of a college dorm, I'm embarrassed that my clothes are damp and wrinkled and that I'm tired and hungry. How I long for a bath! Only that.

Tonight, the dorm seems silent and still, not breathing. I remember that no one will be here except for Mrs. Page, the dorm counselor, and Malinda, the student assistant. And now me. The spring session has ended, and all the Tuskegee University students have gone home. Relief floods through me:

The bathrooms will be empty, and I can dawdle and drift, reading a book in the tub for hours.

And yet when I knock—the dorm is locked—Malinda, a pretty Black college student, opens the door, greeting me with the news that Mrs. Page, who has the keys, is away and won't be back until later tonight. Since Malinda has no keys to the rooms, she directs me to the lounge, a dark, cool interior place filled with plush sofas and chairs. "Oh, goodness," Malinda says, realizing she doesn't know how to turn on the lights in this room, but I assure her a comfortable chair will be perfect and I sit in darkness, my stomach growling, reminding me that I have the metabolism of a flea. I haven't eaten in four hours.

Just as Malinda returns with a flashlight—*"Let there be light!"* she giggles—Mrs. Page bundles through the door, carrying two sacks of fresh peaches from Chilton County. "You're here," Mrs. Page says curtly, her mouth bunched in annoyance, her eyes fixed on me with irritation as if I've arrived too soon, interrupting her perfect night of peaches and milk. Looking past me, she jostles the bags, rearranging them as she walks stalwartly toward her suite of rooms.

Uncertain, I wait, watching the shadows tug at the night.

"Well, for goodness' sake," Mrs. Page gripes minutes later, hands on her hips like a small-town general. She's standing in the doorway, a short, stout woman with dark brown eyes and a fierce, directed gaze. Thank God, I'm not the problem. No, she forgot to buy milk just as I forgot to bring a washcloth and towel from home as if I could dry off after my bath au naturel. *This is a dorm!* I remind myself. Again, it's Malinda who comes to the rescue, offering to accompany me to Calhoun's Grocery in the center of Tuskegee to get supplies. "Not far," she says, "Just a skip and a jump down the road."

Eagerly, I get my car keys, hoping the purchase of milk will restore me to Mrs. Page's good graces and that tomorrow she might smile.

It's one of those southern nights, velvet dark, the air thick with humidity, cicadas chattering, the moon in hiding. Leaves flutter in the light breeze and the streets of Tuskegee are deserted except for an occasional possum caught in the headlights. My mood eases and I chat easily with Malinda, who tells me she's putting herself through school by assisting the mercurial Mrs. Page.

"But really, she's okay," Malinda says, laughing. "More bark than bite. You get used to her."

When we arrive at Calhoun's, a small mom-and-pop store in need of a paint job, it looks uninhabited except for a man sitting in a wheelchair out front, his head lolling to the side. "Hi . . . hi . . . hi," he shrieks, and Malinda stops to talk to him, chatting and laughing though I can't make out his garbled words. Inside, I'm surprised to see several customers milling about, middle-aged men and women getting quick supplies, a child sneaking a Moon Pie into his mother's cart, an old man with gray whiskers buying cigarettes. Though I'm the only white person in the store, there are polite glances and nods as I follow Malinda down the narrow aisles, listening to her comments. "It's right here, well, I swear, it *used* to be!" she says as we search for a towel and then some cheese and crackers. Dutifully, I stack things in the cart, moving behind Malinda, careful not to knock items off the shelves. A washcloth. Peanut butter crackers. Sliced cheese. A small dish towel. Soap.

It's in the milk aisle that two lanky teenage boys, their ball caps worn backward, turn from the refrigerated shelves to stare at me. To my surprise, their eyes are sullen, their gaze hostile. One boy holds a quart of buttermilk and despite myself I smile, glancing at the slender shape of his fingers around the quart and thinking how much my seventy-five-year-old mother loves buttermilk, one of the few happy reminders of her childhood. She likes to drink it at night, pouring a glass as she stands in her pink fuzzy robe at the kitchen counter, always taking full swallows. As Malinda and I inch closer to the refrigerated shelves, neither boy moves aside to let us get a quart of milk. I feel a prickle between my shoulder blades. A tightening of breath. Though they don't say a word, the boys' faces are stone. Their narrowed eyes make me wonder if they see me as an outsider, a foreigner invading their turf. And for the first time, I see myself *being seen*, a white girl fixed by their gaze.

"'Cuse us," Malinda says confidently, elbowing her way past so that the boys move slightly, giving way but mumbling, still eyeing me as they let her though. "Listen," Malinda says to me, ignoring the boys as if they're irrelevant. "Mrs. Page likes whole milk, but we gotta pretend, *we really do*, that we thought we was getting skim." She laughs.

I try to laugh too as we walk toward the counter to pay, but I've become self-conscious, startled by a shiver of fear, every nerve in my neck beginning to burn. I can hear myself breathe. See my shadow falling across the floor.

There's the taste of metal in my mouth. I realize I've never been in a situation where my skin color inhibits me, indicts me.

And this, I realize, is all it takes. Being watched. Being wrong.

As we drive back to the dorm, the darkness thickens and all I see is blacktop with no white or yellow lines, nothing to guide me but the headlights and Malinda's voice. "Turn here," she says, then tells me she wishes only for a "cold, cold Coke, not that diet kind." Somewhere among the trees an owl hoots, a sharp, haunting sound, then the husk of an armadillo flashes at the side of the road, its legs stiff and splayed. When I see a night animal dart into the bushes, anxiety floods my body, a blend of fear and guilt as I think about those boys, about myself. I worry that I'm a woman on a fishing expedition in the heart of Macon County. What can I know about those boys' lives? Only that young Black men are easily saddled with stereotypes that target them as dangerous and criminal, their lives constrained, their hopes narrowed by our history of racial injustice, their fears amplified by drug arrests directed at certain communities, false accusations of rape, and police harassment.

Myself? I feel bleak.

I remember the photograph from the Alabama State Archives I stared at for hours last week, a picture of Black adults and children holding hands while standing in a circle on an unpaved street in Montgomery in the sixties during a civil rights demonstration. One little girl—I couldn't help but notice her—had drawn her hands close to her chest, linking arms with the others, her gaze searching the late afternoon sky while the other kids turned to each other. She looked fragile, impressionable, her long, thin legs so exposed beneath her girl's dress. What was she thinking? Did the presumed safety of those joined hands lighten her fears, make her believe that family and community could protect her? Or was she both indignant and scared as a ten-year-old might be whose world was seriously threatened, white hate biting down like teeth?

I've come to Tuskegee as if I too can join hands, as if I know how to make a difference in racial relations. But what do I really know about a race hatred so deep mobs attacked civil rights activists with bicycle chains, blackjacks, steel knuckles, and even bombs in Anniston and Montgomery and Birmingham?

Has that changed? Changed enough?

While at my desk in Iowa City, I thought of a writing class in Tuskegee as an offering, an opening.

But an opening to whom?

It might not seem so to the two boys in the grocery store. Would they see me as judging them? Misjudging them?

I stare into the inky dark, wishing for a breeze, for moonlight, for clearer sight.

"It's too dang hot," Malinda interrupts, as if reading my thoughts. She shakes her head, frowning. "That's one of the problems here. Heat and bugs and, well, not enough fun. This is a slooooow town." She laughs, staring out at the trees. "And not enough change. But that's *Al-a-bam-a*." She sighs. "Stuck in the past. What we need is a big boost of . . . *women!*" And she laughs again, her voice easy and true, a natural optimism that says we just gotta keep on pushing.

In the distance, I see the lights of the college, barely a shimmer of brightness, but a relief from the dark.

As we drive through the gates, Malinda gathers up our bags of groceries. "And here we are! *Hello, Mrs. Page.*"

When I hand Mrs. Page the quart of whole milk, I watch her shoulders relax, watch her lips soften and part. I watch as Mrs. Page tilts the paper bag, letting the Chilton County peaches tumble onto the counter, a cascade of soft-skinned peaches bunching up in a pile, their ripeness filling the air.

"Mmmmh-mmmh," Mrs. Page sighs with pleasure, closing her eyes. When she opens them, she looks at me, nodding, as if I've passed some invisible test. "Girl, you sit yourself down and eat some of these peaches," she insists.

She almost smiles.

I laugh. I can't help myself. I glance at Malinda. And then I get a bowl and a spoon from the cupboard Mrs. Page points me to, and I sit across from them in a kitchen chair, the three of us eating peaches, letting the juice run freely down the sides of our mouths, cold and sticky and sweet.

After we finish our peaches, Mrs. Page gives me two soft sheets to cover my rock-hard mattress. "You gotta have *sheets,*" she says, shaking her head with maternal finality. Embarrassed and grateful, I thank her. Now, I lie in my bare room, the AC cranked up, the windows clouded with moisture. I've turned out the lights, hoping for sleep, but behind my closed eyes I see the two boys watching me, their gaze disapproving, myself smiling, then glancing away.

Last year, when I made a short visit to Tuskegee University to do historical research, I'd felt self-conscious about my whiteness, sitting alone in the cafeteria, students at the historically Black university talking, laughing, and flirting all around me. And yet even with that awkwardness, I presumed acceptance, as if my identity though different was recognizable and valid. Now I have double vision: me seeing the two boys seeing me. A new frame of reference.

I also see Mrs. Page, grumpy when we first met, then inviting me to share her peaches. In her kitchen, I was no longer Mrs. Foster, no longer a white woman visiting from Iowa, a woman interrupting, perhaps even sabotaging, her routine but the familiar "Girl" who could pull up a chair and join in.

Can I? Is it possible to be a casual but interested participant in this town, to join that "big boost of *women*," Malinda advocated on our drive back to the dorm? Maybe all I have to offer is a willingness to move beyond the familiar, discovering parts of myself I've never acknowledged and following my curiosity while encouraging my students to follow theirs. Of course, I'll make mistakes, but this will be a beginning.

What Needs to Be Needed

STUDENTS SWARM DOWN THE STAIRS, through the halls, feet stamping, shuffling, in and out of the office of Booker T. Washington High School, where I sign in with the secretary. She glances grimly at me, then puts her hand out to stop a boy from going into the office. "You can't go in there yet!" she barks. The boy stops, starts to argue, "But I'm supposed—" then sees me, a white woman, and goes silent, still.

"You here to talk to the girls?" the secretary turns to me, and I nod. It's 2004 and I've come to talk to girls in Tuskegee, Alabama, hoping to pry into the secret web of their educational desires, to ask about their dreams, their despairs, to peek beneath the surface of their ambition.

"Mrs. LaPread says for you just to wait in her classroom and she'll send them in."

Months ago, when I asked Mrs. LaPread if I could interview girls in her English classes for an essay on what "smart" means to girls in the twenty-first century, she sized me up, a sharp, quick glance, then laughed. "Oh, yeah, they'll tell you," she said. "And more." Now, while I wait, sitting in a student desk and glancing at the familiar posters of Maya Angelou and Martin Luther King Jr., I wonder if I'm being presumptuous. Is it possible for a girl to imagine what kind of faith in the self and the system she'll need to overcome her personal anxieties as well as the constraints of poverty and place in order to cast herself into a larger life? Is it possible for any of us?

"A man's possibilities depend on the possibilities of the place where he finds himself," V. S. Naipaul once wrote. And yes, I've come here to take the temperature of place.

Tuskegee is a quiet, dusty town, rural and bleak, a town that looks like a Walker Evans photo of the 1930s with its abandoned houses and weed-choked yards, its empty streets and cracked sidewalks. In the last thirty years, the Black population has moved—like some grim fable—from disenfran-chisement to Black power to accommodationist politics, its economy hi-jacked by white flight (with the accompanying gutting of the tax base) and the dominance of state government (decision-making bounced from the county courthouse to the capital). In 1968, after a violent desegregation of the town's public school system, white residents fled to Auburn and Notasulga, and the town settled into its first giddy fling of Black power. Johnny Ford, a Demo-cratic campaign strategist for Bobby Kennedy in 1968, was elected the first Black mayor of Tuskegee in 1972. He grabbed the reins of power and ran with it, founding the Tuskegee Optimist Club, the National Conference of Black Mayors, and the World Conference of Mayors and launching a Model Cities Program and a Summer Youth Employment Project that pumped economic opportunities into the town.

Twenty-two years later, Johnny Ford is a Republican. Twenty-two years later, the town is simply poor. Broken sidewalks. Potholed roads. A crumbling library. No jobs.

Will the Smart Girls please meet Mrs. Foster in Mrs. LaPread's classroom!

When the girls arrive, their faces are shy, eager, curious, shadowed, wary. Chasity with her doe face, almond eyes, and mass of tiny braids sits across from Shana's wide-open gaze. Brittany giggles. Karenthear idly twirls the tas-sel on her purse, then stops abruptly, looking sheepish. These are the sixteen-and seventeen-year-old ambitious girls Mrs. LaPread has chosen for me, girls who chat easily with me about the heat—*"it just wants to beat you up!"*—the coming storm, about class work and basketball until our ordinary topics give way to the personal: the risks we've taken, the things we're proud of.

"I'm proud of my voice," Chasity says in a voice so soft and feminine I intuitively lean forward, "and proud of being in the Miss Junior Teen Alabama Contest."

"I play basketball." Shana speaks simply, as if this is her essential story. "I like doing that." Loose-bodied and easy, her hair knotted at the base of her skull, she shakes a leg as she talks. "You oughta come to one of my games."

"Well," Brittany sighs, looking pensively at her knees. "I'm not sure, you know." She's all dark eyes, pointy elbows, and skinny legs. "I got sent to an alternative school for two weeks for doing something . . . something I shouldn't have." She's trying to be sober, but a smile sneaks through, dissolving into giggles. "I'm just glad to be back." She grins. Her "crime," I'll learn later, was buying liquor underage, a crime a few kids in my own family have committed, though with lawyer fathers they negotiated that landscape quite differently.

Karenthear shakes her head, not ready to speak while Deneithra studies me with dark, hooded eyes before saying slowly, solemnly, "I'm proud I stayed in school. I got a sister dropped out in ninth grade, but not me." They all nod in unison as if this is the collective risk they've taken, the thing Deneithra has so boldly revealed.

They have stayed in school.

Their humble desires make me sweat. I look beyond them to the world outside the window where the wind is picking up, where a loose paper bag dances in the grass and fall leaves shiver on the trees, where a vital and unpredictable future awaits them. I think about the project I'm working on, a book that explores the various plots of female ambition in contemporary America. Last year, I interviewed juniors and seniors at Harvard, girls who talked easily, even glibly, about studying in Paris, in London, in Buenos Aires and worried about prepping for the MCAT, the LSAT, and the GRE while finishing honors theses on de Tocqueville and Emerson and applying for grants and grad schools. They know that Goldman Sachs will be recruiting in late fall, that their interviews for coveted slots on the *Advocate* are scheduled next week. "*Everything's a competition,*" one of them singsonged in the middle of our discussion, and we all laughed at the terrible truth. To the girls at Harvard, ambition is assertiveness, visibility, networking, a woman's rite of passage to careers and success, abundance and respect, a mind soaring into space. But here, in a place so deeply marked by poverty and racial tension, what can ambition possibly be?

The girls at Tuskegee are the first high school girls I've talked to, and together we sit crouched over student desks, fidgeting in the circle we've drawn, the windows rattling, the buzz of talk and shuffle of footsteps drifting in from the hall. "I'm the knee baby of four kids and I *know* I gotta do well," Deneithra says prophetically. "I got to finish school and go on to junior college." The others nod, faces hopeful, shy with pride. The girls tell me they want to go into sports medicine or into the US Air Force but can't remember the bones of the leg in anatomy class, don't know exactly why our armed forces are in Iraq. They don't know who Carol Mosely Braun is (though she's the first female African American senator and a presidential contender), don't know whether Osama bin Laden is connected to Saddam Hussein or just "some mean man." They don't know if the world is safe anymore. "Except nobody wants to bomb Alabama," Shana says, and despite ourselves, we all laugh.

I try to imagine them hiding out in the library, reading fat Russian novels or buried in science fiction or fairytales or scanning articles about the Iraq War in the *New York Times*. But I can't. And yet their voices are so full of innocence and urgency, so thick with girlish hope as they imagine themselves going to college, then getting good jobs, that I chide myself for my pessimism. Without prompting, they assure me that Black women's lives are no more troubled than white women's, even though there's still racism in the culture.

"The problems for women are single parenting and not enough money," Shana says, a reality she knows intimately. She's from a biracial family, her mother white, her father Black, a fact neither Shana's grandparents nor the KKK left undisputed in that small Alabama town where she was born. To make matters worse, Shana's father ran off, leaving the mother and daughter stranded, barely able to feed themselves.

"And trouble with men," Chasity adds, nodding at Shana, as if explicitly they understand that this is how most women's lives are diverted.

"But women gotta be strong," Brittany says, thumping the back of her desk with her fist, her eyes brightening. "Strong like my mama."

To my surprise, a thrill runs through me.

When the bell for next period interrupts us, the girls say, "Thank you, Mrs. Foster, for talking to us," as if my coming here is their bonus, a favor to them rather than the other way around. As I watch them leave—brown arms gathering up books and purses, skinny legs in blue jeans and flowered pants—something changes in me, loosens. Though I've come here to pry into their lives, to ask intimate questions, to write down their words and follow them to classes, ball games, the library, and lessons, I didn't know that I'd be moved. All of this seemed merely part of the research when they were just names on a page in Iowa, but now they're real flesh and blood girls with sly grins and careful frowns. Now they have shape and form, worries and desires, individual problems that nag and perplex them. I touch my skin, stroke the side of my arm, to see if I too am real.

Back in my motel room I watch the wind thrash the trees, a sudden squall splashing rain against the windows, drops streaking, then smearing the panes. I think about myself and worry about these girls. Though I'm not Black, I'm a small-town southerner and know viscerally the constraints of a provincial life. I remember my own boredom with high school, the slow tedium of classes, thick Alabama heat like a cloak over my brain, then the sense of relief when my mother whisked me out of school every Wednesday, driving an hour to a Jesuit college so I could take a writing class. In the evening we drove home in silence, night blackening the highway, the groves of trees bulky shadows looming near the road. I didn't need to talk. I was carrying something inside me, something I could not express, though I know now it was *hope*, the beginning of a dream. Little did I know that the class was a rite of passage, a place where I could learn the stepping stones of a discipline, the footpath to a bigger world. I was learning that meaning comes through expression and that expression can be nurtured, advanced by a focused effort. I was learning to push myself, to strive for something just beyond my reach.

I see now how firmly the pattern was set: Writing class led to expression, and expression, eventually, paved the way to identity. Behind that pattern was money and time and family expectation, and behind that, a validation of self so intrinsic I can't begin to unravel it, though its main asset was whiteness.

Unable to sleep, I lie down on the bed and stare at the ceiling as if it's breathing. I see the girls sitting around me: Chasity in her pink T-shirt and dark, faded jeans; Shana in navy sweats, her hair slicked back in a tight knot. Brittany's ponytail sticks straight out like a bottle brush. Deneithra wears hoop earrings that brush against the shoulders of her red T-shirt. "Boys," Karenthear said shyly, leaning towards me, "get in my way because they demand so much."

As I listened to them, I wished I had something concrete to tell them: *Do this! This is how you succeed. This is how you grab hold of your brain.* But I know only the bromides of a culture: *Study hard. Take yourself seriously. Think big.* Fairy-tale words in a middle-class romance.

More important, I have to ask myself, what *is* success? Is it only assertiveness, public visibility, financial independence, or is it something more allusive, more paradoxical, something that connects the head to the heart? Is success believing in yourself? Or is that both too simple and too unrealistic?

Shana, I know, is obsessed with basketball. She loves it more than she loves anything else. And yet she admits she's not tall enough to be taken seriously by most colleges, though she's willing to try out and take her chances. She's certainly ambitious, compelled by the game, "pumped," she would say, but is she unrealistic? Probably. But since realistic constraints have played only a small hand in my own choices, I'm not one to court the high road, to say no to desire. *Go for it, Shana!* I want to say. *Use everything you've got!* Because passion is the best reason to try anything, the only guarantee there is.

The next day I sit in a student desk in the back of the classroom, listening to the lesson. "What's the capital of Colorado?" the teacher asks. She's a large Black woman in a raspberry print outfit with a necklace of fine gold chains. Her voice is dramatic, insistent, full of quips and aphorisms. Still, the question startles me. This is a tenth grade English class, not sixth grade geography. "What's the capital of Missouri?"

"St. Louis," a kid says, eager and sure.

The teacher puts her hand on his forehead. "You are not well."

"Jefferson City," another kid finally raises her hand.

For five minutes, there's a relay of states and capitals: Arizona/Phoenix; Kansas/Topeka; Alaska/Juneau; Mississippi/Jackson; Idaho/Boise, a low drone of interest before the class moves to antonyms, synonyms, and pseudonyms, which prove equally problematic. "What is a pseudonym?" the teacher asks.

No one volunteers. Eyes glaze. Hands fiddle with pencils. There's a flight of crows out the window.

The teacher puts her hands on her hips. "Tell me where this hole is y'all go into?" She sighs and says flatly, "Mark Twain is a pseudonym for _____?"

Samuel Clemens, they say in unison.

Later in the afternoon, another class considers the distinctions between denotation and connotation. The students seem desultory and confused, sitting slack in their desks, notebooks closed, pencils strumming idly on their books. "Denotation," the teacher says as she walks among them, "means to mark plainly, to write down, to describe, whereas connotation is something else." She looks at them as they stare idly around the room. "Is there *anything* in your heads?" then she walks back to her desk. "Connotation is an inference. What would you *infer* if I came into this room and said, 'Mmmh-mmmh.'"

"That you smell something," one student says.

"That you see something bad."

"I think it's that you see something good."

"No way. She looks like she's seeing something she don't like."

The teacher sits down. "But you don't really know, do you? You can only infer what I mean from saying 'mmmh-mmh.' That's the reason for language. We can infer many things from a gesture or a sound, but we don't know specifically what someone means until they tell us in language."

What the girls infer from the larger culture is that staying in school is a good thing and that being a Black girl in Alabama—no longer a stigma—can translate into success.

"Success for women is *all* about having options," a sophomore at Harvard told me last year as we gazed at the maple trees coming to leaf in Harvard Square. "It's not enough to be smart. You've got to have choices. You've got to have more than a jam jar full of desires."

I remember my own girlhood in a small Alabama town where at age fourteen I knew only a negative ambition: *I don't wanna be a nurse, a teacher, or a librarian.* I remember being upset and standing in a mud puddle, its perimeter spreading as rain fell steadily into the grass, onto the dark shiny roots of trees humped up out of the ground. I was angry and confused because my world seemed so small, so ordinary, a world constricted by Daddy going to work and demanding and Mother deflecting, by a fleet of men organizing the library, the hospital, the ballpark, the church, men in maroon blazers, blue blazers, sometimes mustard blazers, men in pin-striped suits and wide ties, men in khakis, large stains of sweat under their arms, a deer tied to the tops of their pickups, men who fixed the washing machine, the air conditioner, and the telephone, men with hairy ankles and big feet who clumped through the den with mud on their shoes and sat in chairs waiting for someone to bring them a drink, men who were almost never teachers, nurses, or librarians. In the early 1960s, white middle-class men made the rules and ran the town while white middle-class women tended kids, fixed meals, shopped for the family, and volunteered for the community.

The struggle for me was emblematic of a time and a place in small-town America, a rural outpost that claimed intimacy and safety but presented few options for an imagined female life. Choices were elsewhere, in New York, San Francisco, Denver, and Philadelphia. Now, we subscribe to the myth that we're all linked together, that the modern world is one large Internet family, informed and intact, an imaginative grid. But this new democratized view also has sealed borders, fixed boundaries. The inside and outside still exist.

As I'm leaving Booker T. Washington High School that day, I learn that the school is in "caution" because only half of the class "walked" last year at graduation. The other half failed the exit exam. And then I understand: state capitals, synonyms, antonyms. The Bush doctrine: Rote learning. Pass the test. Move from caution to clear.

I drive through the deserted town, past My Mama's, a little fast-food joint with its boarded-up windows and empty parking lot, past Fred's BBQ, the Country Store, Rockies' Billiards, and Vel's Trendsetting and Styling until I'm outside the city limits. Here cotton grows in nearby fields between groves of forest, an endless sprinkling of white. I'm in the country now. Giant oak trees. Wide ditches. Trees green with shiny leaves. As I stare out the window at the beauty of the land, I know that I long for a heroic story, perhaps the old story of overcoming, "pushing that rock up the hill," and what I see around me is an ordinary story of predictable poverty, of girls growing up in small wooden houses on dirt roads out in the country or on the back streets of Tuskegee— old cars in the yard, no flowers, no beauty—girls who still have trouble with double negatives and verb tenses, girls who worry about the demands of boys more than the demands of academics, girls who will go into the US Air Force and help fight our wars. These are the girls whom no one notices, whom no one writes stories about. These are the girls who have not yet learned to dream beyond the immediate glory of winning a basketball game or going to junior college. These are not the Black girls who have "challenged" their backgrounds nor the middle and upper middle-class girls courted by Harvard and Yale. Their biggest hope is to see a super-mall, to graduate high school, and go to junior college.

Here the American Dream of success is a dirty joke.

Will the Smart Girls come immediately to the library!

What can it mean to them that the announcement over the loudspeaker calls them "smart?"

"It means you know things," Shana tells me.

"What things?" I ask.

"It means you've been *educated,*" Chasity says. "That you want to go to college."

"What about passion for a subject?" I ask. "What about the thrill of creation?"

"Oh, that would be *good,*" Brittany says, her eyes bright with interest. She leans toward me. "How do you get that?"

"I wish I knew," I laugh, thinking that passion for a subject, a profession, even a hobby is what so many of us seek, an intrinsic connection fueled by desire. Most of us cut our teeth on education because mastering a discourse has been the traditional claim to power, a jump-start to the middle class, to jobs and respect. It's the way we gain a vocabulary, learn to critique texts, to articulate ideas. And yet for me, as well as for many people, the path to intellectual passion was less direct, more eccentric, less dependent on the will. Often my own life has been defined by crisis, by a political or psychological trauma that made me see through the veil of circumstances to a deeper reality. For many women—both Black and white—it's the battle itself that leads to subjecthood, a crucial gathering of instinctual forces to push against the status quo. I can't help but think of Rosa Parks, of Ida B. Wells, of Harriet Jacobs and Sojourner Truth, of a lineage of Black women who stayed in the battle until something insistent was won. Would we even know of Rosa Parks, already a fine seamstress and anti-rape advocate, if she hadn't refused to move to the back of the bus that afternoon in Montgomery in 1955?

I look at these girls. Their current battle is to face down the tradition of dropping out when school gets too demanding, too "crazy." "We gotta push on through," Brittany says, "studying instead of making burgers at McDonalds."

In white middle-class America, success demands distrust of the good girl image—the acquiescent, trusting girl—and depends on assertiveness, risk, a hint of rebellion, but ironically, in this Tuskegee high school, the tables are turned: Assertiveness means following the rules, trusting the system. Assertiveness means putting your faith in school, risking hope.

"Is it okay to be a nerd?" I ask, curious if the term has any credibility here.

"Yeah, as long as you don't act *odd*," Shana says. "You know, dress weird, wear your pants up to here." She puts her hands up to her chest. The other girls giggle at this absurd characterization.

"It's okay," Chasity says. "All the leaders in the school make the best grades. And most of them are girls."

As I sit in my motel room with a Big Mac and Diet Coke, I can't help thinking that whatever these girls are getting, it's just not enough. They do not have computers at home, do not read newspapers or national magazines or have AP classes. They have almost none of the "extras"—the lessons, the tutors, the camps, the group outings—available to many other girls. Then, as quickly, I chastise myself: This is a white, middle-class assessment of what is required for success, and in truth, the world is open to anyone who can read. Isn't it? In frustration, I pick up pages of the girls' writing, a twenty-minute session when I asked each one to write about a single day in Tuskegee during the past year. I scan the pages until I come to this sentence: *My life is almost beginning but I have no starting point. There has to be somewhere for me to begin. Somebody has to recognize me. Somebody must be able to see that I am what is needed. I am what needs to be needed and needed is what I need to be.*

I get up from the bed and pull aside the curtains. The moon hides behind a skirt of fog. The sky looks untethered as if I could reach up and pull down distant stars. It's true that ambition begins wherever it begins. In the crevices of desire. In the ache for applause. In the recognition that the self can't do it alone. The self needs to be needed. How simply this girl has stated the problem. I look at the name on the paper: Chasity Grace, the girl who said she likes to sing. I think of Chasity with her head bent over the paper, braids spilling across her shoulders. What she's written is not only smart but poetically true: each of us longs for a starting point, a liftoff to the next phase of our lives. Each of us needs attention. What needs to be needed is faith that the world will open itself and that somewhere inside we'll feel worthy of being heard. It seems such a simple transaction—a call-and-response—but each of us knows it is a long arduous journey and what if there is no one listening on the other side?

It's late afternoon when I take Chasity to her vocal training lesson at Tuskegee University. As we turn from the shabbier part of town into the college with its red brick Georgian style buildings, its groomed flower beds, Chasity tells me about being in a play this summer. "I tried out and got a part," she says shyly. "Speak up," I heard one of her teachers say to her today. "Do you think I can hear you if you don't speak up?"

"I want to be famous," she says, barely a whisper. "I want to have pretty clothes and be seen on TV." I look at her caramel skin and black liquid eyes. Her smile is magnetic, and yet I can't help but think about the hard knocks of a creative life, how pushy you have to be. *You have to yell*, I want to say, but I only nod my reassurance and follow her through the maze of rooms to Dr. Barr's studio.

It is when Chasity opens her mouth to sing that a different voice emerges: a strong, powerful soprano, vibrant and rich. There's a change in the air, a sense of purpose and focus. I can feel it in the room as if there's an infusion of energy, a high wind of excitement. She listens to the teacher, no longer demure or small, but standing taller, straighter. She practices sighing, humming. She sings a series of scales, her voice sometimes breaking. "Don't worry about how you sound," Dr. Barr tells her. "Worry about how it *feels* inside. We're trying to build a sense of what your mouth and internal structure feel like so you can gain control of it." Chasity nods, then begins an assigned piece. "Again," the teacher says, and they both laugh when her voice strains on a high note. "Let's start here at this phrase." He gives her a few bars and she sings, the sound rising, spilling into the air, her voice clear and holy like the ringing of a bell.

"Again," the teacher says. And she sings.

An hour later, we take the back roads out of Tuskegee, through farms and empty fields, cows grazing in the pastures, dogs rushing at the car, barking as we slip by. The sun as it sinks toward the horizon is bloodred, gorgeous.

"How did you begin these lessons?" I can't help but ask, still surprised by the power of Chasity's voice.

"Because of the play last summer. I was in *Purlie*."

"Really? What happened?"

"I fell in love." Chasity smiles and her face changes. Perhaps it is the late afternoon light slanting through the windows, a flicker of evening. Her eyes are the same liquid black but there's something more confident, more assured in her gaze. The shy girl seems to have melted away and a bolder one climbed aboard. "The director taught me to see the play in my head and to look out at the audience like it's your window. She thought I could sing so she pays for my lessons."

When I turn into a lane, an old wooden house sits beneath a canopy of trees, the front porch leaning slightly to the left, a dog sleeping on the steps. Her mother, she's told me, works two jobs, seven days a week.

"My house," Chasity says happily, shifting her backpack as she gets out. "Bye-bye and thanks for bringing me home," she waves as she walks back-wards toward her house, the dog whining as she nears.

I wave back, watching.

There is a beginning after all. One girl has stepped outside the circle.

It's true I see only glimpses of these girls' lives, not the heart. The heart lies in daily struggle, in small moments of attention, perhaps like the one that occurs as I'm leaving Booker T. Washington High School on Friday morning. My arms are full of their gifts—a sweatshirt with the school logo, a coffee mug, a T-shirt, a book about the murder of Martin Luther King Jr. I'm walking down the hallway past students and faculty, nodding to those who smile back at me. Out the windows I see the morning has turned windy and gray, the sun eclipsed by scattered clouds. I am keeping counsel with myself, still brooding about the future of these girls, when Brittany rushes up behind me, Karenthear in tow. "Mrs. Foster," she calls, slightly winded, her sweatshirt bagging over her jeans. "Mrs. Foster. *Please*." She stops and holds up a camera. She wants a picture of the two of us together, shoulder to shoulder, arms loose, heads tilted toward each other. I stand next to her, feeling self-conscious and silly. "Now smile," she says, bumping me with her hip. And for a single instant, I forget myself. I am not a researcher, a witness, or a spy. I am a girl again: shy and hopeful and clueless about the battles ahead. What I see are pansies and bluebells blooming in a neighbor's yard and a two-lane road that leads to somewhere.

If I Could Write Postcards to Mary Hamilton

I.

WHAT I LOVE ABOUT YOU is your fierceness, the way you lived within the blurred lines of history. I like to imagine the day you faced down a Gadsden, Alabama judge, a white rooster of a man, small and squat, his feet propped up on the table as he muttered *what he'd like to do to you if you worked in his kitchen*[1] while the prosecuting attorney repeatedly asked why you were riding a bus through Alabama, disturbing the peace, "our peace," and invading our state. But the thing is, he kept calling you "Mary," a twenty-eight-year-old Black woman who'd had the audacity to be a Freedom Rider, to which you replied, "I won't respond until you call me *Miss* Hamilton."[2] When I read that, I could barely breathe. I loved it! I'd like to think that I would have uttered just such a demand, though, as a white southern girl brought up to defer to male authority, I'd probably have held my tongue, looked down at my shoes, embarrassed and scared, and yes, been terrified at even the thought of becoming a Freedom Rider. But your words so infuriated the judge, he dropped his feet to the floor. "That'll be five days in jail," he snarled, then added a fifty-dollar fine.[3] And the rest is history: Your request was upheld by the Alabama Court of Appeals and the Alabama Supreme Court, and then, as *Hamilton v. Alabama*, it journeyed noisily up the ladder to the US Supreme Court where, in 1964, the decision was unanimously reversed, acknowledging that language is a means of equality and that respect resides in the details: *Every* person who appears before the court should be addressed with an honorific, Miss, Mrs., or Mr.[4]

One small step for womankind.

II.

What are you? *Who* are you? This was inevitably the rub for a light-skinned Black woman as you stood in line to be processed at a Jackson, Mississippi, jail in midsummer where, even in the hallways, there was the reek of sweat, the stench of urine, the overcrowding of bodies. When you were marked as White by a jailer and corrected him, telling him "No, I'm Black," he erupted with righteous fury as if you were messing with him, trying to fool him, trying to get him in trouble for putting a white girl in a cell with Black girls. When you assured him you were Black, he wondered aloud what else you might be, thinking he'd had enough of this agitator-ambiguity, these confusing pigments, willfully ignoring what his great-granddaddy might have done to your great-grandmother without her permission.[5]

"Put her down as Black, Mexican, and white," he barks, taking control of your ancestry. Then, for added bias, "and a member of the Communist Party."[6]

What he doesn't know is how *what you are* and *who you are* have become intrinsically, ruthlessly bound: You are a fighter, a resister, a high-spirited woman with such a keen sense of mattering you kept irrefutably quiet out of sheer spite when a former jailer "threw you in an elevator and ran it up and down again and again," hoping you'd scream in terror because he knew and you knew that "no one would hear."[7]

What he doesn't know is that as a civil rights activist you've been kicked and beaten, been dumped in ugly, sweltering fifteen-by-fifteen-foot cells with mice and insects and a foul, barely working toilet, been given unnecessary, sometimes painful Lysol-based vaginal exams, been disrespected and cursed and taunted, your clothes taken away, your toothbrush taken away, and even when lying on a hard steel bunk beneath barred windows in sweat-soaked darkness, you've managed to raise your spirits by a single liberating thought "We're finally fighting back! We're not gonna take it anymore."[8]

Defiance, you've discovered, is a verb.

III.

For six weeks, I lived in a rental house in Fort Morgan, Alabama, a cozy gray cottage on stilts surrounded by saw palmettos and ragged seagrass, three short blocks from the Gulf of Mexico where the noon sun seared my fair skin. I lived there to be near my family, my ninety-five-year-old mother, my brother, my brother-in-law, my nephews and niece, and their clever, demanding children.

What's absent in that sentence is really the center of that sentence: my sister. Like you, she died of ovarian cancer.[9] She in 2017. You in 2002. She at seventy-one. You at sixty-seven. Both of you died too soon, too young, both of you suffering agonies from that horrible disease, pain becoming your grim, attentive guardian.

And yet during the six weeks I lived in Alabama, a part of me secretly believed that if I could live near where my sister had lived, even for a short time, I might recapture a small part of what had been lost. Of course, this was fickle, even absurd. Instead, I walked around in a daze, staring at tiny green lizards drowsing on the porch railing and giant lily pads in a nearby alligator slough as migrating geese soared above tall, skinny pines. Endlessly, I watched the horizon and swatted at gnats.

We called my sister, a doctor, "The Queen Bee," because she was the first female doctor in this town, her head held high enough to meet the male gaze. "A novelty," the other doctors said, grinning, until their patients left them to be under her care.

What I found instead of my sister was you, a woman who, like her, was a *force*, intolerant of bullshit, willful, ornery, impatient, and dramatically inclined to demand center stage, resisting anyone who tried to silence you. "Don't you dare . . ." is the sentence I hear on both of your lips. Even writing this, I laugh. I imagine that when the two of you weren't insisting or defying or challenging what you considered "just dead fucking wrong," you both flashed a smile big with enthusiasm, one that promised intimacy and affection and was a preface to a casual-but-never-to-be-refused favor. Only rarely did either of you say, "Please."

IV.

"Go on. *Try it*," my sister used to say, both encouraging and frustrated if I showed the least intimidation toward whatever hallucination she considered a bold plan. *Try singing alone in the dark. Try eating five pieces of coconut cake in one sitting. Try running for President of the Science Club. Try sleeping until the very last minute before the algebra test.* Though we'd grown up in a small provincial town in the very toe of Alabama, my sister decided in fifth grade she'd live someday in New York. It wasn't a girl's hopeful wish. It was a formal decision, and she engineered it right after college, not overly concerned about what work she did, only that she have the *experience* of living in Manhattan and discovering something new and liberating, something she hadn't known about herself and the world.

To her—and of course, this is partly because she was young and white and middle-class—the world had no boundaries. Every act, she assumed, depended on her insight, her resilience, her cunning and clarity. And when she ran into restrictions, she simply sidestepped them, diverting into another path, avoiding the backlash of depression and sustaining her forward momentum. It wasn't, I discovered much later, that she was smarter or prettier or more talented than other people. It was simply that she trusted herself, certain that her decisions mattered and that whatever happened would complicate her, even if it added a new burden.

Now, from my reading, I see that you too were bold and directed though you didn't have my sister's options, her white, middle-class privilege, her protective safety net, her economic advantage. What you had was perhaps more profound: a rebel's demand for agency and the irresistible heat of a consuming idea—to disrupt the old order and demand the new. There's the story of how you and the other Freedom Riders, after being tossed into Parchman prison (the oldest prison in our country) for daring to ride that bus, began singing freedom songs to settle yourselves and lift your spirits. Maybe you were singing *"On the road to freedom / We shall not be moved / Just like a tree that's standing by the water side / We shall not be moved."* On hearing your young, vibrant voices, the guards went nuts, became so furious they swore they'd take away the damn mattresses if you didn't stop that infernal singing. *Oh, deep in my heart / I do believe / We shall overcome, some day.* You sang words suggesting optimism, determination, an acceptance of hardship and anguish, words promising that the spirit, so barefoot with longing, so fevered with need, can be stronger than the body.

"You bitches, we'll *take* them," the guards threatened.

Laughing, you girls grabbed those torn, filthy mattresses—so old they were as thin as light—and piled them at the door. "Take them, take them, take them," you called out cheerfully before you turned back to your singing *". . . been a long, a long time coming / But I know a change gonna come, oh yes it will."*[10]

V.

As the hazy yellow light fades from the day, I'm still reading about your fearlessness, still searching for my sister, but what I see is myself: My boldness is reactive, a shattering of my carefully constructed self, even though I wear a tight girdle of anger, barely glimpsed beneath my clothes. In controversy, I've most wanted to duck down low and watch, secretly protected, slyly anonymous, allowed to witness without choosing sides. It's this timidity I find despicable. It's the part of myself I intentionally hide.

In many ways, I overcame it by fighting with my sister, by disagreeing with my sister, by watching my sister when she was furious with someone else as if I were being mentored in fierceness, my mind inscribing her explosion of anger, the knee-jerk tongue-lashing, eye-searing body language of attack, and then practicing it myself.

Lucky and unlucky for me, my best trait is surveillance.

VI.

And it's this I've wanted to tell you, Mary, this small and yet large thing: Often we need another woman's boldness to startle us to attention.

Native Daughter

WHEN I GLANCE AT MY bookshelves, a dark rose cover catches my eye: *Outside the Magic Circle*, an autobiography by Virginia Foster Durr, a white southern activist who fought long and hard against the poll tax, championed Rosa Parks and the Montgomery bus boycott, and opened her house to SNCC volunteers arriving in Montgomery in the 1960s to work on voter registration.

I didn't discover her until the early 1990s, when I began writing essays about Alabama, a time when I desperately needed to know that white southern women had joined Black southern women in the fight for racial equality. How had I missed her, this native daughter who was as voiced in the world of class-ridden, race-haunted Alabama as in the world of power-hungry Washington, DC?

No matter. I found her. I read her. And yet for many years my life of teaching and writing pulled me in other directions even as her book sat prominently on my study shelves. Then, quite suddenly, I came back to her in the spring of 2019 after I taught a graduate class, "History and the Sense of the Tragic," a seminar on Black southern writers for MFA students at the University of Iowa in preparation for a trip to the National Memorial for Peace and Justice (my third visit) and the Southern Poverty Law Center in Montgomery, Alabama. Excited about the class, I wanted it to be both critically provocative and personally rewarding, but to my surprise, two weeks before the class began, students questioned the authority of a white woman to teach the story of southern racial trauma. They preferred a person of color. Though I longed to be admired rather than dismissed, I knew my students had a valid point: I was culturally buried not only in whiteness but also in middle-class whiteness, my credentials resting only on canonical preparation, a writer's intellectual and emotional curiosity, and a conflicted southern identity. And yet more important than my own validation, I believed, was the need for students—mostly East and West Coast students—to have the opportunity to visit the National Memorial for Peace and Justice in Montgomery, a city that had once been the center of our nation's apartheid, the capitol of the Confederacy. No one else at Iowa had stepped up to teach this class.

And yet by the end of the semester, I was tired, more patched together than whole. *Who had I become?* As I put away my syllabus and class papers, I longed for another woman's words to give me grit, to bear witness to the hard slog of political work, to instill me with more patience for myself and my students. Stubbornly, I wanted to teach the class again. A better class.

And so, in late May, I flew to Alabama to visit my mother, then drove a rental car to Montgomery in search of Virginia Foster Durr in the Alabama State Archives, hoping that something in the stack of files and correspondence with her name would tutor me in endurance and resilience, and yes, instruct me on how to bear defeat and to change.

At the archives, I sat at an oblong table, articles and folders fanned out around me, taking frantic notes and iPhone pictures of letters to read later, while worrying that my trip might be futile, as I had only five hours before going home to take care of my ninety-five-year-old mother. After two hours, I was interrupted—my mother had fallen in the kitchen—so I grabbed my notes and rushed down the interstate.

It was on the drive back to my mother's house that I began thinking about Virginia Foster Durr's story, letting my mind drift to her upbringing, her marriage, her temperament, her rebellion, and her work with Eleanor Roosevelt, meditating on how she'd internalized the mythology of southern women, then broken free. After she left Alabama in 1933, something happened to her, something sharp and merciless, something that lifted everything up from the inside and made her take off her white gloves and dirty her hands with politics.

I tried to imagine *how* she changed, what loyalties shattered, what self-discoveries interrupted her day, what battles, perhaps like mine, she'd painfully or humbly fought. Waking up, after all, is always a battle with the self. How could it be otherwise?

To my surprise, I realized that I needed to write about her, needed to both dissect and *reimagine* her story in the hope of understanding my own. Who was Virginia Foster Durr to me?

A journey then. An exploration.

RETURN, 1951

I've decided to start in the middle of her life—yes, in that sticky, uncertain center where her momentum flattens, then irrevocably shifts. For sixteen years, Virginia adored the hungry tumult of Washington, DC, those New Deal years so full of urgency and possibility, the world slowly edging away from the brink. Here, she was wide-awake and desperately alive, born with a social personality to love parties and champion causes, to gossip and petition and believe in reform.

Now, here she is at the Sunday dinner table in Montgomery, forty-eight years old and determined to be pleasant and cooperative because she and her husband, Cliff, and their daughters must live, like refugees, with Cliff's mother in his childhood home. Cliff's uncles, cousins, and his mother—a "true Southern lady"[1]—sit across from her, finishing the midday meal. Of course, the food couldn't be better, especially the peach cobbler with a perfect scoop of vanilla ice cream melting on top. I imagine the maid has just put a dessert plate in front of her and is now pouring the coffee into china cups while a young Black girl follows behind with a pitcher of cream. Relieved that everyone's on their best behavior, chatting about this and that, Virginia takes a little break from her worries and glances out the window at the oppressive afternoon heat shimmering on the grass, glittering on the ivory front steps just as Cliff's uncle says, "I declare, if Cliff had just stayed in Alabama, he probably would've amounted to something. But going up *there* and working for the government—here he is flat on his back and broke too."[2]

She turns quickly, wanting to laugh at the absurdity just as another uncle perhaps nods vigorously. "Big mistake. Mighty big." So, she takes a bite of peach cobbler, indulging in its tart sweetness and tries not to think about the purgatory that is Montgomery.

"Down here" everyone lets loose what they think: Cliff's family hates the New Deal no matter that Cliff was a "brain truster" for almost sixteen years in FDR's administration; they hate the idea of "mixing up the races," insisting that Black people need "looking after" by the white race as if they were children; they hate labor organizations and protests and union people and disapprove of Virginia and her rabble of liberal friends with their meddling ideas. But lord do they love Cliff and their three daughters.[3]

At least that.

As she stirs two teaspoons of sugar into her coffee, she wonders how long she can stand it, though what a silly question since what choice does she have? Cliff's uncle is right: She and Cliff are broke, dead broke, three-kids-and-no-hope-of-a-job broke. Cliff is in bed recuperating from back surgery—spinal fusion—a recovery that will require six months; their three girls are registered in the Montgomery schools; all their savings have been drained to pay for the surgery and a month's hospital stay; and Cliff's mother has graciously taken them in, in effect rescuing them. Right now, Virginia's big ambition is to learn to type well enough to become a proper secretary and start making money, though this seems so small, so suffocating, so dull it's like being shut up in a closet, struggling to breathe.[4]

How did this happen? How did everything shift under her feet? How can it be that she—a woman who fought tooth and nail against the poll tax, side by side with Eleanor Roosevelt, who talked weekly to congressmen and senators—is, here in Alabama, a pariah, a burden, resigned from all the organizations she loves: the Women's Division of the Democratic party, the Southern Conference for Human Welfare, the ACLU, as if atonement is required?[5]

She drinks her coffee and eats her peach cobbler. Through the partly open door, she sees the Black maid stacking the dirty dishes while the uncles worry if the "durn" Communists are going to overrun the country. She both listens and doesn't, the conversation all too familiar since she grew up one hundred miles up the road in Birmingham.

BEGINNINGS, 1903

The one thing I know: Virginia Foster Durr didn't start out a rebel. Oh no, she was raised inside that same holy belief that wealth and whiteness were ordained by God. Born into the aristocratic South with white people high on cotton, investing in coal and steel, the "Black laws" in place, sharecroppers stripped of possibility, and the "best" people singing with money. "You were born to be either wealthy and wise and rich and powerful and beautiful and healthy or you were born to be poor and downtrodden and sick and miserable and drunken and immoral."[6]

She wrote that. She believed it. To her, it seemed inevitable, sacred, a given. It was what her powerful daddy taught, her seminarian father—not a preacher, but a Presbyterian *minister*—who'd studied at Princeton and the University of Berlin, a man wedded to books and privilege, a registrar with the Birmingham Board of Registrars who bragged he'd "never registered any black man" even if that man "had been to Harvard."[7] His philosophy wasn't to her simply an idea, a plot created by men determining who gets what and who doesn't, but the capital T Truth.

Everyone knew it.

She did.

Until, that is, she didn't.

And that's what interests me, how her ideas about privilege and justice began to wobble, how that holy belief jiggled loose, becoming merely an idea, an assumption, a premise that could be critiqued and resisted, seen for its economic presumptions and social capital.

How does *the inevitable* for any of us become obsolete?

FORTUNE, 1918

Perhaps it was Virginia's good fortune not to be her daddy's favorite—he chose her older sister, a pretty, more conventional girl who married Hugo Black—and this choice pushed Virginia to develop a more independent spirit, a mind quick to align with imaginative friends who were great talkers and readers, lively girls who liked to laugh and shunned all that glossy female perfection.

And perhaps it mattered that she was sent to New York to attend Miss Finch's finishing school, where she was curious and loquacious, and then to Wellesley College where more liberal values prevailed. As my friends often say, "You southern girls should be sent to boot camp in New York, if nothing else so you can learn to be rude."

I don't know if Virginia learned to be rude, but she certainly brushed up against ideas very different from her family's, and though she resisted many of them, that aristocratic "Truth" began to crack in the corners, to tear and fade.

HISTORY, 1961

It's a big leap to move her from a privileged girlhood or even from that or-dinary typing class in Montgomery to the arrest of Rosa Parks and the

Montgomery bus boycotts, to she and Cliff and E. D. Nixon and Charles Gomillion working together to further racial integration in Alabama. So, I won't
move so fast. Let's allow that part of her life to gloss the story, shimmering at
the edges, breathing quietly, waiting to emerge. Before this happens, there's so
much she has to learn, so much growing up she has to do.

EXPECTATIONS, 1921–1922

Though she takes her daddy's high-ceilinged rhetoric to Wellesley College,
it's here that she has a taste of what it might mean to be intellectually independent, surrounded by books and friends, studying anthropology and geology,
reading about the Russian Revolution and the reproduction of frogs. It's here
that she learns to kiss and dance, rubbing elbows with Harvard boys and even
Rockefellers and Vanderbilts, feeling the exquisite shimmer of stockings on
her legs, until quite suddenly during her sophomore year that life goes flat and
dark when the cotton economy crashes and all she can say is *"the boll weevil
ate up my education."*[8]

I see her that last month at Wellesley, the end of her second year, realizing
it's over, all the fun and study slipping steadily from her grasp before she returns to Alabama. Still, she's learned a thing or two, had some of her "presumptions" exposed. Early in the year when she saw a Black student sitting at her
assigned dinner table, she went straight to the head of the house to complain,
insisting that "my father would have a fit" and asking to be reassigned.[9] Of
course, she expected to be accommodated. She was from Alabama, and people there didn't do such things, but to her surprise this New England woman,
very proper, very curt, but with expressive eyes, explained that the rules of the
college determined you were to eat at the table to which you were assigned for
a month and you could change after that. She then assured Virginia, her voice
quiet, that if she couldn't accept the terms, she could withdraw. She wouldn't
be expelled, but the college would allow withdrawal.[10] I imagine that Virginia
stared at her, mouth agape as if she didn't understand, though the woman's
gaze was direct and steady. And then, understanding, she closed her mouth,
realizing that what her daddy didn't know couldn't hurt him.

Six months later, she had no choice. Unmarried and unmoored, a tall,
myopic, raw-boned girl, she must go home and do what was expected: make
her debut, which meant parties and balls and afternoon teas with crustless
sandwiches and petits fours and eligible men . . . especially men. Young,

appropriate men. Marriageable men. I can't help but laugh—she's denied an education, but her family will move heaven and earth to finance parties and gowns and tiny beaded purses, satin shoes and garlands of roses, the boll weevil be damned.

POLITICS, 1933–1938

And yet she marries. Marries well. Virginia meets Clifford Durr, a young lawyer, at church and then at the county bar association law library where she just happens to be the librarian, where some invisible pull between them vibrates in the air. Maybe it's her eyes that draw him or her small bow-like mouth. Maybe it's the way she shakes her head, making her auburn hair shimmer in the light. But I imagine it's how easily she talks, the feisty certainty of her thinking, the wry humor drawling beneath her drawl, the quickness with which she sizes up a newcomer. Now everything is as it should be: a wedding followed by parties, dinners, a home, membership in the Junior League, and then the birth of children. Happiness, for her, is living as a young married woman in Birmingham, Alabama, until Cliff 's boss—who hates Virginia's brother-in-law, Hugo Black—fires him (or he resigns) in the midst of the Depression and they're suddenly dumped in the heap of the unemployed. After some months of casting about, Cliff is officially pulled into FDR's administration in Washington, DC, a place and a time like no other.[11]

"Some women fight, and others do not," Joan Didion writes persuasively in her essay on Georgia O'Keeffe. And yet Didion says nothing about *learning* to fight, as if the instinct has to be inborn rather than learned and unleashed, as if loss can't put iron in the soul.

And Virginia knows a thing or two about loss.

With her Rhodes Scholar lawyer husband now working as assistant general counsel of the Reconstruction Finance Corporation for the New Deal, they settle into a pretty house in Seminary Hill—in the "genteel" countryside just outside Washington, DC—with their three children, a cook, a nurse, and a part-time gardener and wash lady, servants Virginia takes for granted. She can't deny that this life is thrilling—all the talk, the ambition, the important people, the gossip, the dinner parties—until quite suddenly, she's trapped in the icy winter of grief.

Their three-year-old son, so blond and beautiful and named after Cliff, has just died three days after surgery from a burst appendix (before penicillin) and she's unable to lift the cloud of depression, unable to think, to feel, to do anything but walk around the house, saturated with sadness.[12] I imagine she is pacing back and forth across the living room, wearing a path in the rug, unable to stop. What to do? Where to turn?

Months go by. She continues to walk. Silent, inconsolable. Nothing eases the pain, slows the throb of her pulse.

And then abruptly she decides to claw her way out of mourning by distraction and diversion, a restless mind's descent. The La Follette Civil Liberties Committee hearings are underway, a four-year investigation into the interference of the rights of labor unions to organize and to exercise free speech. She stares at the schedule. Though she knows nothing about labor unions, it's as good a distraction as any.

And so, one morning in early May, the oak leaves a bright green, the mist rising on the Potomac, the smell of ambition and change thickening the air, Virginia rides with Cliff through the blur of DC traffic. Until now, almost everything in her life has followed a predictable path: education, marriage, volunteer work, childbirth, mothering, a resilient social life and Sunday afternoon get-togethers where she, who loves parties and people, talks easily to friends. The worst of the Depression, thank God, is over, but it's not smooth sailing; the country, having put the brakes on laissez-faire capitalism, is struggling through a recession.

I imagine Virginia sitting inconspicuously in the Senate gallery, a sad, tall woman with deeply curious eyes. She watches and listens. And yet even as she listens, occasionally taking notes and letting her bare feet rest on the cool, wooden floor, her shoes slipped off, her toes flexing, she remembers her son's hair—soft as silk and so blonde it was almost white. His eyes were shaped like hers, large and dark-fringed, narrowing at the edge. When he was born, all her friends congratulated her on having done "something really great for humanity." Briefly she closes her eyes, remembering, and then she stares out the window where the air is balmy, the sunlight crisp, while in the chambers there's only the harsh shadow of anger and bitterness. She hears contempt and despair in a miner's voice as he calls out someone's a liar. And she shakes her head and stares at the accused, perhaps some deputy sheriff from Kentucky, a short, wiry, cunning man in a broad-brimmed black hat saying, "We-llll now, listen, I always carry a pistol. The law obliges. I's just following the law."

She listens, glad for the shouting and accusing until one day men discuss what they call the Steel Police, a private police force hired by TCI in Birmingham, Alabama, to fight the unions, and there's a sharp click in her mind, sudden, irreversible.[13] She leans forward, listening intently, her feet cool on the floor.

That's the subtle change, isn't it? *Leaning* forward, no longer detached, her mind alert, listening instead of distracted. Here's the first time I really see her. Not the brooding, mournful mother or the warm, funny, ambitious wife, but a woman with an intellectual force running through her, a jolt of aliveness, a keenness. This, I think, is where she lives.

The next day she sits again in the gallery while some bigwig from a mining company is on the stand. "We treat our workers nicely," he says in a friendly, thoughtful voice, his shirt white and crisp beneath his dark, expensive suit.[14] He looks like he could be sitting in the front pew of the Presbyterian Church where her daddy is the minister. "We always treat our people nicely," implying they don't *need* to join a union.

"But they have a *right*," I imagine a senator interjects, not quite pointing a finger. "That is, a constitutionally guaranteed right to join a union."

"Listen," the older man leans forward, his voice now with an edge, "my grandfather *built* the town. My father *built* that church. That was my church."[15] But he stops just short of saying what's implied: *He owns the town. He owns the people. He is the town. It's his to do with as he wishes. He can hire and fire whomever he wants. And whose business is it if the company store returns a huge profit and no independent store is allowed to compete? It's just business. His business.*

He's followed by a miner who tells about being tear-gassed during a strike, another miner about being beaten by strikebreakers, his arm broken, then another saying how his phone was tapped and his mail read by company police, "and they tttttried"—he can barely get out the word—to shut up his wife and his children and now "he's done been fired." The men testifying are countrypeople, wary and self-conscious and dressed in overalls and dungarees, not certain what to do in an elevator, a contraption they've never seen, or how to sit comfortably with all these people staring at them.

Virginia stares at the miners too, some with hair thick and wild and as gray as her heart. "It was exactly like slavery times," she writes in her notebook, "except they paid the workers."[16]

I can see her scribbling these words even as a ruckus of noise erupts around her, the gavel pounding, somebody yelling, somebody coughing, her mind humming with new thoughts as old ones fade into silence. There are always two realities: a glimpse of summer trees, lightning bugs at dusk, the laughter of children running through the house, one of them always trailing, calling out "wait!" And then the other: the slow drag of sadness, the house cold and dark, a shoe caught on the middle step. She's lived for most of her life in the former. Now she's taken up residence in the latter.

But the truth is, she knows next to nothing about labor unions or laborers, about countrypeople and their woes or the political machinations of their bosses. Not even the vocabulary. Not yellow-dog contracts, blacklists, open shop, scrip, deputized mine guards. She doesn't know anything about industrial espionage, about strikebreaking mercenaries hired by companies to disrupt a strike, or private police accountable solely to the employer. She doesn't know that labor organizers were sent out in droves to organize all over the South, men and women who were beaten, gassed, and sometimes kept incommunicado in a small-town jail for up to six months, their health broken, TB rampant, their whereabouts unknown to friends and family, alive but buried.[17]

She listens to these men's stories, but she's no ready-made progressive, no blooming liberal though she deeply admires Eleanor Roosevelt. She's still a provincial, the force inside her waiting to catch up. As she listens to the accusations about the mine owners and prominent citizens, about churches dynamited, houses ransacked, sympathizers gassed, she swears *this* doesn't happen in Birmingham. Not by the men she knows. In Harlan County, Kentucky, well, these kinds of things happen, but the men now being maligned by the union organizers "had been so sweet to me all my life and were leading men of Birmingham, the men I'd been brought up to think highly of."[18] There is still, she believes, such a thing as gentlemanly honor, and these men wouldn't allow such horrible acts, would die before they'd allow children to be killed in anti-union explosions.

As if she can't help herself, she rushes off telegrams to these men, her friends' fathers, telling them they're being demeaned by lies and presumptions in Senate hearings and asking them to refute the claims because, well, it's just too absurd. But to her surprise, they send back the most paternal, deflecting letters. "My Dear Virginia, I do not think you understand what has gone on here in Birmingham. Our only objective has been to maintain law and order" as if she's a child, a nitwit, and should not trouble herself because politics is best left to men.[19]

"Oh, such a bunch of pious lies," she writes, her jaw tightening.[20] Fool me once! She's beginning to understand, to see a larger truth: the South is and has always been an oligarchy ruled by and for these privileged men. And they'll do anything to keep it this way.

I can see the old codes of southern life slowly fracturing in her mind, and yet she still holds tight to white supremacy. When her friend Clark Foreman hires a Black secretary, she accuses him of "betraying the South," telling him he's forgotten what the South fought for in the Civil War.

"You know," Clark Foreman retorts, "you are just a white, southern, bigoted, prejudiced, provincial girl."[21]

And it's true. All of these things.

TEMPERAMENT, 1937–1938

She's got a long way to go before ideas of racial justice will shake loose in her, before there's an internal reckoning. When it comes, it will mark and surprise her, quicken and intensify her behavior. She goes hot with anger, quick with happiness. Her husband, Cliff, is calm and rational, devoted to clarity, and never has tantrums. But Virginia, a woman taught to please and defer, likes a fight.

STORY, 1937–1938

Sometimes it's not only what one hears, but the shape of the telling, the way narrative can tighten the bones, come alive in the mind, unraveling character, plot, mood, and epiphany.

Is that why Virginia gets hooked on the story of what happened to Joe Gelders, a teacher of physics at the University of Alabama, while she's at these hearings? Is it his undeniable transformation that grabs her, how this apolitical academic unmade and remade himself, lifting the blinders from his eyes when the Depression hit, becoming so alarmed by all the desperate people—unemployed and hungry and sick—that he educated himself in economics, reading all the way back to Adam Smith, Charles and Mary Beard, the English Fabians, the socialists, and finally Marx and Engels? And of course, being the man that he is, his reading catapulted him into becoming a member of the National Committee for the Defense of Political Prisoners.[22] A smart, gentle man, he's walking home from the bus line in Birmingham one afternoon, just another ordinary day, the sky overcast, a light wind rustling the leaves on the oak trees when three men rise up from nowhere, jam him into a car, then punch and beat him as they drive far out into the country, sixty miles beyond Birmingham into the sticks where the roads are barely paved, the towns sparse, spindly pines reaching for the sun. Here, they stop and toss him from the car, kicking him in the ribs and stomping hard on his chest before dumping him in a ditch in his underwear.[23] One less troublemaker! One less commie parasite! Better off dead.

But the story is just getting started. He can't be dead. It just won't work. And he's not. Somehow, jaw skewed, ribs crushed, he manages to crawl, dragging himself out to the road where he gets a ride. God knows what he tells the driver, Gelders's front teeth knocked out, blood leaking from his wounds. One thing for sure, he's not spouting Adam Smith.

When she first hears about Joe's assault from a labor leader at the La Follette hearings, he's still in the hospital, his story of kidnap and torture acting as his proxy; later it will be revealed that one of his kidnappers is no other than "Crack" Hanna, head of the private police force of TCI, a man who will be indicted but never convicted.[24]

But what's beneath the story, behind the story? What exactly is Joe Gelders's horrible offense, the motive for such torture? To Virginia's surprise, it is this: Joe Gelders had a meeting with three ministers and the mayor of Bessemer about a prisoner, Jack Barton, who was put in jail under Bessemer's anti-sedition laws for possessing what they considered Communist literature, which might be a copy of the *Southern Worker* or the *Nation* or the *New Republic*.[25]

Magazines.

That's it.

Magazines. And she can't get the insanity of it out of her mind.

But why *this* story? Why Joe Gelders? Why not the other labor organizers or strikers, angry and bullied and fired, men who lost children or wives, whose jobs were imperiled, their misfortunes as dark as a midnight sky?

Maybe it's as simple as the fact that she knows Joe's brother, that he's someone like her, a middle-class Birmingham native whose siblings went to school with her. Familiarity is where many of us start, the lurch of recognition. Maybe after seeing her child struggling to live, such intentional violence to another body severs her remaining constraint about the ethics of the Big Mules and the mine owners. Or maybe Joe's choices sink deep into her brain, firing an epiphany, the startling realization that she too can and should take part in the world.

After she hears Joe's story, Virginia stands on the sidewalk in the darkening afternoon, the Capitol behind her. She is waiting for Cliff to pick her up, the sky thick with clouds and the promise of rain. She remembers a day in the early years of the Depression in Birmingham when she was newly married. She was driving a Red Cross worker out to Ensley where the poverty was thick and ugly, a wretchedness she hadn't yet seen. She was part of the Junior League effort to get nurses to areas beyond the streetcar routes, places unknown to her.[26]

Now, staring at the shadows dimming the magisterial whiteness of the Capitol buildings, she sees again that small child bent over, struggling as he tries to walk, his severely bowed legs not strong enough to hold him as he grabs for the hand of a woman whose skin is disfigured by red, scaly blotches. When the mines closed, many miners and their families were thrown out of their company houses and lived in the coke ovens, no more than brick beehives, company guards stationed near the houses to make sure they didn't attempt a return.

"Ricketts," the nurse said as Virginia drove back toward the lights of Birmingham, past men walking the roads, out looking for work. "The child, that is. Lack of vitamin D. The mother's got pellagra." Alongside this misery, the local dairies were pouring milk in the gutter because they couldn't sell it.[27]

She had never seen poverty up close. But now as she glances up into the cherry trees, she thinks the real tragedy was the guilt these families felt, believing they were responsible for their destiny, unemployed and unable to feed their families—*"if we just hadn't got that radio"; "if I hadn't bought that old Ford"*—rather than being victims of the reckless speculation of corporations and banks that had caused the stock market collapse.[28] Instead of becoming indignant and rebellious, they believed they deserved their history. And thus, they were trapped in a feudal perspective, a transgressive story of class without the philosophical means to escape. They'd become double victims: of deregulated capitalism and social Darwinism.

She feels the first drops of rain, but she doesn't shield herself. She wants to be exposed, to feel every disturbance of air.

For the first time, she understands that within her history, there is another history, and within that, another, and then another, like a nest of Russian dolls.

A beginning.

One reason Virginia is important to me is that, though years apart, we've swum in the same soup of resentment. Resentment over the marginalized, fetishized status of southern girls: girls taught to be pretty and pleasant and accommodating and, God forbid, to cause no trouble. If you're a talker, well, entertain, but don't dominate or critique or interrupt, and don't expect to run the show. At least, out front. I'm talking about generations of white women born and raised throughout the twentieth century, women applauded for being loyal and subordinate as if submission is a virtue.

"I was also slowly becoming something of a feminist," Virginia insisted in an interview, acknowledging that she had "great resentment . . . of the role that Southern girls had to play."[29] Though I came of age during the women's rights movement in the 1960s, a philosophy that liberated southern girls like me, Virginia, in the late 1930s, had to bushwhack her way through the trenches, fighting against the poll tax, furious that it disenfranchised so many of us.

I like to think this was her way in: the disadvantage of southern women.

Even before the La Follette hearings, I can see her as a volunteer in the Women's Division of the Democratic National Committee, a group led by Eleanor Roosevelt, who insisted that all Democratic committees should be 50 percent women and 50 percent men.[30] *What?* This single decision made

Virginia lean forward, her mind flushed with heat. It stunned her: *what had been man-made could be un-made.* In the South, she knew "no Southern women on *any* Democratic committees—local, city, or state."[31] I like to think of Mrs. Roosevelt as Virginia's women's rights movement, the poll tax the spark to ignite her consciousness-raising.

Ah, the poll tax! Is there anything less sexy? Southern states had implemented the poll tax after Reconstruction to disenfranchise Black people, but it also disenfranchised poor white people, especially impoverished women. And during this period, the Democratic National Committee's goal was to get rid of it so that white southern women could vote, increasing the Democratic voter rolls and empowering women, a fight they thought they could win. The committee wasn't yet concerned with civil rights. And though Virginia found congressman after congressman to introduce this bill and get it passed in the House, it was "filibustered to death" by Southern Democrats in the Senate, who saw its repeal only in racial terms and as a threat to their survival.

CONFERENCE, 1938

What can she do? The anti-poll tax fight is a big, fat mess. Hopeless. Discredited. But she never stops. It's not in her nature, at least at this point in her life. She and Cliff are still young and vital and believe in the possibility of a resurgent South, a changed South, perhaps a parallel to her own remaking. She's so obsessed with the repeal of the poll tax she becomes a delegate from the Women's Division of the Democratic National Committee to the Southern Conference for Human Welfare in Birmingham, Alabama, a meeting that will have unforeseen consequences.

I try to imagine that day, November 20, 1938. After the hot wet season of summer, the cool briskness of November is a relief, a solace to the senses and perhaps to her memory. *Birmingham,* the boomtown of her childhood—a place that pays equal homage to the Roman fire god, Vulcan, and to Jim Crow laws—where she remembers big fancy houses with chandeliers and servants and soft, drawling voices, where she raced in backyards at birthday parties and watched women seated on lawn chairs with great wide hats, where Nursie, her beloved Black maid, bathed and dressed and put her to bed every night.

This, of course, was before the Depression, before Birmingham lay "prostrate and exhausted," its steel mills and blast furnaces shuttered, its streets flooded with destitute families desperate for work and forced to live in shacks and under bridges, in Hoovervilles and hobo jungles. Though the New Deal's massive economic reformation tried to revive the city, it will take World War II to transform it completely. Still, on this day, there's cause for celebration as more than two thousand liberal delegates descend on Birmingham's municipal auditorium for the first and biggest attempt at a progressive revival, men and women from all over the South ready to tackle issues of social justice, human rights, and economic and electoral reform.

I imagine Virginia is already talking—certainly, absolutely talking—greeting friends as the crowd converges before the open door of the auditorium where even the segregation protocol begins to break down as two hundred Black delegates mingle with the throng of white delegates. In the exuberance and chaos of the moment, some Black delegates move through the main portal, that wide-open front door, avoiding the side door, up a flight of stairs, marked COLORED ENTRANCE. Though white attendees still claim the best seats inside the hall, the ones near the stage, there's a relaxed atmosphere, and people begin to sit anywhere they can find empty seats.[32]

What better harbinger of change for a resurgent South?

Something big will happen. She just knows it.

Like all southern meetings, this first Sunday night begins "with a lot of preaching and praying and hymn singing . . . just a whole meeting full of love and inspiration," followed by Frank Graham's introductory oration on "equal and exact justice for all."[33] I imagine the crowd like an impressionistic film dissolve, a blur of happiness and hope, a southern liberal love story, the clapping, the ovations, the "amens," the smiles, the blissful equivalent of today's rock concert.

Graham, known as Dr. Frank, beloved president of the University of North Carolina, known for his endorsement of racial integration and workers' right to join unions, is preaching freedom as the enlightened way. The crowd cheers when he says, "Let us show that this Conference stands for the Sermon on the Mount, the American Bill of Rights and American democracy."[34]

But inevitably, this romance will prove hallucinatory, for the very next morning the delegates are met not by hosannas and hymns and thunderous applause but by Black Marias and every police van in the city and county surrounding the auditorium. Already the arch-bully Bull Connor stands at the threshold, scowling, his small mouth stern, his body brutish, here to remind everyone of the ultimate southern taboo: integration. Nobody breaks the segregation laws in *his* town, and if this group has any ideas about trying to integrate the seating, they'll be "arrested and taken to jail."[35]

Darth Vader's come to the party.

And just like that, the open door is shut. The first slap to liberalism administered. Because the auditorium has a pronounced center aisle, Connor directs Black people to sit on one side, whites on another, and thus, a new metaphor is introduced: the aisle, no-man's-land, the space between.

Everyone adheres to this new dividing line.

Except when Eleanor Roosevelt arrives the next day, "she got a little folding chair and put it right in the middle of the aisle," Virginia writes in her notes, refusing the metaphor. *No one was going to arrest her.*[36]

What interests me isn't what this says about Eleanor Roosevelt but what this says about Virginia: how the racial divide is suddenly on her radar, how she—a segregationist for much of her life—interprets the aisle as a moral and necessary challenge. Where other people at the conference fight about ideological concerns, she focuses on two things: the open door and the aisle. Who gets admitted and under what conditions?

It's no surprise that she's selected to be vice president on the subcommittee—the Civil Rights Committee—to get rid of the poll tax. And for the next ten years, she'll try to change the voting rights in this no-man's-land, though the poll tax won't be repealed until 1964.

In 2018, when my plane descends into a wild greenness of trees and a wide slice of blue, I know I've arrived. Alabama. Here, the air is a wet sheet of softness, a blur of heat and moisture. The land is flat, the pace slow and meandering, the people all shades of black, white, and brown, their hair cornrowed, ponytailed, buzzed, clipped, and shaved, their ideas nuanced and diverse. I step off the plane, assaulted by a low-slung depression and a surge of exhilaration, and wonder what it means to be a native daughter. Do I still consider myself one? Did Virginia?

Many people I know claim they're "not from anywhere and have no close ties to place." They tell me they've moved around a lot or grown up in a suburban area that feels like anywhere and nowhere. And yet place crawls inside me. It's like an inner skin, painting my psyche. There's no way to displace or dismiss it. I can't slip out of it and often I can't slip deeper into it. Instead, it's as if I'm stuck. And being stuck, I'm always fighting with Alabama, trying to understand and transform it, trying to pry my way into its more slippery core. Maybe this angst is a result of moving away and never returning, the fight internal and intellectual rather than visceral and present.

But Virginia . . . she moved back to Alabama. She had no choice.

DIVISION, 1952–1954

What Virginia wants now, she notes, is to be a first-class secretary and not have to type her letters over.

Ha! I laugh, certain of her irony.

What I can imagine is Virginia drinking endless cups of coffee, her brain electrified by caffeine as she practices these new typing skills until sure enough, by 1952, she's ready to work for Cliff as his secretary at his newly established, beleaguered law firm dependent on the most low-end cases of the law. But worse than their financial and professional woes, the two of them are at odds: Cliff adores Montgomery and wants more than anything to make it his home, regardless of the political and social constraints, while Virginia chaffs under this isolation along with her dependency on Cliff's mother, whom she must live with for three years.

Sometimes she rails at Cliff, her eyes dark and resentful, insisting that, unlike her, he's never felt like an outcast, a misfit, but has "always belonged." He likes to be cautious and sensible, embodying his Rhodes Scholar scholarly self as he patiently works up a case, while she prefers to explode. Cliff doesn't openly fret about the elitism, the segregation, about the unfairness of it all, believing the law will provide.

Maybe he looks at her, his wife, with dismay. He loves the land, the trees, the rivers, the birds, the soft, humid air. He loves the way he can be so alone fishing from the bank of a river or walking in the country, introspective, quiet, thinking. He believes in the goodness of people. Across the room, she stares out the window onto a green lawn, a single dragonfly fluttering above the azaleas. Beyond this lawn is another green lawn. And another. A prison house of torpor.

And then to her surprise, this life of smallness and despondency is challenged in 1954 in such a peculiar, cynical way, it's almost demonic: She is "subpoenaed to appear before the Senate Internal Security Subcommittee chaired by Senator Eastland at a special hearing in New Orleans."[37] The hearing, staged as a stunt on the eve of the *Brown v. Board of Education* decision, is Eastland's attempt to "link the civil rights activities of Virginia Durr and Aubrey Williams (editor of the *Southern Farmer*) and others to the Communist party."

"That polecat . . . that cottonmouth moccasin, that rattlesnake . . ." Virginia calls Eastland, a southern demagogue, because the idea of her as a Communist is absurd.[38] So absurd, it's funny . . . except, well, it's not. The main witness is a guy named Paul Crouch, "an ex-Communist psychopath and liar," who claims all sorts of outrageous things, even that "Mrs. Roosevelt was passing on Cabinet secrets to Virginia who was passing them on to the Communist spy ring."[39] What the hearing attempts to do is to prove that the Southern Conference for Human Welfare in Birmingham, which supported integration, was subversive, disloyal to the United States. And though it fails spectacularly, the hearings are so well publicized in all the newspapers, Virginia's "cover as a nice, proper Southern lady" is blown.[40]

I clap my hands. At least that straightjacket is removed. No more pretense. No more gloom. She's no subversive. All she's done is fight an unending battle against the poll tax and rally support for such liberal causes as voter registration.

And now, released from the bondage of propriety, she picks up the threads of her old life and begins attending meetings of the Council on Human Relations, the only interracial group in the city. As her involvement with the local NAACP branch deepens, she becomes friends with E. D. Nixon, Montgomery's head of the NAACP, along with Dr. Gomillion, president of Tuskegee Institute, and in turn, she's asked to speak to the Youth League (headed by Rosa Parks) about the importance of voting. In this simple way, she gets to know Mrs. Parks as well, though in Montgomery's segregated etiquette, they must always call each other Mrs. Parks and Mrs. Durr, never risking the personal. Virginia learns this the hard way. One day, she sees Ed Nixon in the post office and says, "Why, hello, Ed," and offers her hand. He ignores her, nodding and walking past her, though he later insists, "Look, don't call me Ed again. If I called you Virginia, I'd be lynched. And to shake my hand in public that way, that's going to get me in trouble. Now when I can call you Virginia, you can call me Ed."[41]

She's been impulsive, stupid, insensitive. Nothing has changed. This is still Montgomery, Alabama, home of the Confederacy. Later she looks up from her typing to gaze out at the heat-soaked streets. There's barely a hum of activity, a Black man sauntering by, his head down, the jangling refrain from a radio nearby, a car's motor revving.

Nothing else moves.

Montgomery sleeps.

BLACK LIVES MATTER, 1955

And then, unexpectedly, this quiet, somnolent city explodes.

It is 1955.

First, Claudette Colvin, a fifteen-year-old girl, small and thin, is arrested for refusing to give up her seat on a Montgomery city bus when ordered to by the driver. Though her companions promptly comply, she remains seated and is subsequently dragged off the bus by three policemen who handcuff her, bullying and cursing her as they haul her to jail. What Virginia admires is the girl's courage, her willingness to say "no," to stand up to the meanness of segregation, the white anger and violent response. Claudette's audacity ripples through her. She types more furiously. Though Cliff agrees to work on the case with the Black attorney, Fred Grey, the Colvins ultimately decide not to pursue a court battle. And the story dies down.

Next, Autherine Lucy, a twenty-six-year-old graduate student, becomes the first Black student to integrate the University of Alabama in Tuscaloosa, an admission that results in riots by thousands of white students and townspeople, provoking a kind of reckless violence that shocks everyone: death threats, injuries, mobs thronging the streets, chanting, shouting. At first Autherine Lucy is asked to leave in an effort to protect her, but later she's expelled after she accuses university officials of conspiring with the mob.

The attempts at racial change seem tidal—an act of protest, a hostile, dangerous reaction, followed by months of quiet.

Everyone waits.

And then on December 1, 1955, Rosa Parks, tired after her day's work as a seamstress, refuses to move from her seat on the city bus when ordered, and she's promptly arrested. When E. D. Nixon calls the police station to request the charges against Rosa Parks, the police, recognizing a Black voice, rebuff him. Undeterred, he phones Cliff Durr for assistance, and the police readily tell Attorney Durr that Rosa Parks is booked on the city segregation ordinance, chapter 6, section 11. Within the hour, E. D. Nixon, Virginia, and Cliff arrive at the police station to bail her out.[42]

In many ways, the rest is history: Rosa Parks's decision to fight the arrest becomes the catalyst for the Montgomery Improvement Association's famous meeting four nights later at Dexter Avenue Baptist Church to organize a boycott of the city buses where the newly installed pastor, Dr. Martin Luther King Jr., arouses the congregation with his soaring rhetoric, binding them together as a community. "If we are wrong," King says, "the Supreme Court of this nation is wrong. If we are wrong—God Almighty is wrong! If we are wrong—Jesus of Nazareth was merely a utopian dreamer and never came down to earth! If we are wrong—justice is a lie! And we are determined here in Montgomery to work and fight until justice runs down like water and righteousness like a mighty stream."[43]

Is it here, after bailing out Rosa Parks and listening to Dr. Martin Luther King Jr. that everything about race changes finally and irrevocably for Virginia? Certainly, her frame of reference shifted during her time living at Seminary Hill and working on the Southern Conference for Human Welfare, but now the fight for racial equality isn't abstract or symbolic. It doesn't matter where Eleanor Roosevelt puts her chair. Now the fight is immediate, moral, perhaps even lethal as lives will be compromised and lies will be told about what transpires. Here, you're either on one side or the other.

Little do the people of Montgomery know that this movement, the formation of the Montgomery Improvement Association's boycott, will be a defining moment in the civil rights struggle and that sleepy Montgomery will be one of the places where the battle for racial justice will be fought. Who can know that this long slog, this 367-day boycott, will inspire not only the local Black community but also the rest of the nation?

"It has the quality of hope and joy about it that I wish I could give you," Virginia writes optimistically about the boycott to a friend, describing the movement. "I feel like I am in touch with all the rising forces in the world and the end of fear and slavery is in sight. I know this is just a moment, but . . . it only takes a moment for a new world to be conceived."[44]

But of course, there are always two realities, the pledge of optimism and hope, then the fierce counterattack. By 1960, Virginia's optimism is overshadowed by entrenched white resistance and a schizophrenia of hate. White

Citizens Councils, the KKK, and the state and county governments' reaction are arrogant and righteous, swift and frightening. First, there's the "Southern Manifesto" signed by southern senators declaring that *Brown* is unconstitutional. Then, the attorney general of Alabama issues an injunction that bars the NAACP from the state. The zoo and all public parks are closed. All the chairs are removed from public libraries, a presumed deterrent to integrated reading. Snipers fire on city buses and there are numerous threats and bombings as well as a blacklist of any white person who supports the boycott. "These were the people I was living among and they were really crazy,"[45] Virginia writes, more realistic now. "We live on a narrow edge of tolerance,"[46] she continues, though she and Cliff have been isolated and rejected for years, taunted and sneered at, the recipients of death threats. "In any case," she continues, "it is a real collapse of the law and you know that you have no protection against people that hate you and want to do you evil. Of course, the Negroes have had this a long time, but I am just beginning to know what it is like."[47]

Regardless of the threats, they continue with their work, Cliff helping with the legal aspects of Montgomery's Black community while Virginia types the briefs and volunteers to drive women to and from work during the boycott. It is a difficult time, volatile and violent, but the commitment of the Black community, the tenacity to fight the abuse of segregation one day at a time, both thrills and sobers her.

And to her surprise, the boycott pushes beneath the surface of her life to affect her marriage, binding her and Cliff together, creating a new level of closeness. How stunning, how revelatory this must be, two people long married whose lives are thickened and made more intimate by their connection to racial justice. Cliff assists Fred Gray in drafting the legal challenge to bus segregation in Montgomery, the case that Gray will take all the way to the Supreme Court, the case that will overturn the statute of segregation on city buses, the statute that will change Montgomery and inspire more protests, Sit-ins, and Freedom Rides.

I imagine one late afternoon Virginia sits at her desk, tired but oddly happy as she looks past her typewriter at Cliff. He is writing notes on a legal pad, his hand steady as always, his mind focused, his brow slightly furrowed. I imagine that she smiles, a private, lingering smile, introspective, thoughtful. Cliff no longer believes so fiercely in the goodness of people. And she believes a little bit more. They have both come through a wilderness to define what matters: love and respect and the unending fight for justice. And in of all places, Montgomery.

Ten years later, when Virginia, aged sixty-five, steps off the train from Chicago where she's attended the tumultuous 1968 Democratic Convention, Cliff and their youngest daughter wait for her on the platform, anxious to hear her version of events, to listen to her vivid stories, the sly details she's noticed.

When he sees her, I want to imagine Cliff says to their daughter, "She still takes my breath away."

Mine too.

I want to believe a native daughter learns to tell the truth about a culture: learns to love what is loveable, to challenge what is bigoted and mean and at variance with morality, and to face the uncomfortable. *To face the uncomfortable.* Ah, this begins to get closer to my own story, my terror of being wrong, irrelevant, or worse, being passive, a bystander, a person who does not stand up. In teaching my graduate class, I wanted to believe that I too was interrogating history and wrestling with my privilege as a white woman in America, but perhaps, in the end, exploring racial discomfort (my own and my students') was the real lesson I had to explore. Only by teaching this class did I recognize that students of color, legitimately upset at having an all-white faculty in the MFA program at the University of Iowa, felt both highly visible and simultaneously invisible in the classroom and in clinically white Iowa. They desperately wanted someone less culturally defined by whiteness to navigate the sensitive discussion of race and trauma. And they began to push for this, helping to initiate a more diverse faculty.

In the 1960s, Virginia Foster Durr stepped back from the civil rights campaigns, believing that the movement "belonged to the Blacks running it." Instead of direct political action, she opened her home to voting rights activists, feeding them and giving them a place to sleep while she wrote letters to officials protesting the appointment of candidates who openly supported segregationists. Though no longer on the front lines, she always tried to deepen her thinking about the paradox of democracy and racial injustice in America.[48]

On my phone, I stare at a picture, one of the few things I managed to salvage from my visit to the Alabama State Archives. It's a newspaper print of Virginia Foster Durr and Rosa Parks, two women in their late sixties or early seventies, both dressed in white blouses and dark jackets, Parks also sporting a white cloche hat. Though my notes don't convey the occasion for the photo, I confess that I feel encouraged each time I look at it: two warhorses, two southerners on a mission, two women together. Native daughters.

Club from Nowhere

OIL SIZZLES, A SPRAY OF bubbles rippling across the pan, then the flour-coated chicken dropped in, first a thigh, then a leg, a breast, a wing, another leg, the hiss and sputter of crisping, edges ruffling, browning, the juices drawn in as a hand deftly turns and shifts the pieces in a hot pan in a hot kitchen, somewhere a fan droning, then the curtains fluttering, inviting the sharp smell of summer trees. That hand might be Georgia Gilmore's, a Black hand that's salted and floured and tossed plenty of feasts in this iron skillet, presenting plates of crusted gold for family and neighbors, for anniversaries and funerals, for friends and activists supporting the Montgomery bus boycott. It's 1955, then 1956, and money is desperately needed to fund the hundreds of cars and trucks that ferry Black workers to and from their work across town, the buses defiantly ignored, empty of people, the harassing drivers driving alone. And all this while Georgia Gilmore fries chicken and fish, bakes pound cakes and pumpkin pies, stews greens and plumps rice, selling her food to beauty parlors, cab stands, churches, Saturday meetings, both Black and white hands reaching for the goodness and gladly paying the price, all that money coming into the coffers of the Club from Nowhere. Is that right? What kind of name is that? What kind of club? Oh, it's a sly, clever name to fit a sly, clever way for Georgia Gilmore and her sisters and grannies to contribute, helping the cause without raising a flag, without making white employers suspicious or white landlords feel the itch of eviction if they knew they housed such fighters. But no. This is just Black women cooking. Black women baking and selling cakes and pies. Black women doing what Black women have often done to add a little extra money to the pot. And who needs to know this pot will help keep that boycott going for 381 days, months and months of paying for insurance and gas and wagons and repairs, supporting the system of resistance, the right to say I sit wherever I want to sit.

Where did you say that money came from?

Why, goodness, "it came from nowhere."

A Dark, Unruly Space

IF ONLY MOTHER HAD COME, I think, as we drive toward Africatown in the tiny community of Plateau, Alabama, where the last American slave ship, the *Clotilda*, arrived in 1860. Its captives survived not only six weeks in the Middle Passage but more than four years of slavery during the Civil War. I imagine leading my hesitant mother through the modest museum I expect to find, a place with soft lighting, detailed brochures, displays of old photographs restored by curators and perhaps a video, the female narrator dramatizing the brutal story of this place. I have a pamphlet about Africatown stuffed in a book back in Iowa.

And that's when my husband makes a left turn into a side road, the GPS telling us we're here. I stare at piles of trash exploding into what once must have been a driveway: moldy boxes, fallen branches, blocks of Styrofoam and rotting garbage bags glittering with shiny bits of plastic.

"This can't be the right place," I say as green lizards scamper in and out of the mess.

David looks beyond the trash to a patch of grassy field, then points to a high brick wall where two gold-painted busts, minus their heads, sit mounted on raised platforms. "No, I think this is it."

Almost instantly, I see the white wooden sign—*Africa Town, Welcome Center*—its large red letters faded and warped, the R and second A nearly obliterated, the name divided. How can this be? Where is the museum? Where is the story, the necessary references to the horrors of the slave trade, details I've planned to recount to my mother tonight? *See? See how bad it was, and who knows, might be again?* As the sky goes gray, threatening rain, I imagine my mother standing impatiently beside me, frowning at the neglect, the ruin.

Even as I think this, I worry that my elderly mother will be exhausted today, her legs aching as she navigates her kitchen tasks, her arthritic fingers cramping as she scrubs potatoes and marinates meat for our dinner, keeping herself busy as she awaits and dreads my return. As do I. There's a new rift between us, a dark, unruly space we've made together.

Last night, as Mother and I dawdled, putting leftover shrimp and green beans and salad into plastic containers, then fixing a snack, chatting easily about the long delays of my flight and the raw, burning pain in her legs, I was glad to be here. *Home. I had come home. Home to my mother.* But after she drank her glass of milk and took her pills—one at a time because of esophageal stricture—she turned to me as if we were in the middle of a discussion. "I'm just disgusted with the people of Ferguson," she said, her face pulled tight in displeasure as if with the aftertaste of a pill. "Such disruption. Such hate. I saw it all on TV."

Surprised by this outburst and uncertain how to react, I noticed the loose, puffy skin beneath her eyes, a new bruise darkening her wrist, the thinning of her hair. At ninety-three, she'd normally be in bed by nine o'clock, the covers tucked up to her chin, but because my husband and I had just arrived from Iowa, she'd stayed up to be with us. She's tired, I thought. Overreacting.

"Oh, I know," I said, putting out fresh linen napkins beside the placemats for tomorrow's breakfast. "The Ferguson Police Department and the court practices are *horrifying*. I mean—"

"No." Her voice cut like a knife.

I paused, still holding a napkin. I looked up.

"Those protests, so unnecessary, such an aggravation. I'm sick of seeing people marching." Her face knotted at the thought as she pushed aside her empty glass, the rim cloudy with a film of milk. "I can't stand to see such behavior."

"Whoa, Mother . . . I mean, *really*—" Surely, she didn't believe proper deportment was the essential ingredient in the redress of grievances. Still holding the napkins, I gazed at her, surprised by such vehemence. The truth is, I hadn't watched the protests on TV, but I'd read about Michael Brown's death (an eighteen-year-old Black man killed by a white police officer after a scuffle) and the outrageous violations of the Ferguson Police Department and municipal government in the *New York Times* and the *Washington Post.* I knew the people of Ferguson were angry, so angry that alongside peaceful protests there had been violence and looting and trouble, and yet I'd been so overwhelmed by teaching I'd barely made notes in my journal except the fact that Officer Darren Wilson wouldn't be charged with a prosecutable violation. "I think it's more complicated than it looks," I hedged. "TV sometimes replays the same sensational clips as if that's the only thing that's happening."

My mother shook her head as she washed out her glass. "You can think what you like, but I'm sick of seeing them out there, demanding, always demanding."

Them. Maybe it was that word, the lumping together of everyone—Black people, white people, ministers, civil rights workers, students, journalists, rioters, looters, losers—into a catchall generality, a nebulous slur that ignited me. *How can she be like this? She's my mother!* Yes, my mother, frightened and fearless and often bewildered by the endless spectacle of the twenty-first century where change accelerates impartially, revising and collapsing the known. She'd grown up in the 1920s and 1930s in northern Alabama, a miner's daughter, during an era of strict apartheid and white supremacy, her own people poor and powerless, pushing and shoving as they clung to their fragile status, one shaky rung above Black people. Yes, that tired old argument, that familiar class analysis, the oppressed hating the despised, the exploited dismissing anyone on the other side of the color line, a relentless guerilla war. Though my mother insisted she believed in racial equality—*"of course I do!"*—she wanted the process to be orderly and polite, the progression methodical as if exploitation could be addressed dispassionately, incrementally, without too much fuss. Oh, try that out on history, I longed to chide. In truth, my mother had disliked white college students protesting in the 1960s. "So unkempt!" she'd said. Clearly, protesters got on her nerves.

Leave it alone, a voice inside me said. You're tired. She's tired. She's ninety-three and this isn't just about Ferguson. But as I casually tossed the rest of the napkins on the table, one floated to the floor, unfolding, a corner flipped up. When I didn't immediately pick it up, my mother stared at the napkin, then glanced sharply at me.

I stepped away, closer to the sink as if I needed distance, my own resentment rising. "Well, regardless of how messy it is, the right to march, to protest is a *constitutional* right," I said in my teacher's voice as if she were a contentious student in my university class. "I mean, our country literally began that way. You know that."

"Of course, I *know* that." She drew herself upright.

"And even if it's a spectacle, even if the protestors seem offensive—and maybe *are* misbehaving—the people have a right to protest the injustices of the police force and the city government, and—"

"Oh, you don't know everything." She wagged her index finger at me, revealing its crooked slant. "They *don't* have a right to be violent. To tear everything apart."

"No, they don't, but maybe they've been furious about what's been happening to them for a long time. I mean, the Department of Justice is investigating the city of Ferguson and the police force, and the city, Mother, has a system of citations and arrests and fines so racially biased, so perverse and manipulative they're practically a scam."

"Then the people should go home and wait for it to be resolved." She nodded, pleased with this; then she leaned over and picked up the napkin from the floor, smoothing it, refolding it carefully before she placed it on the mat.

"I wish you wouldn't say things like that," I said as I too glanced at the napkin, knowing she'd ironed it, had probably stood over an ironing board this very afternoon, laying it out carefully, sprinkling it with water, then tapping the iron with a finger to check the heat, pleased that I was coming home. Tonight, she sounded uncharitable, but as a teacher I knew she'd worked hard for many years to help Black girls get into nursing school, Black girls who needed recommendations and guidance, someone to help with the process, Black girls who said "yes, ma'am," and "thank you" in quiet respectful voices.

Now I watched as she moved to her white chair, an upholstered chair beneath the wall phone in her kitchen, the place where she talked to children and grandchildren and great-grandchildren, where she'd probably watched the Ferguson protests on her little kitchen TV, hot packs wrapped around her legs to relieve the vascular pain. She looked undaunted.

I felt a thickening in my throat, a constriction, and turned away, staring out the window into empty darkness where I couldn't see the moon. Why, I wondered, were we having this argument? Was I projecting my resentment at being an outsider in this town and sometimes in my family onto the protestors in Ferguson? Was my mother projecting her fear of change and need for harmony onto them as well? What *was* happening to my mother? Hadn't she always been the most thoughtful, conscientious teacher, the one who helped struggling students, both Black and white, who saw through their raw tempers and misbehavior to their inner needs and talked them through bad times? Hadn't she been the one who stood up for them, who opened our house to anyone in trouble? "Oh, now, settle down, he'll just be here for dinner," she'd say to the rest of us, setting an extra place. Hadn't she had students, always the difficult ones, the ones close to the edge, ride their bikes to our house just to have a word with her? I could still remember her rushing outside to talk to a tall, wiry boy, clearly a loner with big glasses and an unfortunate crew cut while he stared down at his unlaced tennis shoes until she said whatever words of comfort or encouragement he'd come to hear. And then, he lifted his face to her with a gaze of such faith and relief, such recognition, I could only call it worship.

I turned back, still distracted by my thoughts, and glanced at the table where shiny red apples were piled high in a bowl, apples I knew my mother had bought just for me. *She knows I love apples.* I closed my eyes, my mind stalled. . . . I needed to sleep, to relax, to be able to think. *And she always does that, buys them when I come home.* I glanced at the apples, then at her, surprised at how small and vulnerable she looked sitting in her kitchen chair. Only then did I notice her left eye drifting, the eyelid twitching.

"Mother?" My voice was tentative, but it was my normal voice, a daughter's voice. Behind me, the clock ticked loudly, punitively, as if marking the silence. It was nearly eleven.

She didn't answer. Her face, drained of color, was haggard, shrunken, her cheekbones pronounced, her mouth slack. She looked suddenly old: lips colorless, body slumped, eyes vacant. It astonished me. In the silence, I heard water dripping from the faucet. Had it been leaking all this time?

"Mother?" I said again, this time softer, less certain.

I stepped closer. A rush of worry spiked through me. Was she having a stroke? *"Mother?"*

And then, as if it had been a trick of the light, she shook her head and her eyes refocused; she blinked several times and sat up straighter. She pushed her hair back from her forehead, sighing.

"Are you all right?"

"Of course." She frowned. "Just tired. I get tired like that."

Suddenly, the room felt warm and stuffy, the lights too bright. "Are you sure?"

She nodded. And in that moment, we entered a way station, an impasse, all our scolding words coiled back inside our throats, not forgotten but less urgent, a residue of our difference. I wanted to touch her, to make sure she was okay, but as I stepped closer, she shook her head. She didn't like to be helped.

"You should go to bed." I tried to say this gently. "It's late. Really late."

Agreeing, she pressed her hands against the chair to push herself up, but her arms trembled, and she sank back, closing her eyes. Usually it was her persistent vitality, her startling strength and resilience, that flummoxed me. Now I stared at the veins latticing her hands, her arms freckled with sebaceous cysts, darkened by ugly bruises from the Coumadin she took every day.

"Really, Mother, don't be so stubborn. Let me—"

"No."

And so, I watched as she rocked back and forth, her face focused and determined, until she gained the momentum to stand. For a moment, she wavered, a frail, unsteady apparition, her balance wobbly, her expression guarded, and then, she straightened and took small, mincing steps across the length of the kitchen toward the hallway, her back bent, her head tilted forward, her hair muzzy, separated at the center, revealing a patch of white scalp that always embarrassed her.

How had I forgotten her frailty?

I didn't move.

Staring at the trash, I stand still, stupefied, and then, jolted from my inertia, I thread past the muddy piles to the curved brick wall where the gold headless busts look brassy, absurd. From the collar of one, wild sprouts of a blooming weed soar into the air, little white flowers like bits of popcorn caught in the branches; from the other, there's merely a jagged neckline, the interior packed with loose, red dirt. A dark metal plaque affixed to the brick wall spells out two men's names followed by their countries and their nation's flag: *Thomas Azinsou Akodjinou, Benin; and Felix Yao Amenyo Eklu, Togo.* Dutifully, I copy this and take a picture, hoping I'll discover their identities. I never do.

While my husband clicks photos, I gaze at the empty field, at the dried mud that crunches underfoot and the nearby ditches overgrown with brambles as if I can take the temperature of this place. *Hogweed. Dandelion. Torn cardboard. Jagged pieces of brick. Rusty junk the color of ox blood.* It looks abandoned, desolate, a place of danger. *Danger.* I shiver at that word because Pritchard (which includes this community of Plateau) has always been characterized by white people in southern Alabama as violent, "backward and impoverished," a "rough, mean place" with a high crime rate. "Oh, honey," a neighbor said. "Nobody goes there." A Black town. Them. I shake that thought away.

"Maybe there's something more," I tell my husband. "Let's drive to that neighborhood up the hill and ask." I point to bungalows and small frame houses tucked into the trees.

Driving up the steep slope, we enter an eerie quiet as if the neighborhood's deserted, though cars are parked in some of the driveways. It's a bit scary. Weird. What are we doing here? "Kinda quiet," I say just as a crow caws, roused from a telephone pole, a scrap of black in the air. Startled, my senses prickle, alert, a darting fear traveling its invisible route through my body, a fear that feels defensive as if the crow has just spoken: *You do not belong here.* Instantly, I'm ashamed, a gap opening in me, a gap between the writer curious about this place and its history and the girl tutored in privilege, the girl taught to be afraid of the other as if the other hadn't been denied many civil rights, legal protections, and economic possibilities. Even as we idle up the hill, I'm reminded of riding as a child in my mother's Cadillac through the segregated neighborhoods of my small Alabama town to take our maid, Ora, home. What I saw in those neighborhoods was a physical and psychological separation, a hardness and a helplessness, a difference so extreme it seemed tribal, formal, though this was all a consequence of white control, a political and social construction I didn't yet question. With a child's eyes, I saw the Black part of town as frightening, different, everything dragged down and ugly, the houses little more than shacks (rarely brought up to code by white landlords), some yards sporting an azalea bush and coffee cans full of gladiolas and pansies, others barren, coarse grass scuffed away so that only red dirt or mud puddles remained. As my mother's car moved slowly over the graded dirt road, I watched the old men sitting on their sagging porches, their bodies stooped, their hair white and grizzled. They watched us too. Everything here felt separate, taboo, an impotent aggressiveness lying just below the surface.

I always believed that the girl schooled in segregation could be overshad-owed, even destroyed, by the writer, believed that by asking questions, by interrogating myself and the larger world, I'd acquire an immunity, a clean slate. *But that's ridiculous.* No one does. With this jolt of awareness, I know the girl is alive. She's here, inside me, and I don't know how to get rid of her or how to live with such contradictory realities. Who am I if I haven't loosened the constraints of my southern past, lifting the veil of whiteness? How can I admit that I've come here today not only out of curiosity but also to goad my mother, as if visiting Africatown will make my views authentic?

As we wind our way up the hill, such thoughts bite and mock me. I'm si-lent, watchful. Around us, the houses look bleak, the street empty except for a trashcan overflowing with garbage in the middle of the driveway. Then, at the top of the hill, I'm relieved to see a man in jeans and a pullover outside a white frame house working on his car. His face and hands are hidden as he works. "There," I say to my husband. We stop, and I step out of our car.

Hearing us, the man straightens, his expression unreadable. He stares at me, not moving.

"I'm sorry to bother you." Already, I'm uncertain, apologetic. "But we're looking for Africatown. I thought it was nearby, but all I see is a plaque on a brick wall near the highway."

The man studies me in silence, then he glances back at his car.

Because he doesn't speak, I worry that this is a bad idea, an imposition. I realize I haven't even introduced myself. "We're from Iowa," I blurt, "my hus-band and I and, well, we came down here for family. My folks live across the bay."

The man takes a step forward. "Iowa?"

I nod. No one takes Iowa seriously. And yet it's so irrelevant in the culture wars, it carries no threat.

To my surprise, he grins. "Well, I just got back from Iowa."

"You're kidding." And then we're both laughing, pleased to meet some-one in Alabama from a place like Iowa as if it's the most absurd coincidence in the world.

"We're from Iowa City." I move closer. "And you?"

"Was working in Des Moines. Just got back a few days ago."

"Well, you're gonna miss the cold," I tease. "It'll be freezing when we get back."

"Not a bit!"

Before we leave, he tells us there used to be some kind of center, but it got vandalized. "I don't think there's anything left."

What's left are the graves.

It's only as we drive down the hill that I notice a graveyard meandering across a wide grassy slope divided by a swampy ditch, probably seepage from the autumn rains. Tombstones jut from the lush green grass like toadstools, small and erratic. Most are broken, caved-in and cracked, mud-splattered and scribbled on. Some circle the thick trunks of live oaks scattered across the field, shaded by a wide canopy of branches. Piles of leaves, mottled oranges and reds, blanket the ground along with sprouts of dandelions and wild, unruly vines. Some graves are decorated with small ceramic vases full of withered flowers while others sport a simple embellishment: a cross made of glassy beads. I wander among the graves, searching the older graves for dates I can read—1883, 1913, 1915—then angle toward higher ground, past a wrought iron gate wedged between tombstones. Though rusted and warped, the gate is oddly beautiful with its lopsided arc and ornamental rosette, the spokes fluted at the top. As if passing through that gate into another world, I see the graves here look bleaker, are sunk deep into patches of weeds. Impulsively, I kneel in front of one that's badly damaged, its rounded arc shattered, the dates partially obliterated, though I see *May 22* clearly and *18-something*, but not the precise year. Though my choice is arbitrary, I place a hand on the damp, rain-stained stone as if I can swing open that gate, as if I can touch the unknown. Here, there's only the sound of a bird calling in the distance, the twitter of insects in the weeds, the light filtered through gray clouds. It's a simple moment, and yet for the first time today I'm neither angry nor defensive. *This*, I realize, is the museum: this burial spot, these graves disintegrating into the wet, soggy ground, ignored by history, unseen by people who drive past on the highway. A record of survival and death.

As my husband and I drive back across Cochran Bridge, I realize how insufficient the Wikipedia site about Africatown was, the pages I printed out in Iowa. Of course, I had no idea I'd visit Africatown on this trip, and yet as we turn our car towards the dusky water of Mobile Bay, it's not Africatown I worry about but my mother. At breakfast this morning, we said very little, as if tacitly agreeing to leave last night's argument in shadow. Once again brisk and efficient, my mother puttered around the kitchen, plugging in the coffee pot, rinsing and drying cups, whisking eggs while I sliced kiwi, treating last night as an aberration. After I finished my scrambled eggs, I pressed my linen napkin to my mouth, aware of our careful politeness, as I told my mother that David and I were driving to Africatown. "It's a historic site." She gave a slight nod, then cleared the dishes. And yet now I can't help but wonder if we stopped talking, choosing an uncomfortable constraint, because we were afraid of breaking each other's hearts, or worse, of *not* breaking each other's hearts.

When I glance out at the bay, the water is flat and smooth, pelicans standing sentry on wooden pilings while islands thick with marsh grass dot the surface. Only the seagrass quivers, nudged from the living life below. As the gray sky gives way to a weak yellow light, the water shimmers, silvery and still, until a fish leaps, a sputter of waves, then disappears in a froth of white. "Oh, look!" I call out, but what I've seen is no longer there.

What is there, I'll discover once I return to my desk in Iowa, is the history of Africatown, a heritage researched and referenced: books, unpublished manuscripts, articles, recorded interviews with former Africatown residents, even a community history museum called The Den. It is no secret. What was secret—or at least cleverly hidden from authorities—was the scheme devised by Timothy Meaher, the wealthy steamboat captain and plantation owner, and his accomplice, William Foster, to smuggle 110 men, women, and children, aged five to twenty-eight, from West Africa on their schooner, the *Clotilda*, to Mobile, Alabama, in 1860. Everything was necessarily clandestine, as this occurred decades after the United States had abolished the international slave trade in 1808. A risk and a dare. Sneaky and immoral. An economic venture. Timothy Meaher "bet a large sum that he could bring a 'shipful of niggers' to Mobile and not be caught," Sylviane A. Diouf writes in *Dreams of Africa in Alabama*. Because of his wager, these men, women, and children were enslaved on plantations and steamboats during the Civil War. And though they spoke different languages and came from various parts of West Africa, the endurance of the Middle Passage and the horror of being hidden from authorities in Alabama swamps with snakes, mosquitoes, and no sign of rescue bound them together, creating a community. It was a loyalty forged in suffering, a bond perhaps thicker than blood. After Reconstruction, the survivors of *Clotilda* longed to return to their homes in Africa, but when that proved impossible, they bought land collectively and created a town, "the first continuously controlled by blacks, the only one run by Africans."[1]

As I read about their lives—their struggle to survive the inhumane treatment of slavers in a place so near my childhood home—I feel sickened, ashamed. I want to show this story to my mother, to say, "I hope you'll read this," and leave the room.

My mother.

Any thought of Africatown circles back to my mother, to our unfinished argument, to words said and thoughts withheld, to feelings I want to both bury and explore. Some romantic part of me longs to love my mother purely, the way I did as a child, my hand held tight to her skirt, and also to make her revise her ideas or at least to be repentant for disappointing me, which, of course, says how little faith I have in anything other than my own indignation.

The night I finish reading Sylviane A. Diouf's marvelous book, I gaze out my study window, staring at the katsura trees stirring in the wind and the sky's restlessness, which might mean snow. Beyond them, in my mind's eye, I see my mother stirring in her Alabama kitchen, stacking up plates and glasses from the dishwasher, dutifully carrying clean linens to the credenza, perhaps refolding one of the napkins caught in the middle of the pile.

She will always iron her linen napkins.

And I will always notice.

Those linen napkins represent not my mother's inheritance but her accomplishment. Her inheritance bore poverty's painful lessons, its shame carving secret channels in her psyche, buried traumas I'll never be able to fathom. And thus, her story to me is legend, a story of great sadness and ambition: a young woman who escaped a violent family and a mining community through the orderly structure of a college education and marriage to a doctor and who then settled in a small coastal town where, for years, she taught biology and ninth grade science, believing in reason and logic and the power of learning. Like many who jumped class, she feared running afoul of the cultural rules of the South, distrusting any organized resistance to them, binding herself to the status quo and believing that change came from personal diligence and persistence: avoiding obstructions and accelerating at every opportunity. More than anything, she trusted the southern middle-class tradition of rewards and constraints, a structure that gave her life stability and control, its hierarchies defined by race and class.

As branches brush against the eaves of my house, the wind rising, a neighbor's light breaking up the darkness, I can't stop thinking about my mother and me. In many ways, I was groomed to join that middle-class southern life, to claim and value it as my story. And yet its maze of social and political stratifications, so defined by wealth and whiteness and a deep loyalty to tradition, so infused with politeness, ceremony, and rank, lay like a shadow around me. I didn't understand it. I didn't fit; I didn't know how to fit. And it was only when I realized I didn't want to fit that I packed my bags and left. Left what my mother had wanted for me.

Though my mother and I never return to our argument about race, it's entwined in our story, suspended between us, a taut thread tying us together. Initially, I blamed myself for not being more eloquent and less righteous in my mother's kitchen. I imagined that had I been articulate about the grievances that so often lead to angry, chaotic protests (police brutality; discriminatory acts of institutional power), I might have swayed her, made her reconsider her attitude as if all that was needed was a more enlightened tone. But now, sitting at my desk, I know this is foolish. My mother and I are tied to our personal pasts and bound to radically different visions of America, ideas separated by a generation in which the perceptions of authority and power, racial equality, and social justice have dramatically changed. And I know this too: my trip to Africatown was as much an attempt to hide my own inadequacy at addressing racial progress as to challenge my mother.

And yet I like to think of Africatown as a precursor to Ferguson, the Black citizens of both places exploited by racial bias and discriminatory treatment, their civic and constitutional rights curtailed by public officials. After all, the men and women of the *Clotilda* had worked hard at independence, buying land and creating Africatown, and were so dedicated to forming a community that Meaher declared that "the Negroes" had become "uppity." But even with success, they couldn't escape the trickster world. When they tried to vote in the elections of 1874, Meaher, having got wind of it, subverted them at three different polling stations, declaring to the officials, "See those Africans? Don't let them vote—they are not of this country."[2] Though he'd purchased and enslaved them, ensuring they'd be *of this country*, he feared "they were not going to vote right" and must be prohibited. Unable to cast their ballots, the men and women of Africatown pretended to disperse in defeat, drifting away only to regroup and walk six miles to a fourth place, the St. Francis Street voting station in Mobile, where, after each paid a dollar (the equivalent of a day's wages), they were allowed to vote. Though payment was a clear violation of their rights, they were so determined to be a part of the political process that they agreed and kept "that piece of paper proving they had voted . . . for decades."[3]

Maybe in outwitting the immoral, unpatriotic Meaher, they proved they were not outside of history but here to enact the most American ritual of enfranchisement.

When my mother calls, our talk, at first, is tentative, careful. It's late February, and we commiserate about the cold weather, complain about the need for fleece jackets and long robes, about the starkness of the trees. "I miss the blooms of my cherry tree," my mother says, and I know she's gazing out her kitchen window at the tree where in summer the bluebirds swarm. At ninety-four—she's had a birthday—I see her standing there in the low, slanting light, her hand on the chair for balance, her expression wistful, uncertain, and I feel such a deep affection, I wish I could be there too.

It's a misperception to believe that familial love depends only on loyalty and congruence, that it can't survive controversy and change, though there may be new constraints and expectations, a sticky pause. Eventually, my mother and I find a rhythm, my mother continuing her litany of anecdotes about the great-grandchildren, about cleaning out the hall closets of old clothes, about a book she's just read. "And then, there's the ironing." She sighs.

But beneath her exasperation, I hear pride and fortitude. I'll never forget the precise way she folds her napkins into smooth rectangles before stacking them neatly in the pale blue credenza in her kitchen, ready for another day, another meal.

"Good," I say, though I no longer know if the ease of our talk is a daughter's love or my acquiescence to a contradictory world. "That's good, Mother." Then again, I have not yet told her about the graves.

Fingering the Scars

I.

IT SEEMS ODD TO ME that I should care about Tuskegee, a shattered but historic town in Macon County, Alabama, a place I know only fleetingly, a place I've gone to intentionally for reasons both urgent and fickle: to read the lynching files at Tuskegee University, to teach writing classes at the public library, to interview high school girls about ambition at Booker T. Washington High School, and to ride around the county in a pickup, passing pine forests and sun-dried pastures and faded historic signs while talking with a local man after he's bush-hogged his property.

Each time I visit, driving down the long stem of Highway 81 and arriving at the sharp curve that announces the town's entrance, I feel a tightening in my chest, ambivalence compressing my excitement. *Why am I here?* Today, as I pass boarded up storefronts, then the familiar Burger King and Church's Texas Chicken, seeing weeds and faded billboards and a clutter of beer bottles half-buried in the dirt, I tell myself to watch closely, to notice everything, as if only by such scrutiny can I dissolve the boundaries between self and other. But in many ways, the person I've come to observe is myself, the obedient, frustrated girl who grew up in a segregated southern town transformed into a less-than-obedient, frustrated woman who's trying to learn to talk honestly about race and the shifting boundaries of cultural identity.

Self-recognition, it turns out, is a first principle.

❦

If the primary act of storytelling is to reveal what it means to be human, to unravel one's conflicted desires, fingering the scars and protections held close, then my coming to Tuskegee is both an act of revision and return. Let me explain.

Because I grew up in the lush, coastal land of southern Alabama with its rigid caste systems and hierarchies of race, the borders between Black and white were so explicit I knew no one in my childhood who'd flouted them. Even now, in the small Alabama towns I visit, Black women who work as domestics often call their white employers Miss Annie and Mr. Harold as if echoing a plantation past, while Black men, even professors, confess they drive carefully, still wary of being stopped for "driving while Black."

I left the Deep South in my twenties, moved to the West Coast, then the Northwest and the Midwest, and finally back to the South to finish a PhD. I live now in Iowa, a state so white in population as to be almost clinical, and in a college town that appears open and progressive and friendly. It was only in Iowa that I felt bold enough to confront my past, to let myself be haunted by a place that had very nearly crushed me. And it wasn't until I understood I wasn't maimed and had, in fact, survived and in many ways flourished that I gathered enough faith to look at other people. To want to hear their stories. During this time, I read V. S. Naipaul's marvelous book, *A Turn in the South*, which profiled six southern cities, from Atlanta to Tallahassee to Chapel Hill.

The afternoon I finished Naipaul's essay on Tuskegee—"The Truce with Irrationality, II"—I went into my study and impulsively booked a flight to Montgomery, the nearest airport to Tuskegee. Once my flight was confirmed, I made plans to stay at Tuskegee University to research the lynching files and to interview students and faculty, about what I wasn't yet sure. It was 1995. How naive I was back then, some part of me secretly believing my trip would be a life-changing experience, my anticipation fueled by elation, a new "me" in the wings. And yet, how could it have been otherwise? I'd been brought up to be afraid of Black people, to assume my superiority in some fundamental but nebulous way, to believe we'd have no common ground, no conspiratorial laughter over bad lovers or awful summer jobs, no shared sadness or grief over illness or a father's loss; instead, I was educated to assume respect and resentment from Black people, and occasionally a sly menace I'd instantly recognize. To go to Tuskegee was, in this sense, a taboo. Of course, I would go.

❦

For two days, I sat in a basement room of the library reading the lynching files, newspaper cuttings so physically and emotionally reprehensible my mind began to numb to the particulars as if being dragged into that hell of rage and brutality acted, ironically, as a narcotic. Though I took notes, small cramped paragraphs on a legal pad, they would later turn out to be almost incomprehensible. While in that basement, I felt confused and guilty and furious, haunted by one particular image: a mob using a hot poker to gouge out the eyes of a Black man before burning him alive over a slow fire while hundreds of people watched, eating deviled eggs and drinking lemonade as if at a picnic. Blood rushed in my ears. Sweat prickled under my blouse. And yet oddly, it was the mention of the spectators "drinking lemonade"—a festive, cooling drink—that kept reverberating through my head.

The second day I came out of the library and stood beneath a leafy oak tree waiting for a student who'd agreed to an interview. It was late afternoon, the sun hot and flat, the air so still and stifling it was as if my whole body was wrapped in a warm, wet blanket. There was no breeze, no relief. A cloud of gnats floated idly by. After twenty minutes, I doubted whether the young woman would show, but I could not move from the shade of this tree, the nearby pavement glittering in the silent heat. Students walked past in a slow, languid way. No one hurried. No one paused. As I waited, I began to think that it was inevitable and right that I should be here, standing in a place where I'd expected to feel uncomfortable but where, despite myself, I was beginning to relax, to know that everyone was hot and sweaty and there was no reason to be apologetic about it. "I'm just so hot," I kept muttering, feeling the relief of saying it aloud. That seems like such a small thing, but for me its implications were larger and more encompassing. In that moment I sensed that everyone around me had witnessed and experienced suffering, had faced disillusionment and trouble, and yet they were still getting up in the morning and going to work and classes and the library, each day strengthening the self to live beyond dread and suspicion, to read Shakespeare and grow scrub roses, to bring up children and pay taxes. I gazed at the red dirt beneath the grass and the roots of the oak that buckled and twisted above ground and felt that here, right here, was a belief in resilience.

Maybe that's what Tuskegee became in my imagination: a projection, a place broken but never beaten, a community of people whose humor and wit and simple endurance had helped them survive the darkness of poverty and segregation. The nights I sat in that quiet dorm room I'd felt alone and lonely, but once I began to meet people in the community—teachers and librarians, social service aides and clerks—they always told me stories, often stories about family and race. Though white families I knew never acknowledged the fact of Black relatives, Black people in Tuskegee told me, "Honey, there's always a white person married in." I remember Paul, married to a white woman, telling a story about attending an all-white funeral as we sat talking one afternoon in the public library.

"When my wife's uncle died up state, of course I went with her to the funeral." Paul is coffee-colored with a scattering of freckles on his puckish face. "And you know," he smiled, "people were so nice to me. Of course, I was the only Black man there, but there was just no tension, I mean, nothing in the air." He paused, looking out the window at the parking lot. When he turned back to me, his eyes, dark behind rimless glasses, brightened. "Then, after the funeral, one of the women came over to me and she held my hand. She said she just wanted to thank me. And I nodded, pleased. It made me wonder if, in the past, I'd been just too uptight, too presumptuous. She was a pleasant-looking, friendly woman. 'You know,' she said, 'I've never known an undertaker to stay through the service and I just wanted to let you know I appreciate that.'"

Paul's face beamed with pleasure.

And we both burst out laughing.

In Tuskegee, there was always laughter about the pretense of good manners and the inevitable misperceptions surrounding race. For the first time in my life, I admitted that stories about race could be funny, even hilarious. In white culture—or at least the culture I'm from—discussion about race is serious, careful. Never have I heard laughter about white pretentions and Black expectations or white expectations and Black pretentions, the very stereotypes that need to be mocked, but here in Tuskegee, stories about race were neither silenced nor secret.

"Nobody's blind to color," Vivian, a teacher at Booker T. Washington High School, insisted, smiling. "I mean"—she raised an eyebrow at my pale blondeness—"around here, you're the white girl, and that's just that."

II.

When I arrive in Tuskegee, the morning of November 8, 2016, I haven't been here in more than three years. And yet the town looks, to my eyes, exactly the same: the same boarded up mansions; the same dazzling heat at midday (even in November); the same graceful brick buildings at the college, surrounded by green, manicured lawns; the same tired storefronts; the same slow talk and laughter. I've come only for a short visit, curious to learn how a town that is 96 percent Black in a solid Blue county in an all Red state views this "unusual" presidential election. For months I've heard and read the racist comments of Donald Trump, listened to him rant about Mexican "rapists," about building a wall to keep them out, heard him declare that an American-born judge named Gonzalo Curiel is a "Mexican" and thus will be biased against him in a legal case, heard him rail against immigrants and refugees, against Hillary and the Democrats.

Of course, I know that Tuskegee will not be "Trumpland"—we'll have to wait a while to know the true power of the Black vote in Alabama—and yet after interviewing people I meet downtown, trying unsuccessfully to query voters as they emerge from the municipal complex (the polling location), and then discussing voting percentages with the newspaper editor, my notes are skimpy and disjunctive, a disappointment. *No one wants to talk to me,* I've written in the margins. Perhaps I shouldn't be surprised at the reticence of Tuskegee residents to share their opinions with a "white girl" who lives elsewhere, a woman they might never see again. After all, 2016 has not been a triumph of interracial optimism.

After leaving the newspaper office, I cross the lush, grassy square to the courthouse, still hoping for a few more interviews. And that's when I see it: a Confederate statue I've never noticed before—*my own set of blinders*—having spent my time at the college or the public library or at someone's house, drinking iced tea. And yet when I see it—a tall man with a rifle—I think not of the Confederacy but of reading in Brenda Wineapple's *Ecstatic Nation* about a time before the Civil War when John Quincy Adams in 1839 offered an amendment to the Constitution that would end hereditary slavery in the United States from July 4, 1842 onward.[1] After that day, every child born in America would be free and slavery no longer tolerated. Imagine! A breathtaking presumption and a legislative failure. But what an auspicious appeal to man's better nature rather than to his self-interest. Of course, leave it to Mark Twain to give the more telling gloss. "What is the chief end of man?" he writes. "To get rich. In what way?—dishonestly if we can; honestly if we must."[2] And is there a better way to codify the institution of slavery: wealth gained from human bondage, from enforced labor, revenue accrued by racial exploitation, Black women used for breeding purposes, their children sold off for profit? All to get rich. Slavery, after all, was economic: an economy built on racial contempt.

Now I look at the statue. Every statue tells a story. One story, I believe, is meant to commemorate the bravery of men in uniform and the historical reality of war. In my imagination I can see a southern boy fighting for the familiar land and customs of his home, for the farms and fields, the rivers and bays and creeks, the small-town stores, the stables, the streets and alleyways, and the green lawns of the nicer homes. Perhaps he's a generous, thoughtful man, in love with a pretty girl, a man decent to his parents and peers. Not just a soldier. And yet each time I consider this hypothetical man, I recognize the schizophrenia of viewing any Confederate soldier as merely a man defending the land he loves for the very reason that he's also implicitly defending the institution of slavery and the rhetoric of racial fear.

When I walk closer, I see that this statue is *not* of a young man. This soldier is an older man with a moustache, a man who stands resolutely straight, his musket at his feet, the barrel held almost reverently in his hands. He doesn't look heroic or fierce. He looks tired. I lean closer and read the inscription:

1861–1865

Honor the Brave

Monument erected in 1906 by the United
Daughters of the Confederacy

In memory of the heroes who fell in defense of the
principles which gave birth to the Confederate Cause

And there it is, the rhetoric, the story: *the principles which gave birth to the Confederate Cause.*

Though there are people who will argue such "principles" refer to states' rights, in the Confederacy, states' rights are irrevocably bound up in the acceptance and extension of slavery. And so, I ask what I ask of all stories: Who benefits from this narrative? What agenda is it meant to serve? It certainly doesn't represent the legacy of Black Tuskegee except as an acknowledgement of the South's defeat. And yet I suspect white entitlement is merely one aspect of the statue's story. It occurs to me that, for a certain segment of the population, Confederate statues have come to represent in the twenty-first century a nostalgia for a simpler world where identity is assigned at birth by race, gender, class, and region rather than as something that evolves in our modern world, complex, self-conscious, and unstable. In that perspective, the statue represents a world that legitimizes caste inequality.

My first instinct is: *Take It Down.* Who needs a reminder, even a celebration, of white supremacy? To my surprise, I also have a second thought: *Why Only This Part of the Story?* After all, there were other southerners who died in battle, other southerners who fought bravely for a cause they believed in, who risked their lives for their homes and families, who fought for the rivers and bays and creeks of the South. If this Confederate statue is to remain, it should be joined by a second monument, a statue of a Black soldier, perhaps a man from the First South volunteers, "the first federally authorized regiment of freed slaves," who fought for a future outside of the perversion of slavery.

These Black men, slaves who volunteered to fight for their emancipation had "a fiery energy about them beyond anything of which I had read,"[3] wrote their commander, General Thomas Higginson, a literary man from Massachusetts. To even command this troop, he was considered a "marked man," as the Confederacy had vowed "to hang all white officers of Black troops on capture."[4] In his journal, Higginson wrote that he "would need to demonstrate to a skeptical North—and a contemptuous South—that a Black regiment was as good, as brave, as disciplined, and as dogged as any white one."[5]

He discovered, of course, that they were.

Why not create a town square that presents a more complicated narrative of the southern conscience and the southern experience during the Civil War? After all, nearly 440,000 Black men and women were enslaved in Alabama during the Civil War,[6] and about 2,700 white Alabama men enlisted in the Union Army while 90,000 to 100,000 white Alabama men served in the Confederate Army.[7] There was no singular narrative. Even Black female slaves served as spies for the Union Army, as did white women for the Confederate Army. Like identity, the South during the war was complex in both its suffering and its heroism.

III.

The day after the election, I walk out of my motel room into the open air, the sky a bridesmaid's blue, the heat finally lifting, crows lined up like gossipy aunts on nearby telephone poles. Beyond the parking lot, there are ditches full of kudzu and yellow wildflowers blooming near a stand of pines. In the other direction, commercial signs blanket a highway busy with morning traffic. I watch cars exit onto the interstate, then look south, toward Tuskegee. It's not true that Tuskegee as a place didn't change me. It simply didn't make me more heroic. By coming here, I've been intuitively pushed in the direction of history and forced to scrutinize my undefined beliefs, which means, of course, that I've tried to ask questions I don't know how to answer.

For years in my discussions about race in Alabama, many white people have insisted, often in aggrieved voices, that they're not personally responsible for slavery or for the current problems of African Americans. Most often they support this argument with the assertion that they've lived their lives in an ethical and prudent way, providing generosity and respect for others and a belief in the American Dream of upward mobility for all. They admit that they now see that segregation was wrong, but "it was the way of things" in their communities, and yet oddly, this argument omits the incredible leverage white people, people like myself, have been given: the benefit of white skin, the privilege of that pigment in a world of white control and power as well as the assumption that our success will be the result of our intellect and talent, our inheritance and ambition, our ability to persevere and make wise choices. Likewise, our failings will not be seen as a racial fault.

In contrast, I often imagine a young Black girl who grew up in the mid-1940s small-town south during Jim Crow segregation, a girl who might have lived in my hometown or in Tuskegee. This girl will most likely have had little access to a decent high school education. She will be the product of inadequate schools, inadequate books, and inadequate transportation to and from school, perhaps studying with a teacher who is overburdened with students. As Robert J. Norrell documents in *Reaping the Whirlwind: The Black Civil Rights Movement in Tuskegee*, Black schools in Macon County often had almost sixty pupils in each class compared to the twenty-two in each white class; expenditure per pupil was approximately one-tenth for Black students what it was for white. Perseverance and resilience will be uniquely required of this other girl. She may have insufficient funds not only for education but also for warm clothing, health care, and food. She will certainly have less access to a higher education, the possibility of becoming a teacher or nurse or a librarian—jobs available to women during this time—and thus, earning a decent, livable salary. Any success she has will be considered an anomaly, while her failures may be expected. In the public story, her lack of accomplishments will be ascribed to her race rather than to the circumstances of her history. Her ambitions and hopes will rarely be considered at all. And yet what exists behind this girl's life isn't just a personal story but a historical story of deprivation and disrespect: the political, legal, and financial disenfranchisement of apartheid, the fear and inadequacy of daily life during segregation, the spiritual persecution of being treated as less, and yes, often the very fact of slavery in her ancestry.

White culture, which often insists on amnesia, fixates on the trope of financial responsibility as a validation for its superiority and conveniently forgets that it denied the possibility of that responsibility to Black people during segregation and fought bitterly to retain that leverage during the civil rights era and beyond.

To deny personal responsibility for slavery or segregation or for the current ghettos of Chicago or Baltimore misses the point. The point is that those who have benefited from a system of racial privilege (*inherited, not earned*) and who in their daily lives have maintained the status quo, either consciously or unconsciously submitting to the values of white supremacy, owe a public debt to society to help amend that inequality and to eliminate systemic privilege. The debt is not personal. The debt is civic. It is a recognition that inequality, especially savage inequality, is not overcome in two or three or even four generations and can be ameliorated only by a continual fight. It does not make white people who answer to this debt heroic; it is far less than that. Instead, it is a duty. A form of reparations.

There is no other way to move forward.

It was only by coming to Tuskegee that I recognized my own systemic privilege. During the first two years I visited, I was often discouraged when a writing class was canceled due to some miscommunication or an interview abridged or disappointing. I always arrived with a project that had been arranged and agreed to before the trip, but when my plans were delayed or changed, I'd sink into a depression. One January, I flew into Birmingham, rented a car, and drove to Tuskegee to teach a two-day writing class at the library, only to discover when I arrived that the dates I'd set had been changed.

I was so discouraged, I wanted to flee, *forget about Tuskegee*, and forfeit the second day's class. Frustrated, I made myself stay, staring morosely at the dense piney woods that bordered Tuskegee as I drove toward the library the next day, wondering why I was here, what the hell I was doing.

When I came through the door of the library, Alana, a tall, statuesque woman who wore a sweatshirt that read ADVANTAGED, rushed toward me, pulling me into a deep, comforting hug, her thick arms wrapping around me. "We thought we'd lost you," she said, referring to the class that had been canceled while I was in flight. "But you're here." She smiled, calling out to the other women at the conference table, "Now look what just come through the door!"

I laughed, surprised and thrilled at her enthusiasm, my mood instantly shifting, my relief palpable. The class went well.

On my flight back to Iowa, I considered these failures as cultural: the difference between academic expectation and a small-town ethos. But now I've come to see my disappointment in a slightly different light. A part of me believed that response and attention were my due. I was offering something—classes, discussion—to try to make up for what my ancestors had stolen, and thus, I should be rewarded. *I was the central benefactor of my quest.* And then later, on election day in 2016, I stood in the hazy light outside of the municipal complex, dusty leaves still on the trees, the murmur of southern voices all around me, the sun flickering just beyond the buildings, and understood that most of my allegiances and expectations had been shaped by whiteness.

As I walked toward the parking lot, I heard Black women talking in that confident, confiding tone I remembered from Alana, a no-nonsense voice of purpose. "That won't fly with me," one of the women said and snapped shut her purse. The other women laughed and nodded. That day, what I couldn't and didn't know was that in a little more than a year, Black women—perhaps these very women—would be instrumental in making sure that Roy Moore's bid for the US Senate "didn't fly" and allowing the entire country to celebrate. But that day I paused. That day I wanted to eavesdrop, to linger, to listen to these women, but they were already jangling their keys, moving toward their cars, returning to work or families, maybe fretting or charged by this odd moment in history and what they'd be called on to do.

PART IV

Lessons of Legacy and Loss, 1996–2020

Who are the dead but unending dreams wrapped tight inside the living? They die, then arrive unannounced and insistent, "C'mon, let's decorate the Christmas tree! Let's make everything pretty!" They slouch on the gray-green sofa, knees curled, arms bent, and ask for a blanket. "The white fuzzy one, please." They wave lightly, fingers fluttering as they turn the corner into shadow, here, then gone. Who but the dead can summon me, opening me to the mysteries of the past, the deep, dark reservoir of memories? It's not grief I feel but a flood of relief. "You're back," I say. "I'm so glad you're here."

Umbilicus

I'M VISITING AN ELDERLY PROFESSOR at an assisted living facility in the college town where I live. I haven't seen him in almost five years, and I'm surprised at how small, almost wasted, he appears. He's lost about forty or fifty pounds and navigates with a midnight blue walker on rollers that looks, to my unpracticed eye, like a miniature shopping cart. He's thin, stooped, creeping very slowly, very carefully toward the inner door but still wearing his signature "driving cap," a rather battered black straw. Because his brown face is now gaunt, his dark, protruding eyes are more pronounced, his lips wide and curved upward in a way I never noticed. He has a tear in the knee of his khaki pants like a ten-year-old boy just back from sliding into third.

"He was one of my best teachers in graduate school," I say a little too loudly to the minder who is returning with him from lunch at the mall. I doubt if he remembers me, just as I've begun to forget the names and stories of the students I taught more than twenty-five years ago.

"I know who you are," the professor says, glancing up and staring intently at me, pausing a moment in his deliberations.

But I wonder. Does he remember my anger, my voice as sharp as a hurled glass when we had a misunderstanding years ago? Does he remember the two of us drinking coffee and reminiscing about the South, empathizing over the shame and despair that saturated our most potent memories? Does he remember the sack of oranges I brought to his home when he was sick or the three perfect sand dollars I wrapped in ivory tissue inside a small box, talismanic support before one of his readings? Does he remember the books he told me to read, the way he pointed to one on his shelf and said so low I could barely hear, "That. You should read that."

When the nurse buzzes us into the unit, I follow behind him like a daughter, a supplicant, an anxious student, wondering why every time I see him, I feel a tug of connection and distress as if between us there exists an invisible cord.

I heard about him before I saw him. He was famous. He was eccentric. He was a genius, a Pulitzer Prize–winning MacArthur Fellow who, it was rumored, rented a room in an apartment just to have a private place to read, separate from his house. He took afternoon walks around town in his bedroom slippers. He always wore a driving cap, wool in winter, straw in spring, each pulled so low onto his forehead he was protected, shaded from view. He grew up in Savannah, Georgia, and so hated the South he once said emphatically he'd *never* go back. He liked greasy food. He loved bourbon and sweet potato pie and movies very late at night. He'd graduated from Harvard Law School but never practiced law. Sometimes he slept in his office. Sometimes he slept on the couch. Sometimes he didn't sleep at all. Much of this was apocryphal, fantasies and gossip cooked up in the overheated brains of writers in a city overflowing with writers surviving the long dark, snowy winters of Iowa City. Whether true or not, all this lore unnerved me, made me see him as a mysterious, unapproachable presence, someone I'd never know.

When I finally met him (or rather found myself in the same room with him), I was surprised. He mumbled. He stood awkwardly at the edge of the room as if he might need to flee. When someone asked a question, he glanced up and then let his gaze slide back to the floor. His discomfort confused and perplexed me, but I considered it as simply another eccentricity of genius. It never occurred to me that he might be shy or self-conscious or insecure. Didn't he have everything a writer could want?

In contrast, I'd arrived at this writing program unprepared, a neophyte storyteller jumping class. My terror at the prospect of being here was eclipsed only by my belief in hard work. This had always been my method: a reckless leap from a cliff and then work, sacrifice, solitude. *Let everyone else play.* Having finished an MFA in art four years earlier, I'd taken only two years of creative writing classes at UCLA Extension while working temp jobs and editing gigs, surviving in a rent-controlled apartment in Santa Monica, writing stories on the weekends and during my lunch breaks at the movie studios where I found work. Now, for the first time, writing would be central.

In my first year in the program, I met with the professor only once. I sat across from him at a local café while he commented on two of my stories, his signature mumble making me lean nervously forward, my brow furrowed, my eyes fixed to his face. "Yes," I'd nod. "No, I don't know." More than anything, I wanted him to *see* me as if his vision might catapult me into being. And yet I sensed that everything about me made me invisible and simultaneously hyper-visible. From the exterior, I looked every inch a middle-class white girl with long blonde curly hair, fair skin, and blue eyes. I looked, I knew, like a cliché of southern womanhood, the very thing from which he'd been taught, in the South, to avert his gaze. That fall day, drinking coffee with him, my blonde hair curling over my T-shirt, my eyes darting to his, I felt trapped in the 1950s of my Alabama childhood when it had been dangerous for Black people and white people to interact. To me, he was a taboo, and I assumed I was the same for him.

If I grow still and close my eyes, I can see myself sitting across from him, anxiously tucking my hair behind one ear, trying to make my face bland, emotionless, resisting even the compromise of a smile. He was to be my liberation from a segregated past, and yet his presence meant something much deeper, something beyond the racial. My connection to him felt personal, visceral, as if he alone—by his presence—was urging me to push beneath the surface of my life to a danger I couldn't yet comprehend. It frightened and exhilarated me. I didn't understand it. Even when I'd catch a glimpse of him in the hallway of the university building that housed the program, I'd feel an insistent tremor, an emotional tug as if I were being pulled into deep water.

After that initial meeting, I didn't talk to him again until the next year, near the end of the fall semester. By then, I understood the competitive terms of the program: Ambition was our currency, confidence our pretense, publication our mantra. One of my friends said casually that, within the program, our literary status was stamped on our foreheads like grades of beef: Prime Rib, Tenderloin, Sirloin, Ground Chuck, Stew Meat. I laughed only because I couldn't argue against the point. Those of us who were Ground Chuck tended to be the worriers, the watchers, the persistent, workaholic ones whose inner lives had become a scattering of nerves. I suspect now that even those designated as Prime Rib—the ones publishing and receiving awards—had many sleepless nights.

In late October, I wrote to the professor, asking to do an independent study with him in the spring. I waited until just before the secretary left the department office to nervously put the request in his box. Such permission—two decades before email—required direct contact or a note.

By November, I hadn't heard from him. Too embarrassed to call or leave another note, I thought, well, that's that, story over. But then one gray, sullen afternoon, after Thanksgiving, I was walking through the English-Philosophy parking lot on my way to the library when I saw the professor not far ahead, his signature wool driving cap pulled down so low, I could barely see his face. It had snowed earlier, a light drift that still blanketed the hoods of the parked cars. Feeling bold, I ran across the slick pavement, calling out his name.

He turned, gazing at me, a quick, forensic look, his large, dark, slightly protruding eyes staring at me as if seeing through me or perhaps seeing all of me. Then his look became guarded, inaccessible. He didn't speak.

"I left a note in your box," I blurted. I tried to put myself in his path, afraid he'd get away from me, and asked him about an independent study for spring. "You said a year ago that the story I wrote should be a novel and I've been working on it."

He looked longingly toward the entrance of the building and took a step away from me. Then he stopped, and without turning to me, said, "I will do it, but I can only meet with you once." He mumbled something else about difficulty and problems, but the sentence itself dissolved in the air. In profile, I noticed that his face looked haggard as if he hadn't slept.

All I heard was *yes*! I felt so immediately grateful, I barely listened when he said, "Send me your work about a month before the end of the term. I'll contact you about a meeting."

That winter, the cold held me in a tight grip. When my fingertips split open, I wore fingerless gloves inside the house. My skin itched and flaked from the forced air heat, the lack of moisture, as gusts of wind battered the house. It was a brutal winter, one of the worst in Iowa. Our car doors froze, our windshield wipers froze; if we ventured onto I-80, we saw jackknifed trucks littering the sides of the road like giant abandoned toys in a gothic tale. Each morning I dressed in two sweaters, a down vest, two pair of socks and jeans and sat at my desk in the upstairs room, working on my novel. The characters seemed difficult but real, leading me into vulnerable places where I often felt stranded, not sure how to progress. I'd pushed myself back into the quagmire of the South, into those small, isolated populations on the fringes of society, communities that could be judgmental and gossipy, places where I'd never fit.

By mid-April, I'd shaped fifty pages for the professor, and I put them in his department box. It was spring now in Iowa, the trees just beginning to bud, the tulips and jonquils flourishing in my neighbors' yards. I could look out my study window on the second floor of our little house and watch the pink and white dogwood trees sprouting blossoms. Two weeks passed. The cherry tree on the corner put on its party dress. Another week passed. It was now early May, nearing the end of the semester and I began to worry. Had he forgotten about the independent study? Was he too busy to see me? Did he hate the work and was simply avoiding me? I put another note in his box, a simple inquiry about possible times.

A day passed. Then another day. One night, late, after I'd finished grading student Rhetoric papers, I rode my bike down alleys and side streets, bats soaring in the night air, stars sprinkled across the sky, an eerie silence settling over the neighborhood. I needed to calm down, to diffuse my anxiety. The alleys were empty of people and yet I found solace in the lighted upstairs rooms where students were probably reading and working, some surely as anxious as I.

When the phone rang the next day, I was startled. "Is this Ms. Foster?" I'd forgotten his voice: low, mumbling, hard to understand, and yet so serious it could have been directing me to a Sunday funeral or a doctor's appointment. "I've read your work," he said. "And I can meet you at two o'clock on Thursday."

"I think I can do that," I said nervously, catching my breath. "Let me check. Just a minute, I need to—"

But the professor had already hung up.

I suspect that all fury is born of past injustices, an accumulation of minor hurts ready to erupt with just the right provocation. It seems odd to me now, my anger at the professor for hanging up, surely a misunderstanding rather than an offense. And yet even now, I remember sitting at my desk, my face blooming with heat, my body trembling with rage. Rage because I'd had no control over the situation; rage because I'd simply wanted a little time to compose myself before agreeing to the meeting; rage because I'd so wanted his approval and feared he didn't like the novel, the dead phone a symbolic critique; rage because I didn't want to be Ground Chuck anymore. And this too: rage because I had so little agency to demand anything from anybody, my life a tangled warp of suppressed feelings.

Without thinking, I called him back. I had no idea what I would say, and I knew that if I let myself consciously think about it, I'd never do it. Listening to the phone's ringing, my brain flashed, adrenaline roaring through my body. When he answered, I said in a voice so clear and direct it surprised me. "I think you were rude to me on the phone just now. You hung up before I had finished. I don't think we should meet." And then I hung up.

There is nothing so sweet to the underdog as righteous triumph. I was half-dizzy with power, thrilled at having said "no" to an authority figure, someone who mattered. I'd yanked free of the umbilicus and barely had time to revel in this triumph or feel the creeping embarrassment that would later haunt me, when he called me back.

"Ms. Foster," he said formally in a quiet voice. "I think we should meet. I've read your work and I think we should keep our appointment."

Both relieved and defeated, I said simply. "Okay. I'll meet you at two o'clock on Thursday."

I put down the phone. I wondered if I had won. I wondered what that would mean.

Now I was adrift, the cord unceremoniously cut. When I arrived at my two o'clock appointment, his office door was open. Glancing around before entering, I saw that it was the most ascetic office I'd ever seen: no paintings or prints on the walls, no easy-care plants near the window, no warmth or color from a rug or a chair. There were four floor-to-ceiling bookcases full of books and an institutional desk that must surely have been in this room since the 1960s. The one window opened not to the greenery of an oak tree or the blooms of a dogwood but to a tiny smear of blue-gray sky.

The meeting lasted less than thirty minutes, the two of us formal to the point of primness. I no longer remember what was said. All I remember is the heightened tension, the professor staring at the door as if reassuring himself that he could escape, while I stared at my manuscript, its crisp pages in a neat stack on his desk.

The cord had been yanked free. But had it? I told no one about this incident until almost a year later when I reminisced with a friend about whether I'd learned more about the craft of fiction or about the vagaries of human nature while in this MFA program. We both agreed we'd acquired a more critical awareness of storytelling, had learned that it was easy to start a story and hell to finish one. During a lull in our conversation, I told my friend about my difficult encounter with the professor, a man he knew much better than I.

"Jesus," he said, alarmed. "Didn't you realize the *strain* he was under?" His eyes flashed in irritation.

"No. What do you mean?"

"It nearly did him in." As my friend told me about the complications in the professor's personal and professional life the past spring, I realized that I hadn't thought about his life at all. I'd thought only about my own. I'd *assumed* a life for him, assumed that his status made him immune to the ordinary problems of being a father, a writer, a colleague, a man. To me, he was invisible, just as I must have been invisible to him. It was such a startling realization, I felt ashamed.

That night I lay awake for hours, anxious and embarrassed, my thoughts circling in a loop. When I finally slept, I was immersed in a disturbing dream: I was carrying the corpse of my father wrapped in a pure white shroud, his body an odd, cumbersome bundle. I believed that I'd killed him and was now trying to find a place to hide him. The guilt was unbearable, making my chest hurt, a caustic burning that spread through my body like fiery wings. I didn't remember any more. I'm sure the dream went through many twists and turns, and yet when I woke, I saw clearly the plot: The professor wasn't the authority figure whose praise I wanted, whose expectations and terseness made me furious, but my father. How neatly I'd superimposed one onto the other. How deftly I'd bound myself to the professor in the hopes that his approval would hijack my connection to my father, as if the professor's fame could undermine my father's demands. How important and futile it had been for me to say no. Thinking this, I sat up in my bed, invisible to both, trapped in a myth of my own making.

Here was the deep water, the danger I'd sensed but not understood.

That very day I wrote to the professor, apologizing for my behavior the year before and confessing my own unconscious projection of one authority figure onto another. Though deeply ashamed of my behavior, I felt again the pull of something intangible, a sense that behind this disaster lay a way of seeing that only the professor could teach. And for the first time in years, I allowed myself to think about my father.

My father, as I knew him, was all upbeat optimism teetering above a bedrock of fatalism. In his small-town medical world, people died every day. They died despite the best medical care. They died accidentally, tragically, slowly, intentionally, heroically, alone, in operating rooms, in trailers, in cars, and in new ranch-style houses. They died with and without his help. But in my family, we didn't talk about death or failure or suffering or even a rare case of "being in the dumps." Of course, we knew there was trouble and anxiety in our lives and in the world, but we understood that only the naive and overwrought gave voice to such worries. Stoicism was the god of our survival and stamina. Stoicism and humor. Make a joke about it, get over it, bury it. And yet secretly my father was a man defined by terror: He was terrified of dogs, all dogs, even the gentlest, most lethargic lap dog, terrified of unknown places, of heights, of forests, of darkness, of the ocean's undertow, of shame, of inappropriateness, of poverty, of failure, of having his children fail. Terror of failure. And we both knew that the only thing that mitigated terror was work. Work meant we hadn't given up.

Now, thirty years later, I think how ironic and how fortunate that I felt the pull of these two men, so different and yet so similar. Though one was Black and one white, both were born into poverty in the American South and raised to believe they shouldn't "get ahead of themselves." Both thumbed their noses at that tired narrative, took a chance, and entered college. Both gained courage from an aunt, a woman whose strong will and good sense instilled in each a belief that they could do the unimaginable: be worthy in the world. Both had tremendous energy and used their hard-won positions not for financial gain but in service to a larger idea—the sacredness of community. Both liked

booze—and I suspect used it to excess. Both had diabetes and had little patience with poor health. Both succumbed to disease and diminishment, becoming small and frail, men reduced to nurses and walkers. Their ultimate
terror, I think now, was the terror of being thrust back into their histories, of
becoming again those small boys, oldest sons, alone in a ruthless world.

I follow the professor to his room in the assisted living facility, a room that
opens onto the hallway and a common room with upholstered chairs and sofas and low-lit lamps. I'd thought the professor would have an apartment, but
he has only a bedroom and bath, a white terry cloth robe hanging from a hook
just inside the door. I sit on a hard chair beside a fold-up wheelchair while the
professor lounges on the queen-size bed, the Sunday *New York Times* spread
out on the covers, the Book Review section on top. At first, we talk about easy
things, about his daughter coming to see him, about my visit to my ninety-
one-year-old mother in Alabama, about the awful winter in our town. I no
longer remember what moves us into more personal territory. It might be that
I tell him about my husband's cancer and recovery and my writing about illness and marriage.

To my surprise, he begins to tell me details about his past, about his father, a master electrician whom he loved deeply but who liked booze and
was put on a chain gang in Georgia for not finishing jobs, about his mother
who believed that injustice and segregation were God's decisions rather than
man's, about marriage to a woman who was afraid of men, about taking care
of her and having a caretaker mentality.

"Did you love her?" I ask.

He said he did.

"Well, there you go," I say.

He nods.

And yet as we both sit in the stillness—he's begun to look drowsy, his
eyes fluttering, then closing, making him look older and more vulnerable—I
understand how profoundly I've misjudged him. For so long I thought of him
as a man shielded from trouble by fame, a man with authority, with pride
and intellect and literary respect, but now I realize that he is so much more
than these things. He is—and was—someone who takes care, a custodian of
creativity.

He opens his eyes and stares at me, trying to stay awake. Then his lids droop and I know he's settled in for a nap.

I nod quietly to his sleeping figure, then leave the unit.

But that night I can't sleep. It's been unusually cold for the past week and I pull the covers closer around me, snuggling deeper, trying to get warm. I'm still thinking about the professor. I remember that just before he drifted off to sleep, he said, "I've been reflecting on my life and I think I haven't done that badly coming from where I did." I remember my surprise at this humble self-assessment, this direct, simple statement. It seemed so personal, so intimate. And he'd said this to me. Again, I felt the pull, the umbilicus tightening. The cord between us wasn't about writing or authority after all. It was about care-taking, about pushing beyond the limits of the self, about finding within a di-minished identity the resources to offer insight or solace or hope to another. It wasn't a blood tie but a human tie.

Amends

"THERE'S SOMEONE IN THE BATHROOM at night who tries to stop me from getting in," my father insists a few weeks before he dies. "I don't see him, but I know he's there."

I nod as if this invisible predator is real, doing his dirty work in the dark. I never challenge my father's delusion, just as I never challenge the certainty that with advanced, untreatable pancreatic cancer, he will soon die. Though my father's been a family physician in Alabama for almost fifty years and for the last three months has dressed in a suit and tie and sat for two hours at his desk, he's never once mentioned that he has cancer. "This problem," he calls it. "When I get over this problem."

I nod at this too.

My father is seventy-nine, and though he will not see eighty—shy only three months—I believe this marker would have suited him, fulfilling a triumphant defiance of his past when, during my childhood, he both secretly feared and ritually announced that he'd be dead by forty. Not thirty-nine. Not forty-one or forty-two or forty-three. No, he would collapse at forty as if this were an inheritance from his father, who died at forty on the way to the hospital from untreated peritonitis. Then again, perhaps this premonition came from the recognition that he descended from a long line of Irish Catholic alcoholics, garrulous, optimistic, reality-denying drinkers who casually dismissed heart attacks, strokes, and exhausted livers, even though the clock was ticking. Indeed, the stories were vivid, sobering: His grandfather (his father's father), once widowed, packed up his three kids and traveled with them by train from Nashville to Mobile, insisting they wait in the Mobile train station and mind the oldest while he went to find work and a place for them to live. He returned twenty years later.

Instead of dying at forty, my father was revitalized, an unexpected reckoning with fate: In the next decade, he became an even more popular doctor in our town—elected president of the county medical association, serving as mayor pro tem of the city council, and named to the boards of hospitals and banks and universities—and, to use his most valued compliment of others, a "credit to the community."

Rather than a coffin, he entered a new sort of daylight.

And yet it was also during this decade and the next, amid my father's vigor and popularity, that our troubles began. At first, our disagreements and rumblings simmered rather than erupted, small storms that never escalated to dizzying winds or damaging hail, never flooded the driveway or saturated the topsoil. What they did was erode the nerves and waterlog the heart. My father, after all, was often tired from his strenuous schedule and I had not yet been dragged down to the bottom of myself.

There's someone in the bathroom at night who tries to stop me from getting in.

"He'll get plenty of offers," my father said to no one in particular as he pierced the yoke of his fried egg with a piece of toast. It was a warm Saturday morning in 1962, and my father gazed out the window where dogwood still bloomed and my mother's ferns shimmered lush and green in the light before he pushed the dripping toast into his mouth. Sitting on either side of him at the breakfast table, my sister and I knew he meant my brother, still sleeping, as Saturday was the only day—no practices, no games—he could languish in bed. Though it was early September, college football coaches from all over the country had been angling for my brother, piling on coded compliments, sending him glossy brochures and stats, and discussing campus visits for later in the fall. My father drank his coffee, scratched idly at his neck where dry skin often flecked onto his collar, then turned to my sister, who'd gone back to reading her book. "Now you," he smiled, "should accompany me on rounds tomorrow and we'll see what you notice." My sister looked up and nodded. "You finish the practice tests?" He meant the prep course my mother had ordered. My sister gave him a sly smile as if even the thought of tests was a noisy intrusion into the sealed, blissful place of her reading. We all knew she read only what pricked her interest, though in the end, after extravagant dawdling, she'd rise to the challenge and devour the tests.

I was eating a second cinnamon roll, peeling it from the outside, attentively licking icing from my middle finger, cleaning it up quite well, and listening carefully, as if beneath the pitch and thrust of my father's words, something critical was at stake. As I pulled the soft, sticky dough from the center, I surreptitiously watched as my father took a last sip of coffee, crumpled his napkin, began pushing back his chair, and then stopped. He gazed at me. "Honor roll," he said, then got up.

In our family, we knew too well my father's priorities: Success, to him, was a transcendent ideal, a transformation that led only to applause. And what he wanted was a grand slam, wanted his two daughters to succeed as much as his son, wanted my sister and me to have the grace and beauty of women and the ambition and nerve of men, to be persuasive and eloquent, clever and resourceful, to succeed beyond his limits and, of course, to be doctors. In many ways, my brother and sister complied with these terms, but I, well, I was too bound up in myself, both urgently stirring the pot of achievement and hopelessly confused by the results. Inside me lived a secret restlessness, a half-crazy feeling of wanting to change the story, to do the unexpected—to swim underwater across Perdido Bay, carried by silty water and the hard thrust of my arms from one marshy bank to the other, to put my head down on my desk and sleep through classes, shushing this life and dreaming another, to say "No" with loud, emphatic naughtiness—but these desires were suppressed by guilt and a diffuse hope that my path would be refined and recognition inevitable as if the way to success followed some natural law. In high school I made As, but not A+s, was slender and mildly attractive but never pretty, was elected to minor offices but never the important ones, the ones that singled you out as a leader.

"You just never *fit!*" a classmate announced cheerfully last year as we sat chatting on one of my visits home. He said this with such affectionate clarity I laughed, as if someone had finally grasped my essence.

And yet, growing up, I carefully plucked and pruned myself, desperately wanting to fit, to gain my family's approval even as I longed to let down my guard and be let "in" for no reason at all. In truth, it wasn't until I divorced at age twenty-four—my world gone dark by failure in love—that my life was upended. Suddenly, I had to put myself back together again, and I did this with a protracted slowness and then with sudden acceleration by moving across country to Los Angeles to begin an MFA in art and design. At age twenty-seven, I'd lived such a provincial life my sense of art was little more than living-room karma. "Now, you make something pretty out there for your mama," a neighbor instructed before I left, and I knew that "pretty" meant art to decorate the living room or grace the entryway, something traditional and ornamental to enhance the aura, complementing the drapes and rugs and adding pleasure. I smiled. Of course.

Inevitably, in my first semester at UCLA such assumptions were assaulted, left gasping in the dirt. In a seminar with Chris Burden, a performance artist, I discovered that he'd once paid an assistant to shoot him in the arm with a .22 rifle at a gallery performance as a way to contemplate pain and suffering and perhaps replicate the trauma of surgery without anesthesia on his left foot at age twelve after his motor scooter accident on Elba. When another art student gossiped about how Burden—*"can you believe it?"*—had done this shocking, risky art piece called "Shoot," I hesitated, then laughed in astonished embarrassment, imagining my parents' alarm if they ever heard such a story.

And yet it was from Chris Burden, who was quiet and unassuming, even shy in class, that I learned a crucial lesson about art: It's the artist who determines what matters. Not tradition. Not familial or cultural aesthetics. Not the fashion or rhetoric of the day. The artist.

I never looked back.

That summer, after my first year at UCLA, I prided myself on having burst free of my small-town chrysalis, having spent the year not only making art but going to museums and galleries, to music concerts, to plays and film festivals and university lectures, to discussions about feminism at the Women's Center, and even sleeping once with a married man, all things I'd never have considered in Alabama but things that had changed me. When I arrived home for a month's vacation in July, my hair longer, prettier, my posture looser, my identity as an artist more confident, my way of dressing stripped down to the bare bones of colorful tank tops, shorts, and tennis shoes like every other art student, I was secretly pleased. *Bringing LA to Alabama*, I smugly thought.

But to my surprise, these little revisions annoyed my father. A career in art seemed risky if not irrelevant to him, a bohemian indulgence (though he wouldn't have used that word) in need of a reality check. What did he care about Philip Glass or Vito Acconci or Judy Chicago, artists who would have seemed, at most, kooky to him? In contrast to me, my brother and sister, a lawyer and doctor, respectively, had followed the narrative line: Admired and settled in professions and marriages, they had new houses and babies and energy to spare. What had happened to me?

When my father saw me burning the edges of a piece of cloth I intended to dye and paint, singeing it erratically for its aesthetic unevenness, his face puckered in a frown. "What kind of job can you hope to get?" he asked, wrinkling his nose at the smell. "I mean, how will you support yourself?"

Surprised, I looked out the window where heat shimmered on the driveway, where the ferns were so big and green and fleshy, they looked monstrous. My father, I knew, had a right to be worried, for though I was a teaching assistant in my department, he still gave me money, insisting I live in a "decent, safe place" instead of "some rat hole," which meant a functional apartment near UCLA. But since his worries constricted my desires, I fought them, denying the premise, resenting his concerns. Didn't he see that I'd been broken by divorce? Didn't he see that I no longer was?

Later, I'd worry that I'd missed the point, the point being that my father wouldn't be here forever to help with the rent and I'd have to risk more than ragged edges of cloth to discover my own relevance. But that July I only parried and dodged my father, maintaining a stalemate until one afternoon the plot unraveled and we collided as we readied for an outside event in 96-degree temperature. "Put on some decent clothes, for Chrissake," my father insisted when I wandered, distracted, into the den. He was incensed that I no longer presented myself in attractive dresses or tailored pants and with well-combed hair, as he thought a respectable southern girl should, but ran around in shorts and tennis shoes without socks, my hair loose and untidy, my face almost bare of makeup. Startled, I glanced at him in his red and green plaid golf pants and tomato red knit shirt, his shape in profile a rounded arc from belly to groin, his shoes a dazzling white. How could I tell him that, well, as a feminist I was released from the obsessive need to please men?

Instead, I burst into tears.

"Oh, stoppit," he said, irritated, and walked away.

In retrospect, neither his irritation nor his expectations should have caused surprise. As girls, my sister and I were forbidden to wear blue jeans or shorts to his office, our bodies as well as our minds meant to be representative of the family. Such decorum was expected.

But now I was defecting.

And yet the day I was to fly back to LA, I longed to make amends. More than anything I needed to explain, to clear myself, to make my father see that what had offended him—the way I looked and dressed—had, in the larger picture, been a good thing. It meant that I could change and adapt, could fit in with my peers in a new place even though such choices were more casual than those in Alabama. This reflected, I wanted to emphasize, a focus on work rather than presentation, a heightening of ambition and a willingness to sacrifice, all things my father approved. As I stood inside his medical office that morning, patient charts stacked on his desk, his stethoscope looped around his neck, he seemed distant, distracted as if anxiety pricked at his thoughts. My father wasn't a big man but was short and compact, light on his feet, with a quick grin and a quicker wit. He had a restless, nervous energy that charged the room and drew people to him, but when irritated, he could explode, veins popping out on his forehead, his words sizzling the air. He could frighten me. He was my father. Not quite God, but close.

Watching his face, my voice tightened, my words rushed and insistent as if I were trying to win an argument. *But this is a minor thing*, I kept reassuring myself. A part of me wanted to say, "Please," while another part dared insist, "Oh, this is silly!" and stalk out to the car. Before I could do either, before I could win my father over, he turned away from me, gazing out the large glass windows at his car parked in its familiar spot beside the office, the hot southern sun splashing diamonds of light onto the polished metal, the vacant lot beyond trimmed and mowed. He seemed to pause as if weighing his thoughts or perhaps considering my words, but when he turned back, his face looked strained.

"I really want—" I began, then hesitated, the air suddenly tense, sharp with silence.

Neither of us moved. Only time jumped forward. I watched a nurse pass his door, a shiny medical tray held aloft in her hands. Someone in one of the treatment rooms cried out in pain, *aaggghhh*, then quieted. The round clock on his wall ticked loudly as if measuring our silence.

"Daddy," I began again.

He held up a hand. "What you say may be well and good for Los Angeles."

His voice was low, and to my surprise, oddly quiet. Though he didn't step closer, I felt his nearness, his presence. "But"—he looked directly at me—"*this is Alabama.*" And then he stepped back, his gaze holding mine. "And don't come home until you can do something important."

It was a sentence I hadn't expected.

A sentence that scalded the air.

There's someone in the bathroom at night who tries to stop me from getting in.

Within three hours, I was on a plane to Los Angeles, my life split in two. I'd arrived in Alabama a daughter, but as I stepped off the plane in LA, I'd metamorphosed into a person beyond a daughter, a woman whose instincts and self-interest were absurdly, indignantly, at war. My instincts had always been defined by loyalty to family, to a sense of us—our history, our jokes, our ambitions, worries, and needs—but now self-preservation demanded an unmooring. *Maybe I'll stay away for twenty years!*

But where does self-preservation come from?

In my youth, I naively thought self-preservation depended on courage or self-confidence or a grand intelligence. I believed it emerged from a solid grounding, but now I sensed it came from something deeper, a secret undergrowth of loneliness and despair, a vital selfishness that you matter.

It's this mattering that becomes your identity.

Then again, how you come to it determines the mattering.

Once I landed in California, I breathed no such higher thoughts: My brain was in panic, bursting its boundaries. All I knew was that I was a stray, exiled from the tribe. Banished. Adrift. Alone. As I walked through the hot Mediterranean air toward my apartment, I marveled at the pitch of my resentment and a new bristling catalyst for ambition: Why not let my retaliation be artistic, a creative stab in the back?

Perhaps it's here, right in this very moment—the ocean breeze ruffling my hair, bougainvillea blazing in the hills, a skateboarder hurtling past—that I found my salvation: a passionate fury that would deliver me *from* myself and deliver me *to* myself, releasing me from the prison of a southern girl's need to please. Such fury, of course, lives in the nerves, thrills with the birds in early morning as they flit from bush to grass to window, burns blue in the thick heat of noon, and swarms in dark corners at night.

And so, each morning, my arteries on fire, my lungs roaring, I took this anger-junked self to work, processing photos in the photography lab, reverse dying fabric to be painted and collaged in the design studio, writing short scripts for video essays. I arrived at the art department in my uniform of tennis shoes, tank top and shorts, stopped at noon for a snack of cheese and crackers and an apple, left the studio for a salad and sandwich at supper, and then returned, staying until eleven o'clock or midnight, binging on cookies from the vending machine.

Sometimes, near six or seven o'clock, another graduate student named Betty would arrive with her dog, Heidi, on a leash, having driven down from Northridge where she taught during the day. She didn't come every night, but always on Friday, Saturday, and Sunday nights when she could stay for at least five hours, working at her loom, brewing pots of coffee, letting Heidi sleep beside her on the cool tile floor. Often, on the weekends, Betty and I were the only ones in the studio, me working in an adjoining room where there were large padded tables rather than looms. Because there were no doors between us, we'd shout thoughts to each other and laugh. When Betty rose to heat up her coffee, I'd take a break with her, opening the refrigerator and taking out a Diet Coke, splitting a bag of Oreos. One Saturday night, Betty leaned on one of the tables, sipping her coffee, glancing out at the Saturday night traffic streaming down Sunset Boulevard, then looked at me. "I know why I'm here. I mean, weekends are my only free time to work on my art, but why are *you* here?"

It seemed too complicated to explain. "I like to work," I hedged.

"On Saturday night?" Betty laughed.

I laughed too. "Yeah, I know. I just can't seem to get it all done." What I couldn't say was that I'd pinned my hopes on making a larger, more complicated piece, a design that confounded me despite all my strategies and experimentations.

Betty looked at several of the sections I'd pinned to the wall—the reverse dyed sections reminiscent of earlier topographical pieces but also a faded peach cloth painted with a lavender grid—and intuited my concerns. "Sometimes sleep is the best resource. At least there's the possibility of dreaming a solution." She drank a big gulp of coffee and grinned. "At least, that's what I keep telling myself."

And then she went back to her loom.

But sleep was inevitably the problem. Sleep meant a release, an unwinding, meant lying down, my thoughts untethered, a labyrinth of anxieties open to darkness. Each night when I came through my apartment door and saw the comfortable but ugly plaid couch and beyond it, the necklace of lights descending toward Westwood, my heart sank. Here, alone and unbuttoned from ambition, the possibility of being a fool, of kidding myself, of wanting what I couldn't have, punctured the armor of my fury. Staring out into the night, I felt stricken. Who did I think I was? What had I actually accomplished? If I meant to defy my father, to "show him," why did I still cash his check? All moral indignation wilted under this scrutiny, for the truth was I couldn't afford to live here on a TA's salary even though I scrimped on everything, even sleeping on three beach towels because I didn't have enough money for a mattress. No, I was nothing. I'd always be nothing. And I didn't know how to stop being nothing. I was just a girl far from home, sleepless on an ugly plaid couch.

It pains me to realize that it never occurred to me to get a second job, to cut back my hours of art work in order to support myself completely, to create my own independence. I'd so convinced myself my vindication had to be artistic that my sole response was to "do something important," as if, even in defiance, I remained the obedient daughter. And this too was part of the war, this battle between obedience and egoism. While working, I felt such a rush of vital selfishness and redemptive meaning, I didn't give a damn about my father's money. I'd use it when I needed it. His loss. Too bad.

But alone in my apartment, lying on my beach towels, the shame of dependence burrowed deep into the crevices of my brain.

To release myself from this trajectory of work and sleep, I often went to the LA County Museum of Art and stood before Robert Motherwell's *Elegy to the Spanish Republic 100*, staring at the thick black rectangles separated from each other by black oval shapes splashed on white canvas. The painting so large and abstract was flat and one-dimensional with only the barest hint of depth in the top left corner, but what I loved was its mood of mournfulness and lamentation. No softness. No shimmer of green, of leaves fluttering in the trees, no imagined sun or wisp of sky. Here was tragedy and death. A recognition of horror. Unassimilated sadness. It was important to me that Motherwell began the series in 1948, the year of my birth, inspired by the Spanish poet Federico García Lorca, who was abducted by Franco's henchmen, taken out on a lonely road, and murdered. On certain days, just being in the presence of the painting, I felt soothed, relieved of my burdens, my body calmed. Standing alone, staring at the farthest black rectangle vanishing into the painting's fold, I entered a silence, an existential pause: It was okay to be me, to believe in art.

There's someone in the bathroom at night who tries to stop me from getting in.

Because I had no home to visit for Christmas vacation, I flew to New York to tag along with my video professor, Nam June Paik, who was performing on Christmas Eve at CBGB's with a punk group. Of course, I had no idea they wouldn't begin playing until midnight or that the band would be such a noisy racket of synthesized sound I'd need to anesthetize myself with glasses of cheap wine, and yet it was here in this noisy club that I contemplated the absurd irony that Nam June had shattered another of my perceptions about art. At a party back in October, I'd been showing off, trying to be amusing as I told Nam June (a visiting professor at UCLA) about the "culture" of small-town Alabama: the water ballets, the drive-ins, the beauty pageants, and of course, the tawdry, sex-edged gossip piercing the fumes of permanent wave solutions at Zade's Beauty Shop where a woman under the dryer would yank up the hood and say smartly, "Oh, for the Lord's sake, y'all talk louder. Can't hear a durn thing under here and I'm not missing out."

To my surprise, Nam June had grinned. "Do Alabama," he said, pronouncing it *Ala-boma.* "Do the Drive-in, the beauty shop and all the stories of your town." Startled, I shook my head. Hadn't I come to graduate school to be introduced to a *higher* order of culture, to leave behind the provincial, the drawling boosterism and regressive politics of my little corner of Dixie? How else could I possibly remake myself?

And yet that night in New York, lying sleepless in a narrow bed in a friend's studio apartment, my mind swarmed with ideas as if I'd slipped free of a straightjacket I hadn't known I wore. I remembered not the familiar, campy things I'd told Nam June but walking at age seven in the stillness of late afternoon beneath a canopy of trees, tangles of moss swaying in the breeze, dragonflies buzzing, their wings iridescent, my flip-flops making a soft slap-slap as I meandered down the middle of the road, attuned to bursts of blue sky beyond the trees and the dank, iron smell of the river around the bend. I was alone and happy as if the entire world was mine. I remembered how a gang of us girls would start out on our bikes every Saturday morning in summer and ride the back roads past soybean fields and farms and wide ditches blooming with goldenrod and dandelions, seven miles to the secret glade of the "springs" where we dropped our bikes and scrambled over roots and down rock-carved steps to the sudden damp coolness of rushing water, pools streaming over moss-covered rocks, tadpoles drifting in the current. I remembered singing with my father in the car, my sister and I in the back seat, my father belting out songs—"Ricochet Romance" and "Here Comes Peter Cottontail"—in the front seat in his off-key, scratchy voice, my sister and I giggling in guilty pleasure as we joined in. As a child, I lived inside this life, never imagining it might dissolve or that I'd ever linger, outside of it.

Alabama. What did it mean? How in the world could I make art out of Alabama?

Though I'd worked mainly in fabric design, creating large wall hangings that mimicked pastel landscapes, ragged topographic maps suggesting elevation and density, fabric dyed and layered and painted, some of the edges burned and unravelling, after taking the video course with Nam June Paik, I began making art videos as well. Like everyone in the late 1970s, I experimented with conceptual subjects, but I also subversively tried to render my own desperation and rebellion. In one video—an abstract, moody piece—a girl is clearly lost in a large empty space, though what the viewer sees is a collage of the girl running—the splash of her flower-patterned dress, her searching eyes, her empty hands, the blur of her feet on a bare concrete floor, a flood of light searing the stark white columns that provided the only architectural grace in the room. The story line and voice-overs I no longer remember. What I remember is that at the end the girl cries out in a plaintive voice, *"Daddy."* It was, of course, a primitive attempt at exorcism. Though my fabric pieces were not directly autobiographical, this, well, this made me understand Chris Burden more intimately, revealing how creative revision could transform pain into something freeing. This wasn't about my father. This was about me.

By the end of that year, after I'd completed two successful fabric pieces (abandoning the unfinished one Betty had seen), the faculty arrived on fourth floor to critique my work, attached now to a white wall with a space cleared for their viewing. I stood beside my work, apprehensive to hear their evaluation and intuit their silences. I was expected, of course, to discuss my own process as well, but we students knew the real status of the meeting wasn't our voice but theirs. *All those hours*, I kept thinking, knowing that time spent in the studio didn't equate with quality. Heroics were irrelevant. Art was fickle, deaf to retaliation. Along with the fabric pieces I'd also set up a video installation in the woods behind the art department: a video piece on penance in which the viewer entered a tall, rectangular box I'd built, painted, and then hauled up a small hill to a cloistered spot behind the Art Department. Once inside, the viewer drew a curtain to become a surrogate priest, witnessing a ritual of blue painted females emerging as if out of ether, their hands clasped, their voices almost a whisper as they confessed the contortions they'd enacted in their desire to be good and the inchoate longings subdued as they struggled to rise. Some heads were bowed; others stared directly at the camera, eyes unblinking. In one scene there was a close-up of my face dripping with honey, my eyes closed, my mouth barely moving as if furtively uttering words, "Ave Maria" playing in the background, the camera moving closer and closer until it settled on the fleshy curve of those murmuring lips and then on the dark, infinite space between the words.

It was a balmy day, the sky hazy with a scattering of clouds, the air dry and still, only the sounds of traffic in the distance suggesting that UCLA was in the midst of the city. The campus often felt like a reclusive enclave, an imaginative cocoon separate from all the commercial hype of Los Angeles. My video in the woods had been available for viewing for three consecutive days, and this was the final day. I'd occasionally seen students or faculty trek into the woods, but I always rushed up the elevator to the fourth floor so that I didn't have to witness their return. That afternoon, not long after I'd finished my critique, I stood alone in the sculpture garden near the art museum, peeling back the plastic wrap from a toasted cheese sandwich I'd crammed into my purse. I began taking small bites, barely noticing what I ate and only wishing I'd remembered to bring a bottle of water. When I glanced up, still chewing, I saw one of the painting professors emerging from the path to the woods. Embarrassed suddenly, and hoping to remain anonymous—I'd never taken a class with this professor and though we'd passed in the hallway, we'd never been introduced—I looked down at the last two pieces of my sandwich, the cheese congealed to a shiny orange, the bread damp and soggy, as the man came closer to where I waited. As if paralyzed, I didn't move until he was near, then I looked up quickly, unable to restrain myself. Instinctively, I imagined he'd pass by, perhaps not making eye contact, but to my surprise there were tears in his eyes. He nodded to me. I nodded back. And then he stopped right beside me. "Thank you," he said softly, staring directly at me before he moved slowly away and began climbing the stairs to the art library.

I watched him ascend, an older, dark-haired, slightly plump painter I didn't know, and yet because of his astonishing words, I could move on too.

There's someone in the bathroom at night who tries to stop me from getting in.

Years pass. With time, my relationship with my father begins to mend, though the patching is visible, jagged in places, smoothed over in others, like tiny, broken capillaries sprinkled across fair, freckled skin. Each time I go home, my father and I hug at the beginning and end of each visit, but we remain wary, no loud sighing or noisy drama. By now, I've moved both my location and my artistic desires. I'm at the Iowa Writers' Workshop in Iowa City, studying fiction and living amid cornfields and writers, men and women who've come here from every part of America, their ambition charged and hungry, the competition visceral. I'd like to say that at this stage of my life I'm grounded and confident, but I've learned that to be a writer is more a collage of loose ends and knotted threads, one's steadiness dependent on the daily work of unraveling and reconstructing a character's destiny, one's confidence a Rorschach of intent and uncertainty. Still, I hold fast to the shape of myself, happy to be able to live this life.

The winter after I finish my MFA, I sit in a narrow upstairs room writing a novel while outside my window, there's a great white emptiness, the plowed cornfields covered in a fine drift of snow. Each day, I put on long underwear, jeans, sweater, boots, hat, gloves, scarf, and coat and walk out onto the bumpy farm road that circles the house my husband (whom I met in LA) and I share with a friend whose wife is teaching in Chicago. Ruts, sometimes two feet deep, run in fissures across the road, but it's still manageable for walking. Farmhouses occasionally dot the landscape, two-story white Victorians with plastic-wrapped windows and wide-open vistas, nothing but fields and a lint-colored sky. Often when I step outside, the wind howls. Automatically,

I hunch over, pulling a woolen scarf up over my mouth, and walk, glad to be stretching, to be part of the elements after sitting at my desk. On one of these walks, I glance up just as a flock of birds stretches across that grayed sky in lyrical formation, a small sudden glimpse of beauty. Probably flying south. I stop to watch, admiring them, and instantly think of my father, musing on how we both like birds, how one summer we sent each other snapshots, almost always blurry, of the birds we'd seen. My father. In my mind, I see him laughing, the way he shows all his teeth, his eyeteeth like mine, long and pointy, his eyes lit up at a good joke, reveling in pleasure. My father. I see him at 3:00 A.M. standing in front of the open refrigerator's halo of light, half asleep but hungry, looking for a piece of Monterey Jack cheese. I see him there because I often wake then too, my body, like his, a metabolic tornado. My father. I see him at the breakfast table, reading the newspaper as he did throughout my childhood, so absorbed he forgets to loosen his hold on the handle of his coffee cup.

Now the birds are gone, the sky empty, but I'm still thinking about my father. For many years, I haven't imagined talking intimately to him or casually laughing as we did when I was a kid and we'd find ourselves staring compulsively into the refrigerator at 3:00 A.M. I haven't imagined the sudden recognition of pleasure we both have when we arrive at Wolf Bay or Soldier Creek, the two of us intrinsically drawn to water. I haven't imagined a fit of uncontrollable laughter, loud and raucous, another thing we have in common. On my biyearly visits, I've kept my arms crossed and my mind shuttered, revealing little beyond the daughter who left, still a partial stray. I've never let him "in." As this thought lingers, I feel a shift, a loosening as if something inside me is unwinding, breaking apart. And then I'm running, flinging off my coat and gloves and hat, anxious to sit down and write.

As my fingers race across the keys, I know I'm writing this to myself as much as to my father, describing the complications I've lived through after the disaster of my marriage and how I've come to understand my choices, how art and writing have provided me a way to unravel the tumultuous story bound up inside me, a story that includes him, that has circled and pushed against him but has never really touched him because I haven't been able to see him seeing me, as if we both exist in shadow. In a flush of revelation, I realize that, like me, my father was the oddball in his family, the one who broke loose from his family drama to define new terms, to make a new life, one different and perhaps incomprehensible to his parents. They expected, at most, that he'd go to work, as they had, at the docks in Mobile or the paper mill in Pascagoula, cooking gumbo and catfish and playing cards in the evenings or watching wrestling on TV. They lived, it seemed to me, in a numbing complacency, perhaps too distracted by the hard buzz of their lives to step outside themselves and ask larger questions. Like me, my father must have been both tied to and separated from his family, a bicultural kid, educated beyond them into a life of different values where respect followed academic and professional achievement rather than maintenance and loyalty.

I write this too.

I have a picture of my father as little boy in 1929 sitting at his desk at school, a picture I've kept in an envelope and gazed at each time I've packed up and moved. Now I pull it out of a suitcase. In the photo, my father wears a white, stiff-collared shirt and smiles shyly at the camera, his hair a nest of curls on top, short above the ears. His eyes look like my eyes—curious but simultaneously suspect, a raw hope held in, not quite ready to explode. And this is the father I write to, the boy in the man whose contained curiosity is my guide.

There's someone in the bathroom at night who tries to stop me from getting in.

What do I want? I ask as I write.

I no longer want to be let "in." That's now beside the point. What I want is to let my father know I'm no invisible night creature, but here, right here, alive and well and defined by the desires and boundaries I've created by scraping against my own moment of history, which means I've pushed hard in one direction, fallen off track, picked myself up, and corrected my course, seeing possibility through the thin sheen of a bubble. And I've followed that possibility. It's what matters.

What I want is to be a daughter again, a daughter who can amend and make amends, can change our story or at least find shelter in a new, more intimate place. When I shove the letter through the mail slot in the post office in Iowa City, I feel a great weight shift from my shoulders.

And yet, a day later as I sprawl on the double bed in the upstairs bedroom, I'm less certain about the letter. I've just laid myself bare. I've exposed what I know of the hard places in my life and the turnings within those hard places.

Read with a certain mind, my letter is an exploration of failure and unraveling.

Read with a certain mind, my letter is an admission that nothing important was accomplished.

Read with a certain mind, my letter is a koan, a riddle, a recognition of what accomplishment might really mean.

For the next few days, I take longer walks even though the cold bites into my skin. I pull the scarf around my mouth and nose and stare at the empty fields and the drift of clouds in a flat, gray sky, the horizon a slash of white in the distance. Then I go back inside and turn on my computer. My choice has been made.

"Your father wants to talk to you," my mother says after she and I have visited for ten minutes on the phone. A week has passed.

"Pat," my father says in his gravelly voice, the hiss coming clearly through the wires. I can see him in his bathrobe and slippers, one foot rubbing his callouses against the smooth pile of the rug, his glasses slipping downward on his nose. "How are things up in the Arctic Circle?" he asks, teasing about the weather in Iowa and praising, as always, the sunniness of Alabama. "Best place in the world." But then he goes quiet, the silence between us thick and awkward.

I wait. Outside my window snow is falling, the flakes light and drifting, coating the roof of the barn and whitening the old dirty snow that spreads like an endless lake across the yard. When the wind picks up, the snow swirls, a flurry tossed against the pane, obscuring for a moment my view.

"Come home," he says, his voice soft and deep. "I want you to come home."

My father and I have both mellowed, even slyly swapped places. Now I want success and my father wants to slow down, to watch the rhythm of the light, the way it glitters at noon and then shadows the water in the pool in late afternoon, deepening the blue. But what surprises me is how my father becomes my biggest fan, the one in the family who encourages my writing and teaching, who revels, of course, in any publication or award I get, but who also asks simply, "What are you working on?" when he calls. Always, he asks about my work. And to free me from the economic constraints of my creative life, he likes to send me "fun money," money he insists I use for pleasure. And yet it isn't through talking on the phone or in person that my father and I become close. It's through the old-fashioned epistolary mode, both handwritten and typed pages sent through snail mail. In letters, I tell him about seeing two deer frolicking in a field across from my house, scampering around the yard like puppies, chasing one another; I tell him my worries about completing a novel, how I'll write in late afternoon, finishing a chapter, but will be anxious the next morning about the next one; I tell him about the dogwood coming into bloom, my brown world exploding into green.

In response, my father mostly sends me short, staccato sentences in his beautiful, slanting penmanship on both sides of a prescription, sentences that often make me laugh.

And yet, it seems another irony that as we become close, my father's health begins to deteriorate. Not all at once. But through a series of surgeries and chronic diseases that require maintenance and discipline, two things he's never mastered in reference to his own body. Because he's lived a workaholic life, a life of service and hypervigilance to others, always attuned to being a "credit to the community," he's depended on an abundance of energy and endurance, choosing rich foods when he gets a chance, drinking too much, sleeping erratically, avoiding exercise and pushing the boundaries in every way. When illness comes, he ignores it as if he can will it away until a crisis sabotages his dismissal. Then, he goes under the knife, complaining and recovering and returning as much as possible to his former ways.

That is, until he's diagnosed with stage 4 pancreatic cancer.

I've been home for a week, sleeping on the couch across from my father's hospital bed, getting up when he wakes for ice chips, for the portable commode, and watching him as he sleeps on his back, the covers drawn up to his chin. He's frail but alert, mostly preoccupied with the small details of bodily discomfort, though he revives for a few minutes with visitors, then slips into a coma-like sleep after they leave. Tending to him is a relief, a ritual, a promise that he's alive. I can't imagine it ending.

And yet it is ending. His breathing is shallower. His words simpler. His sleep longer. What I remember most vividly is that two days before he dies, one of the hospice nurses arrives to bathe and change him. My father lies in his hospital bed in our den, the curtains to the French doors open, allowing him to gaze out at the fenced-in backyard where pansies bloom and ferns hang from baskets, where bright, chlorinated water in the pool glistens in the sunlight. I happen to be in the room that day when the nurse comes into the den, dressed in her white pants and nursing shoes. She's a large, solid Black woman, slow-moving and pleasant, and she greets my father affectionately, taking his hand in hers. I mean to leave the room to give them privacy, but as I step into the kitchen—separated only by a built-in counter and cabinets—I stop and turn, watching as she soaks a washcloth in a bowl of cool water and lifts one of my father's arms. He gazes at her with a look of surrender, a look I've never seen on his face, a face now so gaunt his cheekbones jut below sunken, faded eyes. Though I tell myself to leave, I don't take another step. As I stand half in the room, half out, the woman begins to sing, a soft, low crooning, rich and intimate, her voice lowering almost to a hum and then rising, swelling as she loses herself in the rhythm of her task, as she lifts each arm and washes the loose, wrinkled flesh of my father's body as if the very task is holy, dipping the white cloth into the water, wringing it slightly, then easing it gently around the sinews of his neck, cleaning behind the ears, under the chin, taking out a new cloth and touching his scalp, easing his forehead, smoothing his brows, her voice carrying him, holding him as if he's a little child being soothed after a long, tiring day. I remember that my father closes his eyes as she holds his hand, even when there's nothing else for her to do. I'm surprised when his eyes flutter open again as if he needs to see her, his gaze never leaving her face as she sings the final verse, her voice barely a whisper, blessing him, preparing him for his journey in a way that none of us, so close to him, have known how to do.

It's been twenty years since my father died. Tonight, I step out onto my back deck, the grass dark and barely visible, the sky a dusky blue. It is quiet here, only the faint drone of a neighbor's air conditioner disturbing the night. I see the flicker of a lightning bug over the dying lilies, the leafy shadow of our katsura tree, the gnarled thrust of rose bushes crowding the fence. In the quiet, I think about my father and me, as I often do. Even now, I yearn to amend and make amends. I want to amend the girl I was and the man he was, to make myself more daring and less anxious, to make him more compassionate and less demanding. But of course, I can't. All I can do is grapple with the mystery of us, our similarities and differences, and remember the way we learned to lean toward each other in the most natural, intuitive way even as we sometimes disagreed. I marvel that it took me so long to recognize that healing a rupture requires a willingness to stand alone and to bend toward another, demands a heaping of selfishness and a healthy ration of empathy, and of course, implies that the voice of aloneness risks narrating her story to a willing ear.

Soon darkness will cover the trees and the flowers, will swallow up the sharp edges of the fence, will blot out even the grass. Soon I will be inside with a book, stretched out on the couch, turning pages, a cup of tea within arm's reach. But not yet. For now, I want to breathe in the stillness just a little bit longer.

Pilgrimage

S HE LIES IN SHADOW, THE Christmas tree lights a soft blur, the desk lamp turned low, casting its pale glow on her socked feet, which must, *absolutely must*, be free of the blankets. She's nestled in the "Cadillac recliner"— the biggest La-Z-Boy I've ever seen—with Rusty, the neurotic little rescue dog, wedged in by her hip, the two of them immersed in something like sleep. Until she's not. I hear the chair creak, her throat gurgling, then the rustle of covers, and I'm up from the nearby couch, a trained jack-in-the-box.

"Up? You want to get up?"

She says nothing but holds out both hands, code that she's ready to move. She looks at me not with the old territorial command but with the gentle gaze of the humbled, the desperate, the dying, her eyes expectant, docile, her world shrunken to these late-night ramblings. And yet as I lean toward her, silence and stillness connect us, returning us to childhood, two little girls listening to a song without words, their minds humming.

"Bathroom," she finally says as Rusty leaps to the floor.

I take both of her hands, brace myself on the rug—though skeletal, she can be deadweight—pull her upright, then circle one arm around her waist to hold her steady as we begin our pilgrimage through the piano room, the bedroom—her exhausted husband a wrapped mound of blankets, the hospital bed empty, the IV pole a glaring sentinel. We push past a protruding dresser, she tottering ahead through the bathroom door, my hand on her elbows, afraid she'll fall. "Slow, go slow," I caution, her body pulsing, anxious about *accidents*. Dismissively, she tosses her head, her pace quickening. I catch up and with a quick grab, lift her nightgown in one swift movement. Promptly, she sits.

The bathroom is large, baroque, chilly, painted a dark, saturated gold as if part of a palace. Paintings hang everywhere beneath recessed lights, every room a gallery. Beyond me, a wreath of scarves dangle from a doorknob. Jewelry piles on the counter. I sit on the marble step to the sunken tub overlooking a garden, the Alabama sky black and heavy, the garden overgrown, the tub empty except for the tangled legs of a spider. Outside I hear the faint howl of a coyote, its yellow eyes prowling the outer fields for prey. It's 4:00 A.M. and my brain's imprinted with sleep. I yawn, then smile sheepishly at my sister, but she doesn't notice. She's too busy wiping herself, then bringing the paper from between her legs as if she might see cancer cells, the blur of colors a tarot card of disease. Like a child, she holds it out to me.

I nod approval.

And then, on cue, she thrusts out her hands. "On to more Stations of the Cross," I say, perking up. The lavatory. The Christmas tree. The kitchen chair. Last night she insisted on stopping at the Christmas tree, staring intently at the garland of lights and shiny ornaments as if a wave of dream life and fear were colliding, her mind straining to remember. And then transforming before my eyes, she straightened, her gaze becoming razor-sharp. "If anyone tries to steal my Louis Vuitton," she said indignantly, "I'll shoot them."

I laughed. Her old acquisitiveness had come roaring back. "You don't have any Louis Vuitton, Miss Priss." I patted her back.

She grinned wickedly, then leaned into me, pressing her forehead against my forehead, skin against skin, bone against bone, as if I were her resting post. A gust of tenderness swept through me, a surprising, surreptitious pleasure: *I am the chosen, the beloved, the only one.*

"Kitchen," she says tonight, barely glancing at the tree.

And we walk.

"We're me," she used to say when we were four and five as if I were marsupial, folded up inside her. I didn't agree or disagree. Sometimes her energy would pour over me, shiny and clean, the two of us tangled like roots, though she insisted that *she* lived closer to the sun. Did it matter if she slept closer to the door, got the best doll, the prettiest barrettes, the most praise? For a long time, I felt permissive, generous. After all, she was safe, predictable. I knew the whirs and whims of her mind. I knew what she needed, what she wanted, while I was easily distracted, a squirrel jumping from branch to tree. And yet inevitably, almost unconsciously, I wanted elbow room. I wanted solitude. I longed for my own invisible shelter. I don't remember it clearly. And yet there was some year, some month, some week, some second during my childhood when her weight felt like a fist, and I must have planned my defection. I imagined slicing myself free, a hot splash of blood, a wince of pain. But even as I was thinking this, she snapped, "Get away from me," the golden flecks in her irises flashing, her voice a blade. "You're such a *baby*."

It wasn't her fury that astonished me. It was her intuition, her awareness, my insurrection so perfectly blunted. How had she known? How had she gotten there first?

I stepped away, my own anger reduced to claws pinching and grabbing at air. I was separate but confused. An island far from shore. How quickly she'd tossed me away. How smugly she'd claimed victory. And then I knew. Beneath our closeness lay a hidden world of competition, and beneath the competition, a great need to be loved. And beneath that, two little girls, furious and frightened and spinning as fast as they could. One of us would have to be sacrificed. We couldn't both win. Could we?

"You're such a baby," she repeated. And then she laughed, a hot, dry little sound. She didn't need me.

"Writing is drawing the essence of what we know out of shadow. That is what writing is about. Not what happens there. Not what actions are played out there, but the there there." When I read Karl Ove Knausgård's words, sitting at my desk in Iowa City, something bloomed and collapsed in me. The essence of what we know. What did I know? My botched defiance; the delight of inclusion; mockery at my mistake, then laughter and the warm, sweet pull of intimacy. But how do you transform such feelings into meaning, find the hidden self, peek beneath the skirt of consciousness? For me, the first glimpse came through anger, an explosion of feelings: dark, volatile, murderous. Anger at myself for wanting to please her, to watch her face startle with surprise, burning with pleasure. Anger at her for how much she wanted me to be a mirror, reflecting back to her, a shimmer of silvery light.

"Do *not* write from anger," my first writing teacher said. Yes, of course. It made perfect sense. Anger is the weapon of the victim, an emotion produced by fear. It casts a veil over reality, speeds up and distorts impressions, translating what is boundless and unfathomable into the graspable, the precise. And yet, I hesitated. Why not let anger run its rough tongue over the page? Why not let it saturate and clarify, open wide the mouth of the repressed?

Six weeks ago, my sister lay naked on top of the bed, sick but not yet dying. Dying was still a ghostly abstraction, a blip on the screen, someone else's future. Yes, the chemo had been bad this time. "Very hard," she'd said, but bad was just a temporary condition like Red Man, the name of a monster rash worthy of an impressionist painter, a splash of scalding red circling her waist, her legs, in the secret hollow beneath each breast, and around her anus in a perfect oval.

"Whoa, you have a baboon butt," I said, laughing as I smoothed Vaseline over her skin, the edges of the rash so defined they looked as if they'd been traced.

"Yeah, I got lucky." She rolled her eyes, made a mocking face.

As she turned over onto her back, the sun flashed through the windows and I heard her maid Polly muttering, "Miss Jean, Miss Jean, you not *feeling* right," as she padded down the hallway, a stack of clean towels in her arms. Somewhere a phone was ringing, the microwave beeping. Somewhere other people were answering emails and sipping coffee, painting their nails Love Me Lilac, but here, it was only my sister, Jean, staring at me, naked and anxious as I spread Vaseline over her twig-sized legs, across her waist, as I lifted each breast for a tender swipe. She watched me without the slightest hint of embarrassment though we'd been raised to be self-conscious, even prudish about our bodies, always glancing away. I looked at her and slyly thought, "We're me," as I gently massaged her thigh, trying not to hurt her, feeling the softness of my hand on her skin. And laughed.

"What's so funny?" she asked.

"Nothing," I said. "Everything."

"Everything's *not* funny," she said. "Red Man go away."

But it was only I who went away, back to Iowa, back to a sudden cold snap, a swirl of wind and snow, my husband and I dressed in fleece jackets, flannel pajamas, and woolen socks, curled together under quilts, our heater gone bust, the new one not yet installed. "Apparently, *everyone* in Iowa needs a new furnace," my husband said wryly.

"Not funny," I said, our frozen breaths cleansing the house.

When the phone rang the next morning, I leapt for it, insisting the heating company had succumbed to mercy and bumped us to the front of the line.

"She's doing poorly," my brother-in-law said. He sounded anxious, worried.

"Shall I come?" I'd been home barely a week. "Wait, of course. I'll get a ticket."

"She does better when you're here. If you can—"

Poorly. This was how it began for me, the word "poorly" buzzing inside my head as I waited in the Eastern Iowa Airport for my flight to Alabama. What I felt was a sharp stab of sadness and beneath that an uncanny feeling of not being surprised. *She's dying*, I thought for the first time, her body too frail to survive more chemo, her intestines blocked, then unblocked, then blocked again. And beneath that as I wandered to the window to gaze at the gray, murky sky, as dull as an empty sea, a sense of how incomprehensible suffering is, how theoretical and furtive, how unknowable. And beneath that, a guilt that I could not cry, could not feel. I was dry grass. A leafless tree. An old stone.

"Group Three," the airline attendant called, and quickly I shifted my backpack and queued behind a neat, cheerful, lipsticked woman who was already talking, but I turned my gaze to the carpet, mute and ashamed. With a short layover in Charlotte, I rushed to the women's restroom, anxious about time, imagining the inevitable line for the toilets, the way I'd shift from foot to foot, my heart beating faster, *hurry, hurry*, my body bursting with impatience. But as I entered the room, an attendant glanced at me, holding me with dark liquid eyes brimming with kindness. "This way, *sweetheart*," she said in a soft southern voice, directing me to an empty stall. And it was there in the anonymous gray of an airport restroom, sitting on a toilet, my backpack still attached, that I leaned over and cried, my throat aching, my lap damp, my pent-up feelings released by the tender voice of an unknown woman who had called me sweetheart.

Within hours, I was sleeping on the couch next to her recliner, sleeping when she slept, waking when she woke, talking when she needed to talk, turning on the heating pad, getting meds, cokes, water, ice, pillows, nightgowns, tissues, socks, charging her cell phone, reading messages, joking, pleading. Sometimes I brought little slips of our childhood, dog-eared memories to distract if not to divert the pain. "Remember that year we were mermaids, how we lay, propped up on one arm on a platform onstage, dressed in turquoise leotards, our tails shimmering with sequins. Remember? We unzipped the tails, tossed them aside as if we were Broadway stars and, *voilà!*, we danced!"

She nodded, then grimaced, asking me to adjust the heating pad.

"Remember how *you* started our make-believe games with 'I'll be Rose Red and you be Snow White.'" I watched her, listening to the steadiness of her breath, noting the slight quiver of her hands. "Why did you want to be Rose Red?"

But her eyes only fluttered and closed. She was sleeping, Rusty at her feet. Alone on my couch, I listened to rain crashing into the trees, seductive and alive, water seeping everywhere, darkening the roots of the ferns and the caladiums, the lilies, the iris, the oaks and the pines, the world disappearing, the edges of the self, blurring. Tomorrow the driveway would be full of puddles, but maybe the sky would clear, Snow White and Rose Red turning their faces to the sun.

Lying on lace-edged sheets, Snow White watches Rose Red sleep, her arms and one foot tossed outside the covers, the other leg bent at the knee, making a triangle beneath the sheets. Rose Red's face is turned toward Snow White, her eyes closed, twitching with the blinking of dreams. Her dark bangs are ruffled, exposing a smooth forehead, dark lines of eyebrows, dense lashes. But tonight it's the arms that Snow White watches. Through the light of the bathroom, she stares, engrossed, as they turn a smooth mud-colored brown like the inside of a bruise. Snow White is amazed. Something is happening, something she's keenly interested in. As she watches, Rose Red's arms begin to dry up like seed pods, like sticks, shriveling into the burned arms of a doll. Snow White stares in total absorption, greedy, wondering how Rose Red will manage with such curious arms. She thinks of all the things

she'll have to do for her, feeding her, dressing her, wiping her butt. She imagines picking up Rose Red's favorite blue blouse and wearing it herself, watching Rose Red stare at her with a stunned, furious gaze as Snow White prances, pirouetting around their room, her body so alive with feeling, she's in a world of her own, laughing, in love with herself. Watch me! Watch me! Then suddenly, Rose Red's foot kicks at the air, and Snow White blushes, ashamed. Now she's holding the blue blouse out and trying to fit Rose Red's fragile limbs through the sleeve holes that narrow as she pushes each arm though. It's awkward and Snow White is clumsy. Rose Red begins to cry. Frightened, Snow White tries harder, but the arm catches on the fabric, and when Snow White jerks it impatiently, the arm gives way like rotten cloth. Horrified, Snow White turns away, frightened, waiting. When she looks again, Rose Red has changed positions, both arms under her pillow, hidden. Then she sees Rose Red's fingers curled around a lock of hair, all her fingers pink and plump and whole. Snow White breathes easier, softer. And finally, she sleeps.

Anger isn't enough. It's too much. Anger, I remind myself, is merely a catalyst and must give way to self-consciousness, to a deeper, hidden reality. Nothing is as it seems. Sometimes, not even anger. Though the bridge to the unbearable is feeling, writing must pull conflicting emotions out of the shadows, risk the impossible, unravel the *secret* secrets, explode the chronology.

Nothing *is* as it seems. When I was broken, my sister said, "Come." No hesitation. No whisper of drama. No questions. "Here," she said, and I slept on her couch, on her spare bed, letting her brush my hair, letting her feed me, soothe me, her touch warming something at the very center of me.

For years I tried to write about her, to understand how our relationship both pleased and appalled me, how like Molly Bloom I longed to say *Yes!*, and then like Stephen Dedalus, turn brusquely away. What I wanted, of course, was a room of my own, that metaphorical place from which one says, "These are my desires, my fears, my feelings." In reality, it will take me years to see how upset my sister is with me, upset that I moved so far away—Los Angeles, Seattle, Tallahassee, Iowa City—leaving our difficult family and our provincial hometown, and how burdened she is by all that I left behind.

What I do know is that in our twenties, my life tumbled and swung by its connection to her while she, independent and ambitious, defined the turf. And then, as if we'd grown tired of such corseted roles, we crossed a boundary in our thirties and switched paths. Of course, she was still vital and funny and outrageous, but I escaped to another world, the world of writing and art, of interiority and intellect, a life of quiet reflection. Now I began to listen with a certain detachment, a hint of irony, an anthropologist in sibling garb.

Inevitably, I think about our life together as I'm grappling with a novel about two sisters, creating a character much like her, a girl I call Amanda. One morning as I'm plotting what Amanda will do after her younger sister, Jit, runs away, how spooked and angry and frightened she'll be as she stares with disbelief at her sister's disheveled bed, at the audacious act of leaving, I'm stunned to recognize that beneath my sister's confident persona, wedged deep inside her restless intelligence, she's terrified of abandonment. It's such a startling revelation, I put down my pen. I stare out into the late afternoon light, the heart-shaped leaves of the Katsura tree drifting in the Iowa wind. Of course, she'd wanted my subordination. Of course, she'd insisted on loyalty. It was her protection, her leverage. If I needed her, I'd always be there, wouldn't I? I'd never desert her.

We're me.

"Where's Pat?" she keeps asking the day she is dying, her face pale and gaunt, her breathing becoming shallow, thin.

I see her lying partially upright in her chair, swaddled in blankets, her eyes gentle and frightened and pleading, her hands gripping a pillow, her lids drifting closed, then fluttering open. "Where's Pat?" she whispers, barely a sound. "Where's my sister?"

As if I've heard her, I'm rushing back from an errand, running through the yard where tiny frogs leap in the wet grass. Somewhere in the distance I hear the solemn peal of church bells, a dog barking, the frantic hum of cars. How long does it take me to run through the den, up the three steps to the kitchen, through the breakfast room, the second den, the music room, the bedroom until finally, yes, finally . . . I lean my forehead against her forehead, my skin against her skin. She's chilled, shivering, her arms as dry and thin as shriveled sticks, her body slowly, resolutely shutting down. Only her eyes move. When she looks at me, her eyes are ancient, yielding. I can't stop looking at her, breathing for her, touching her, knowing her, loving her as if we'll always be two girls listening to a song without words, our minds humming.

"I'm here," I say. "I'm here."

The Custodian

"HERE. IT'S ALL HERE." SHE bends over to scrutinize the contents, her desk drawer cluttered with yellow legal pads, insurance policies, old taxes and mortgage papers stuffed tight inside this narrow space. Nothing can escape. "All the paperwork you'll need." When she glances up, her hazel eyes are focused, insistent. At ninety-five, she's so tiny her blue sweater reaches to her knees, her wrists thin and threaded with veins, her fingers crippled and cracked. When she slumps in her white chair, she looks like a child. "I want you to know," she continues, "so you don't have to worry about my funeral."

"Oh, Mother, really—"

"I know, I know, you don't want to talk about it," she interrupts, already rifling through papers, pulling out a manila folder that looks as if it's seen multiple incarnations. "Look, I've got a CD for my funeral. Not much and you'll have to pay taxes, but an old pine box will do."

I roll my eyes. "I'm not burying you in an old pine box as if you were Addie Bundren. I don't know why you say such things."

"Well, people go to all this nonsense about the casket and for what? It's just going in the ground."

And yet I remember how she questioned every choice she made for my father's funeral, anxious about refusing the most expensive casket—the solid mahogany with velvet lining and embroidered head panel—though not skimping either. Still she fretted. Was it good enough? Too good? A waste of money? Would it represent him as he wanted to be represented—respectable but not showing off?

"Don't cremate me." She pushes the drawer closed. "I don't want to be in a vase on someone's mantel."

"Absolutely not." I try to be reassuring. *Do people really do that?*

"But nothing fancy."

I think of the careful placement of decorative pillows on her bed, the way dessert spoons are laid out, the polishing of silver, the necessity of dust ruffles and silk curtains, the linen tablecloths, the crystal punch bowl, the row of high heels still lined up in her closet. Fancy is my mother's middle name.

"Now, I want you to go through the house . . ."

Though I've often begged off this tour—who gets dibs on what—today I scan each room with a speculative eye though I live in a one-hundred-year-old house in Iowa without space for an extra armchair. My mother loves this part of her story, sweeping into each room like a docent, proudly touching the inlaid pattern on a chair, assessing the matching sconces, glancing at the delicate curved leg of an antique end table. "This is an *expensive* cabinet," she says, smoothing a hand affectionately across the wood. "You should consider it," as if I'm a prospective buyer. In many ways, her house *is* her legacy, each item bought with assurance and delight, her furniture and accoutrements her most intentional becoming.

No daughter wants to imagine her mother's death, and as I choose an armoire, a sofa, the inlaid card table, the twin beds with elegant, carved posts, I tell myself I'm acting out a charade. Before each visit to my childhood home in Alabama, I privately brace myself for her deterioration, and yet I'm often surprised, even shocked, by her vitality: she's up at 6:30 A.M., drinking her coffee at the kitchen table and relentlessly cheerful; she drives to the grocery store, the bank, and thirty-five miles down the highway to take cheese straws or red velvet cake to her great-grandchildren; she buys and wraps all her own packages and never misses a holiday. I know I'm kidding myself. I'm like Mrs. Ramsay in *To the Lighthouse*: When confronted with Cam's fear of the animal skull nailed fast to the nursery wall, she removed her shawl, winding it round and round the "horrid thing" until Cam no longer saw "horns all over the room" but only the disguise, the camouflage. *See how lovely it looks, how delighted the fairies will be.*

And that's what I do. I hide the skull. Disguise terror with softness. Clutch at deception. "You might like this," my mother says, turning on the small chandelier in the entryway.

"Oh, yes!" I agree as fairies flit just above her head.

But when the shawl loosens, inevitably slipping, when it sways, swinging freely in the evening breeze, what bleak and unexpected landscape will be exposed?

My first glimpse of this terrain, the shifting shape of things, occurs months later when I return to help my mother with vascular surgery. After the procedure for varicose veins, her left leg encased in a tight support stocking, her face foggy with pain (she refused the valium), the phlebotomist releases us with care instructions: ice packs and elevation; rest, then walking. So quick and easy. What can go wrong?

But after the ice packs and a slow "mobility" trek around the kitchen, the two of us gazing out the window to see if the azaleas need trimming, if the mail has come, if that damn stray cat is back, my mother collapses, slumping deep in her chair, her face deathly pale, her eyes fluttering, her breathing shallow. As I help her to bed in late afternoon, I realize it's the first time I've seen her submit to the frivolity of a nap. "A waste of time!" She's always censored daytime sleepiness as if only work is important. *Get this done. Get that done.* Busyness and bustle, then the respite of shopping.

Now, as she lies on top of the covers, one leg elevated, her arms limp, her mouth fallen open, she looks fragile, shrunken. *Old.* Infirmity has crept in, as sudden as a caress. Carefully, I cover her with a blanket, then stare at her like a helpless child before closing the door and sitting alone in the kitchen, waiting for dusk to arrive, the house eerily still, the TV dark, the phone mute, the air conditioner off. *Is this the beginning?* Theoretically I know there'll be an unraveling, the shawl loosening, darkness creeping in at the crevices, her energy weakening, collapsing. *A sudden glimpse of the skull.*

I look around the kitchen as if there might be other disturbing signs. Last night when I opened the refrigerator, the carrots looked withered, a dirty orange, and there was something soupy in a plastic bag, bleeding a bad smell. Today, I noticed her left eye had narrowed, squinting; as she tried to eat, she spit up a spongy piece of bread.

Has her skin always been this pale? Her balance so precarious?

That night I wrap myself in a blanket on the couch in the den to be closer to her, the house quiet at midnight as I tiptoe into her room. In sleep, she looks exhausted, her face anxious and defensive. She's afraid at night, she tells me, even with the outside lights on, the doors locked, the security system armed. By her bed, she keeps her "getaway" shoes with hard rubber soles "just in case I have to run into the bathroom, lock the door, and call the police." Though I could easily satirize this fictive plan, her deeper torment isn't fear of intruders but pervasive loneliness: no one to listen to the toss and tumble of her mind, the humiliations of aging—a forgotten word; a mis-step, then a fall; strangers at the grocery store; and the absolute worst—never being allowed to finish a story because her children and grandchildren are so impatient they rush her to "get to the point," as if her pace is unendurable, their demands imminent.

What she wants is to reveal her soul, but she doesn't know how.

Like most of us.

The next day while she's napping in her chair, I distract myself by rummaging through her bulging closets: old wool coats, V-necked sweaters, beaded evening gowns, dresses with huge shoulder pads, wide-leg linen pants, blouses pastel and misbuttoned and wrinkled. I'm prowling, utterly bored when *What? Is this possible?* I pull out a pink boa! Immediately, I wrap it around my neck, coyly twirling the ends and sashaying my hips, pretending to be Gwen Verdon even as I sneak back into the kitchen to check on her. To my surprise, she's awake. "Look at this!" I strike a dramatic pose. "Don't I look decadent?" I turn all the way around. "I could be a dancer, a stripper, a cocktail party crasher. This is soooo 1950s. Did you even know you had this?"

Giving her no time to answer, I unwrap the boa and lean toward her, smiling. "Let's do a crazy pic for your great-grandkids. They'll love it!" And before she can protest, I rearrange the pink blanket over her lap, letting it ripple and fold over her shoulders, then wrap the boa softly around her neck, its light pink strands flirting like long delicate feathers with her thinning hair. I paint her lips a bright cherry red, add dark sunglasses and give her my brown LePen to hold in her mouth like a cheroot. Viola! . . . a gangster moll! After taking several pictures, I let her choose the one she likes, and am absurdly pleased when she picks the most dramatically gangster-like: her head tilted coquettishly back, mouth pursed, silver bangles on her wrist—though, dammit, I forgot the beauty mark. Still, she perks up, laughs, and for the first time since her surgery she wants something to eat.

Can it be true that just as words differently arranged evoke different feelings, a body differently dressed can reinvent itself, come alive?

And alas, the opposite.

This fucking thing, I fret, wrestling with the support hose that refuses to behave. Once off her leg, the stocking's a shriveled sleeve, wrinkled, tight, impossible. An enemy! Each time we try, the cloth barely touches her skin before she cries out, astonished, outraged. "Oh, I can't do it," I say, and in exasperation call her grandson, a physician, who lives an hour away. To our great relief, he drives over to help. And yet even he can't coax her leg into this trap. Instead, in a drawer, he finds a pair of support hose from one of my father's surgeries years ago. I'm surprised my mother has kept them, though I shouldn't be. For decades, my dance costumes from fifth, sixth, and seventh grade (all fur-trimmed) have hung like domesticated pets in my girlhood closet. There are Christmas cards in a drawer from the 1990s, brochures from the 1980s, high school commencement announcements from the 1970s, each drawer a memoir to a different era. By the time my nephew leaves—the support hose on—my mother and I are so exhausted, we're cranky and anxious, bickering over food, over what and how much she should eat. After I bully her into taking small bites of toast and drinking a full glass of milk, she naps in her chair and, to her horror, wets herself.

That night I lie in the dark in my old bedroom, tossing and turning, thinking about the merciless demands of aging and how my mother will be ashamed of everything I've witnessed. Independence has always been her trump card. No show of weakness. No loss of control. No fumbling or disgrace. She does not relax the priorities—napkins neatly folded at the table, silver polished, shrimp peeled for grandsons, thank-you notes written on time, her sense of southern life beholden to this old status quo. In so many ways, she *is* a glowing representative of a good old age, of exceptional genes, luck, and success: She texts, uses Facebook, manages her personal and financial affairs, has chronic but manageable health problems, shops and cooks and puts on her own nightgown and slippers every night. But oh, the stress, the discomfort, the blunt hazard of even this small surgery: slow days of repetitive acts, small talk, a sinkhole of fatigue while the larger world seems ever more distant and surreal. I stare at the ceiling, both exhausted and wide-awake: When here, I feel as if I'm carrying the burden of her sorrows, holding them protectively close and simultaneously tossing them into the dark, as if to say, *"And so?"*

To my surprise the next morning, my mother's in the kitchen as if it's an ordinary day, walking slowly to the counter, brewing her coffee, getting out the half-and-half. She turns on the little TV in the corner: the weather forecast, the results of some poll, then a buzz of commentary about Dr. Christine Blasey Ford and her allegations of sexual assault by Brett Kavanaugh, the Supreme Court nominee, when they were both teenagers and attending a private school.

"This is going to be hard," I say, glancing at the TV. I fix my tea and sit across from her.

"It's going to be 'she said/he said.'" Mother sips her coffee. "It won't change a thing."

I nod, agreeing, though I desperately want Christine Blasey Ford to appear credible, to *be* credible. I dislike Kavanaugh not only for his ultra-conservative opinions but also for his priggishness, the hints of aggression in his performance, a buttoned righteousness in his affect. I know it's only his judicial opinions I should care about, but his facial gestures and body language suggest something smug yet attenuated in his personality. A boy-man. A pal.

At noon, while I'm driving Mother back from a brief checkup appointment with her doctor, we catch the beginning of the Senate hearings of Dr. Blasey Ford on NPR. Mesmerized by her testimony, we sit in the driveway, listening. But after fifteen minutes, the heat builds up in the car and I help her inside. Once she's seated in her chair with the ice packs in place, I turn on the TV and we watch the proceedings for almost an hour. And yet listening to the absurd questions by male senators, my mother begins to fret. As she smooths out a napkin, something irritated and intractable lights her eyes. Suddenly, she's not having it, this fickle attempt at justice long delayed, this thoughtful, vulnerable middle-aged woman airing her past in public. "What was she do-ing at that party at age fifteen, drinking a beer with those boys?" she asks, impatient, pointing at the TV.

"Well, they were teenagers and that's what teenagers do," I say, having no better answer.

"And why was she wearing a bathing suit and no underwear?"

These are the kinds of details that irk my mother: I imagine her mind hammering out questions, circling the threat to appropriateness and propri-ety. She's angry at girls who don't take responsibility for their choices, girls who dress provocatively and swear like boys and go to unchaperoned par-ties, girls who should know better. "These girls," she continues, "are partly to blame for the attention they're getting."

"Oh, Mother," I say irritably. "You may think culture should have stayed as it was in the 1950s, but the world of the 1980s for upper-class kids *was* per-missive and often irresponsible, but that doesn't give men the right to assault women. Even if a woman goes to a party, she's not asking to be harassed or raped. You know that."

"Well, it's just too convenient for her to come forward now."

"Maybe so. But maybe *this* reality—his being nominated for the Supreme Court—is the only reason she would *ever* come forward. Maybe it had to be this important for her to endure a hearing. I mean, those men . . . look at them . . . these hypocrites in the Senate are going to make her life hell."

My mother shakes her head, her mouth bunched tight. "They don't know what they're doing . . . these girls."

She's not even listening to me.

Despite my better angels, my own anger stirs. My mother, a product of a Victorian past, is hard on girls as if they alone are the "keepers of morality," while boys can be irresponsible, petty dilettantes in the sexual game. This view of women's sexual roles, oh, how it annoys me! *Will she never change?* "What do you know about young girls today other than what you've seen on TV?" I ask. "I mean, have you read anything about girls in the postmodern era of liberal democracy . . . their goals, their desires, the constraints they feel? What about the statistics of rape and sexual assault? Or contemporary theories of trauma?" I don't pause, don't give her a chance to respond, but keep talking, talking, telling her how trauma "becomes" trauma for the very reason that it's unassimilated, that a victim can both know and not know how the trauma could have happened, and that near-rape may seem benign in the telling but the threat *in that moment* is overbright, often overshadowed with fear, a fear that can be suppressed and diffused until it awakens and repeats itself. "What do you know about women who have no sense of power in the social and political world? Women brought up to be subordinate, who *still* wait on men?" This last, a dig: She waited like a servant on my father and brother.

My mother looks at me darkly. "I know what I know."

"Jesus, you sound like some blowhard in a bar," I say.

"And you too," she says quickly.

We stare at each other, eyes flashing, surprised. There's a pause, heat between us. And then, another surprise, we both laugh.

"No, no, no, I'm not letting you off the hook," I say, but the mood has shifted.

I click off the TV and we both eat a big slice of red velvet cake.

But we don't always laugh.

In late November when I'm visiting again, the pain is different. Again, she sits slumped in her white chair, her leg healed, but her face is crumpled, her feelings hurt by an argument with a favorite grandchild, their conversations tense. My mother feels unwanted and misunderstood, her words misperceived. "Everything I say," she laments, "it's all wrong."

"I know this is hard," I try to soothe, "but telling me about this is important. I mean, giving voice to your feelings. Letting it out." I sound, to my own ears, like a bad therapist.

Her face wet with tears, she lifts her head and says with sudden urgency, "I think I've been numb for most of my life and haven't known what I felt." She begins to weep again, her eyes red and strained. "Usually when someone says something that hurts me or openly rejects me, I try to bury it, try to insulate myself . . . from the anguish."

An odd excitement ripples through me. Her *knowing* that numbness has been her protection is an insight that surprises me. Not knowing, I think, would be the darker tragedy, the worse fate. Staying numb, she's telling me, has allowed her to function, "to get on with it," even as subliminally she's aware of the repression.

"Did you ever let yourself be angry?" I ask.

She looks away, blotting her eyes. "Oh, *yes*," she says finally. "Angry at my mother."

"Really?" I'm surprised. I haven't known this.

"I must have been ten or eleven and living in Praco," she begins. "Oh, I'd done something wrong, I can't remember what, maybe I'd forgotten to hang the clothes on the line, which meant they wouldn't be dry by nighttime, and my mother slapped me. 'I hate you,' I told her, and I wanted to hurt her too. Today it would be a slap, tomorrow the swish of a switch that left strings of blood on my legs." She sniffles and reaches for a Kleenex. "When she came at me with a switch, I used to collapse on the floor and pull my dress over my legs so she had to hit me on my back and shoulders where it wouldn't show. And this day, the day she slapped me, I said it again, said it as mean as I could. *'I hate you.'*"

She tells me that her mother didn't move. I imagine her mother's bare, unlovely face, her eyes alert, her gray-blonde hair escaping from her bun, her fat shapeless body encased in a faded housedress. "All she said was, 'Someday you'll understand.'"

"And did you?"

"It wasn't the slap or the switch that galled me, but that it was the *only* attention I got. She was just too busy to notice me unless I did something wrong. And yes, of course, I understood when I was older, but still, I resented the situation . . . all those children and work, you know, from dawn to dusk."

Her mother had eleven children before my mother left home for college at age sixteen. To make matters worse, they lived in such hostile, impoverished conditions in a company mining town that there was neither time nor inclination for her mother to teach her anything special or spend time alone with her. Not surprisingly, my mother internalized the fury. She might be the sacrificial daughter living in the shadows of her feelings, but she'd leave as soon as she could.

And she did.

I've known for a long time that my mother's way of loving me is, in some ways, a reaction to her mother's way of loving her. How could it be otherwise? She grabbed the form of that childhood and flipped it upside down. Where there'd been deprivation, she promised plenty: My sister and I had a closetful of clothes, a pretty room, a nice house, music and dancing and tennis lessons, books, and travel in summer. Where there'd been *no* attention, she was intently conscientious, driving us to endless lessons—many in a city an hour away—and helped us make pizzas and cakes, overseeing science projects, buying books, making costumes, taking us to concerts and performances. She transcended her own mother and childhood in every conceivable way, even by being pretty and slim and one of the best teachers in the school. She managed everything except—and here's the brutal slap: There is always an "except"—she'd learned too well to repress emotion, to be just slightly detached, to never push against authority, to prize success and resent failure and want desperately to fix those failures. But my failures—a snake pit of despair—couldn't be fixed. Of course, I understand now that the unfinished girlhoods of mothers—especially those denied any respect as girls—often influence the unfinished girlhoods of daughters.

Anger and numbness.

The story beneath the story.

For both of us.

"I'm losing it," Mother says on the phone one night after I've returned to Iowa. "I went to sleep in my chair today and the corned beef burned to a crisp in the oven. And I paid seventeen dollars for it," she sighs, her voice dire.

"Well, I'd probably have eaten it anyway. Burned to a crisp is just my taste," I tell her, but she isn't about to be forgiven and goes on with her list: She forgot to take her medicine at nine o'clock, forgot her doctor's name this morning, forgot what you call that thing everybody's doing on social media—Twitter—and didn't get the right kind of milk at the grocery store. She can't change the filter in the furnace, can't get up on a stool to replace the lights, can't remember words longer than two syllables.

"I'm losing it," she repeats.

I assure her she's not, that she's just made another red velvet cake, peeled two pounds of shrimp, and read the entire issue of *Time*. "If you're losing it, then more of us need to."

There's a pause. She doesn't respond. I feel her silence on the other end of the line like a weight. "Mother?"

"I want pretty music," she says in a different voice. "Nothing liturgical. I don't like that. I like melody."

"I agree. Pretty music is absolutely necessary." I hold the phone tighter, my voice softer. "Something beautiful."

"Yes."

"Like 'Ave Maria'?"

"Yes."

"And personal? Like 'Somewhere Over the Rainbow'?"

"I love that song."

Though our conversation has shifted, I believe I understand. She wants me to be responsible for the beauty of her funeral and the composition of her story. Though she doesn't say it, I know I'm to be the custodian of her unfinished narrative, attending the doors that remain open, the buttons undone, the sheets ruffled, the memories unburied with the buried. She wants me to see the skull, to press my own to its hard, aggregated mass, my fingertips brushing against it, my lips touching it, and then to wind something of beauty around it, round and round and round, until it's both utterly the same and utterly transformed.

I am alone at the cemetery. A flat, unlovely place, the grounds a grievance of green and yellowing grass. The trees, except for the live oaks, are neither voluptuous nor gracious, merely functional, as are the hedges circling some of the graves. The atmosphere is one of quiet indifference. Let the dead rest. Slumber and sleep. Merciful torpor. My mother has always resented this cemetery's lack of beauty, the hedges around our plot skimpy and oddly ravaged as if the sandy soil is rejecting them. Even the green of the leaves appears faded. Large black ants march brazenly through patches of dirt.

Today, no one is here. I look out over the acreage of graves and see only squirrels and birds and tiny green lizards, sublime and still, sunning themselves on the granite. I walk to our plot, my mother buried beside my father—my sister on the other side.

I'd like to say that I kneel and touch the earth exactly there—her place—but I don't. Instead, I sit on the base of my father's Celtic cross, my feet in the grass, my hands on my knees, and glance at the calla lilies on a nearby grave. Unsure what to do, I begin to hum, a soft, tuneless vibration I feel deep in my throat as I lean over and pull loose a weed, and then another, blowing off an ant.

For my mother, I will buy roses.

A blush of red roses.

Part V

Reckonings, 2018

Archive of the Dead

ARTHUR ST. CLAIR, A MINISTER, was lynched in Hernando County, Florida, in 1877 for performing the wedding of a black man and a white woman.

Jack Turner was lynched in Butler, Alabama, in 1882 for organizing black voters in Choctaw County.

After Calvin Mike voted in Calhoun County, Georgia, in 1884, a white mob attacked and burned his home, lynching his elderly mother and his two young daughters, Emma and Lillie.

Ham Patterson was lynched in Callaway County, Missouri, in 1884 for speaking disrespectfully about some white people.

Jim Eastman was lynched in Brunswick, Tennessee, in 1887 for not allowing a white man to beat him in a fight.

Seven black people were lynched near Screamer, Alabama, in 1888 for drinking from a white man's well.

A black man was lynched in Millersburg, Ohio, in 1892 for "standing around" in a white neighborhood.

After a white man attempted to assault Jack Brownlee's daughter in Oxford, Alabama, in 1894, Mr. Brownlee was lynched for having the man arrested.

General Lee was lynched in Reevesville, South Carolina, in 1904 for knocking on a white woman's front door.

William Miller was lynched in Brighton, Alabama, in 1908 for organizing local coal miners.

Will Brown was lynched in Omaha, Nebraska, in 1919 by a riotous white mob of up to 5,000 people.

Grant Cole was lynched in Montgomery, Alabama, in 1925 after he refused to run an errand for a white woman.

Elizabeth Lawrence was lynched in Birmingham, Alabama, in 1933 for reprimanding white children who threw rocks at her.

Ed Bracy, G. Smith Watkins, and Jim Press Meriweather were lynched in 1935 for working to organize a union among sharecroppers in Lowndes County, Alabama.

Jesse Thornton was lynched in Leverne, Alabama, in 1940 for addressing a white police officer without the title "mister."

I walk into the twilight of the National Memorial for Peace and Justice, the oxidized steel columns now high above my head as the floor descends into dusk, a prelude to darkness. Here it's not symbolic trees inscribed with names that confront me but a tableau of stories, a printed reckoning of victims of domestic terrorism in our nation's past: men, women, and children lynched by white supremacist mobs, mobs who, in ignorance and contempt, promoted the pathological myth of racial inferiority. Here, the victims' stories are written in stark white words, embedded on smooth gray plaques, words that speak of unspeakable crimes in short, declarative sentences. Subject. Verb. Place. Date. And yet what I understand from these words is both simple and complex.

You can be lynched no matter your age or gender. No matter your resistance or passivity. No matter your constitutional rights. No matter your courage in affirming those rights. No matter your hope or its cousin, respect. No matter your mind's intent, your will's unflinching hunger, or the inevitable, unfathomable need of the human imagination to enact a self, an identity, a dignity.

No matter.

As I progress down that slanted path, reading each story, the air feels thinner. A stillness descends, a quiet that chills. Outside, the grass is lush and green, the air thick with swirling gnats, a cardinal perched somewhere in the limb of a white oak tree, a mosquito biting. And though there are people around me—there's the shuffle and squeak of shoes, the occasional cough or sigh, an old man's sneeze—I'm wrapped in solitude, roaming with the dead.

As if the day has paused, I stop.

And then, I walk on, reading the words, each plaque an ambush, until I hear, from somewhere deeper in the void, a child call out, "Wait, wait," his voice high and urgent, stitched with a child's insistent demand, and as suddenly I'm back in my childhood in Lineville, Alabama, circa 1953, where Maddy is swinging me, back and forth, her hard, calloused hand nudging the wooden seat of the swing, my curly head tilting toward the ground, my bare feet up in the air.

And then she's not.

The swing slows. I squirm and try to pump my legs. I want to keep going. "*Swing*," I command, certain she's stopped only to get a pinch of snuff she'll lodge deep in her gums, bulging out her lower jaw. Already at age five, I know I'm in control, the master of my fate, that Maddy, a large Black woman who is often in the kitchen when I wake up, is here to take care of me while my mother teaches school. "Swing," I call out exuberantly. "Swing, swing, swing."

And she does.

Even now, I remember only a warm summer day, the fading blooms of the crabapple trees, the slow buzz of insects, a bluebird pecking hard at something in the grass. Nothing but pleasure will shake the midafternoon calm. As I fly through the air, I never think about Maddy except for the steadiness of her hand on the swing and the rhythmic "uh-huh" of her voice. To me, at five, everything is normal and right with the world. A child doesn't yet understand the wounds of history or the horror of apartheid, doesn't understand that Maddy—and everyone who is her color—might live in constant danger and certain damage in the Jim Crow South. A child doesn't yet understand the intolerable truth: that the grotesque psychology of racism claims both the living and the dead.

⟸

How could it be otherwise? Even as late as 1953, after the Depression and two world wars, many states insisted on segregation laws to make Black citizens "stay in their place" accepting the humiliations such submission required. Not only were there the overt physical signs of separation and exclusion—Colored Restroom; Colored Water Fountain; Colored Entrance; Colored Waiting Room; Colored Balcony; Colored Section—but there also were extralegal constraints (the KKK; the White Citizens Councils) and, if necessary, the law.

And of course, that list doesn't include the real and symbolic implications of Whites Only restaurants, hotels, libraries, schools, churches, cemeteries, houses, apartments, phone booths, hospitals, jails, amusement park cashier windows, residential houses for the elderly and handicapped, or the paucity of paved roads, streetlights, and indoor plumbing available to Black citizens, along with a poll tax and voting restrictions (literacy tests given only to Black people) created to disenfranchise them as voters. The raw divide between Black and white.

I have been at this memorial for more than an hour and I want to leave. Not just to leave but to flee, to not-see, not-read, and not-know any more, as seeing and reading and knowing require not just mourning the dead memorialized here but also recognizing the extent to which racism is tied to my inheritance, to the prejudice lodged in my heart. Some selfish part of me wants to say, "But at least I came . . . I showed up," as if paying an entrance fee and walking through the memorial frees me of historical implications when I know too well that "performing" goodness has little to do with the burden of thought.

When I walk out into the hazy summer day, leaving behind the oxidized steel columns and solemn words, I think again about Maddy. Who was she, this woman who arrived at our back door every weekday, already worn-out and middle-aged, whose life I knew so little about? We were not expected to know much about Maddy, to know what she liked or disliked or to concern ourselves with how she lived. To show deep interest would have been a break in protocol, a misstep into another world, a slip into the shadows. We knew only what she did well—cook and clean and tend to me—and our lives went on, constrained and busy, with so many books to read, a piano to play, medical conventions and PTA meetings to attend, new shoes to buy. Though Maddy exists now only in my mind, I try to imagine us sitting beside each other in comfortable, cushioned chairs, both of us too old, and she too frail, for anything less. We will want something cool to drink and yes, some home-made cookies would be nice. Of course, I want to ask about her family and her church and the grace and terror of growing up in Alabama, but how to begin? How to ask what she remembers from living in Lineville so many years ago, what heartbreak or relief pierced her mind as she pushed me on that swing? Did she ever feel the sticky tentacles of fear touch the base of her throat or cherish some distant hope of owning her own home? Did she stand stoically in line to vote, knowing the futility, or watch her children leave on the bus for Detroit and Chicago and Cleveland, secretly relieved? Did she believe in the prophecy of redemption in the heavenly sphere and keep an envelope of burial insurance receipts wrapped in a rubber band?

What could she tell me?

In my mind, I see her settling back in her chair, easing her aching legs, stiff now with arthritis, her feet barbed with corns and bunions. She is patting smooth a wrinkle in her dark blue dress. She is very old. I see it in the set of her body, in the thin gray knot of her crinkled hair and the wiry chords of her neck so prominent beneath her chin. Her bosom is slack. Her ankles swollen. Only her eyes, dark and penetrating, remain nearly the same. Eyes that stare. Hard. She was born, I think, in the first decade of the twentieth century.

I imagine her quiet at first, slowly drinking her iced tea, sucking on a piece of ice, her lips working, with no wish to hurry as she takes my measure. I watch her bite into a cookie, crumbs scattering across her lap, then drifting to the floor. Only as she wipes them away from her dress does she fix those great dark eyes on me, and then, without ceremony or hesitation and with the grievance of the very old, she begins to talk, telling me little pieces of her life, small fragments of feeling that make up her story of what it was like to be a stranger in her own country.

And I listen. The stranger in me is learning to listen.

Acknowledgments

Many thanks to Claire Lewis Evans at the University of Alabama Press for her wise and thoughtful guidance in bringing this book into the world, to Jay Lamar for her insight and generosity, to Kris Vervaecke for her faith and clarity regarding this book's value, to Louise Crawford at Brooklyn Social Media for her invaluable advice in support of this book, to Addie Bolton for her shared curiosity, to Jan Weissmiller for her perceptive responses, and to my husband, David Wilder, for being there as a reader and supporter.

I'd like to thank all the friends who read various forms of these essays, including Jim McKean, Marilyn Abildskov, Kris Vervaecke, Kathryn Ann Ford, and Linda Bauer. I'm grateful to Roy Hoffman for his crucial suggestions in editing "Alabama Triptych," to Lee Martin for his insightful comments, to Mary Allen for her continuing generosity, and to Frye Gaillard for his support. I am grateful to have been a student of James Alan McPherson at the Iowa Writers' Workshop.

Publication credits and awards for this manuscript:

"Prologue," excerpts, *Southern Humanities Review*, 2013.
"What Needs to Be Needed," *Shenandoah*, 2004.
"What Needs to Be Needed," *Best American Essays*, "Notable Essay," 2005.
"The 'Orig,'" *Kestrel*, 2010.
"You Girls," *Fourth Genre*, 2011.
"Umbilicus," *The Spectacle*, 2015.
"Nowhere," *Colorado Review*, 2018.

"Nowhere," *Best American Essays*, "Notable Essay," 2019.

"Fingering the Scars," *Florida Review*, 2018.

"Sleepwalking," *Juxtaprose*, 2018.

"Pilgrimage," *Antioch Review*, 2019.

"Pilgrimage," *Best American Essays*, "Notable Essay," 2020.

"Written in the Sky," *Under the Sun*, 2019.

"Club from Nowhere," *Brevity*, 2019.

"A Dark, Unruly Place," *Massachusetts Review*, 2019, under pseudonym Emily Douglas.

"A Dark, Unruly Place," *Best American Essays*, "Notable Essay," 2020, under pseudonym Emily Douglas.

"Amends," *Missouri Review*, 2020.

"Alabama Triptych," *Louisville Review*, 2020.

"Alabama Triptych," *Best American Essays*, "Notable Essay," 2021.

"Silence," *Alabama Review*, forthcoming.

Notes

Written in the Sky

1. Philip Dray, *At the Hands of Persons Unknown* (New York: Modern Library, 2003), 373–74.

If I Could Write Postcards to Mary Hamilton

1. Camila Domonoske, "When 'Miss' Meant So Much More: How One Woman Fought Alabama—and Won," *Code Switch* (podcast), November 30, 2017.

2. Domonoske, "When 'Miss' Meant So Much More."

3. "Mary Hamilton Wesley, 67; Civil Rights Activist Challenged Segregation" (obituary), *Los Angeles Times*, December 12, 2002.

4. Domonoske, "When 'Miss' Meant So Much More."

5. Mary Hamilton, Louise Inghram, et al., *Freedom Riders Speak for Themselves* (Detroit: News & Letters, 1961), 4.

6. Hamilton, Inghram, et al., *Freedom Riders Speak for Themselves*, 5.

7. Domonoske, "When 'Miss' Meant So Much More."

8. Hamilton, Inghram, et al., *Freedom Riders Speak for Themselves*, 15.

9. "Mary Hamilton Wesley, 67" (obituary).

10. Hamilton, Inghram, et al., *Freedom Riders Speak for Themselves*, 16.

Native Daughter

1. Virginia Foster Durr, *Outside the Magic Circle: The Autobiography of Virginia Foster Durr*, ed. Hollinger F. Barnard (Tuscaloosa: University of Alabama Press, 1985), 241.

2. Durr, *Outside the Magic Circle*, 241.

3. Durr, *Outside the Magic Circle*, 241.

4. Virginia Foster Durr, *Freedom Writer: Virginia Foster Durr, Letters from the Civil Rights Years*, ed. Patricia Sullivan (New York: Routledge, 2003), 23.

5. Durr, *Outside the Magic Circle*, 243.

6. Durr, *Outside the Magic Circle*, 32.

7. Durr, *Outside the Magic Circle*, 102.

8. Durr, *Outside the Magic Circle*, 63.

9. Durr, *Outside the Magic Circle*, 56.

10. Durr, *Outside the Magic Circle*, 57.

11. Durr, *Outside the Magic Circle*, 84, 85.

12. Durr, *Outside the Magic Circle*, 108.

13. Durr, *Outside the Magic Circle*, 109, 110.

14. Durr, *Outside the Magic Circle*, 109.

15. Durr, *Outside the Magic Circle*, 109.

16. Durr, *Outside the Magic Circle*, 109.

17. Durr, *Outside the Magic Circle*, 107.

18. Durr, *Outside the Magic Circle*, 110.

19. Durr, *Outside the Magic Circle*, 110.

20. Durr, *Outside the Magic Circle*, 108.

21. Durr, *Outside the Magic Circle*, 104.

22. Durr, *Outside the Magic Circle*, 112, 114.

23. Durr, *Outside the Magic Circle*, 110.

24. Durr, *Outside the Magic Circle*, 111.

25. William Warren Rogers, Robert David Ward, Leah Rawls Atkins, and Wayne Flynt, *Alabama: The History of a Deep South State* (Tuscaloosa: University of Alabama Press, 1994), 485.

26. Durr, *Outside the Magic Circle*, 78.

27. Durr, *Outside the Magic Circle*, 77.

28. Durr, *Outside the Magic Circle*, 79.

29. Durr, *Outside the Magic Circle*, 103.

30. Durr, *Outside the Magic Circle*, 101.

31. Durr, *Outside the Magic Circle*, 101.

32. Virginia Foster Durr, interview by John Egerton, February 6, 1991, Southern Oral History Program Collection-0337, 36.

33. Durr, interview.

34. Southern Conference for Human Welfare, *Report of Proceedings of the Southern Conference for Human Welfare* (Birmingham, Alabama, November 20–23, 1938), 29.

35. Durr, *Outside the Magic Circle*, 121.

36. Durr, *Outside the Magic Circle*, 121.

37. Durr, *Freedom Writer*, 30.

38. Virginia Foster Durr, interview by Sue Thrasher, Jacquelyn Hall, and Bob Hall, 1975, Southern Oral History Program Collection #4007, 33.

39. Durr, *Outside the Magic Circle*, 261, 263.

40. Durr, *Freedom Writer*, 31.

41. Durr, *Outside the Magic Circle*, 252.

42. Durr, *Outside the Magic Circle*, 280.

43. Martin Luther King Jr., "Montgomery Bus Boycott Speech," December 1955.

44. Durr, *Freedom Writer*, 95.

45. Durr, *Outside the Magic Circle*, 297.

46. Durr, *Freedom Writer*, 99.

47. Durr, *Freedom Writer*, 135.

48. Durr, *Outside the Magic Circle*, 323.

A Dark, Unruly Space

1. Sylviane A. Diouf, *Dreams of Africa in Alabama: The Slave Ship Clotilda and the Story of the Last Africans Brought to America* (New York: Oxford University Press, 2007), 2.

2. Diouf, *Dreams of Africa in Alabama*, 175.

3. Diouf, *Dreams of Africa in Alabama*, 176.

Fingering the Scars

1. Brenda Wineapple, *Ecstatic Nation: Confidence, Crisis, and Compromise, 1848–1877* (New York: Harper Perennial, 2013), 9.

2. Wineapple, *Ecstatic Nation*, 476.

3. Brenda Wineapple, *White Heat: The Friendship of Emily Dickinson & Thomas Wentworth Higginson* (New York: Anchor, 2009), 131.

4. Wineapple, *White Heat*, 126.

5. Wineapple, *White Heat*, 126.

6. *Encyclopedia of Alabama*, s.v. "Slavery," by Keith S. Herbert, 1.

7. William Warren Rogers, Robert David Ward, Leah Rawls Atkins, and Wayne Flynt, *Alabama: The History of a Deep South State* (Tuscaloosa: University of Alabama Press, 1994), 197.